D1327396

THE
HOUSE
WITH
Sixteen
Handmade
Doors

ALSO by HENRY PETROSKI

To Forgive Design: Understanding Failure (2012)

*An Engineer's Alphabet: Gleanings from the Softer
Side of a Profession* (2011)

*The Essential Engineer: Why Science Alone Will Not Solve
Our Global Problems* (2010)

The Toothpick: Technology and Culture (2007)

Success through Failure: The Paradox of Design (2006)

Pushing the Limits: New Adventures in Engineering (2004)

Small Things Considered: Why There Is No Perfect Design (2003)

Paperboy: Confessions of a Future Engineer (2002)

The Book on the Bookshelf (1999)

Remaking the World: Adventures in Engineering (1997)

*Invention by Design: How Engineers Get from Thought
to Thing* (1996)

*Engineers of Dreams: Great Bridge Builders and the
Spanning of America* (1995)

*Design Paradigms: Case Histories of Error and Judgment
in Engineering* (1994)

The Evolution of Useful Things (1992)

The Pencil: A History of Design and Circumstance (1990)

*Beyond Engineering: Essays and Other Attempts
to Figure Without Equations* (1986)

*To Engineer Is Human: The Role of Failure
in Successful Design* (1985)

THE
HOUSE
WITH
Sixteen
Handmade
Doors

*A Tale of
Architectural
Choice and
Craftsmanship*

HENRY PETROSKI
*with photographs by
Catherine Petroski*

W. W. NORTON & COMPANY
New York . London

For information about permission to reproduce selections from this book,
write to Permissions, W. W. Norton & Company, Inc., 500 Fifth Avenue,
New York, NY 10110

For information about special discounts for bulk purchases, please contact
W. W. Norton Special Sales at specialsales@wwnorton.com or 800-233-4830

Manufacturing by RR Donnelley Harrisonburg
Book design by Charlotte Staub
Production manager: Julia Druskin

Library of Congress Cataloging-in-Publication Data

Petroski, Henry, author.
The house with sixteen handmade doors : a tale of architectural choice and
craftsmanship / Henry Petroski ; with photographs by Catherine Petroski.
— First Edition.
pages cm
Includes bibliographical references and index.
ISBN 978-0-393-24204-1 (hardcover)
1. Architecture, Domestic—Maine—Arrowsic. 2. Phinney, Robert Edgar,
1915–1989. 3. Petroski, Henry—Homes and haunts—Maine—Arrowsic.
4. Petroski, Catherine—Homes and haunts—Maine—Arrowsic. 5. Arrowsic
(Me.)—Buildings, structures, etc. I. Petroski, Catherine, illustrator. II. Title.
NA7238.A77P48 2014
728'.370974185—dc23
2014006423

W. W. Norton & Company, Inc.,
500 Fifth Avenue, New York, N.Y. 10110
www.wwnorton.com

W. W. Norton & Company Ltd. Castle House,
75/76 Wells Street, London W1T 3QT

1 2 3 4 5 6 7 8 9 0

*To our friends and neighbors
on the Road,
and in memory of V.P.,
who loved visiting Pineledge*

CONTENTS

PREFACE

THIS IS A STORY about a house and its environs. To my wife, Catherine, and me it is a special house because now it is ours, but it was not always. It was conceived sixty-odd years ago by an amateur carpenter who immersed himself first in designing it and then in building the unique structure. The house may be modest, but it is also a model of thoughtful design and careful craftsmanship.

So much of the house remains in its original state that it has been possible to deconstruct it to tell the story of its making. This deconstruction has not been physical, however, because no nail was pulled, no screw unscrewed, no board removed to look into the house's innards. The nature of its design and the manner of its construction provide ample opportunity to examine the underside of wooden floors, to study the back sides of handmade doors, and to peer into the dark corners of unfinished closets to ferret out much about the man and his house. But as transparent as some of its structure may be, there are also parts of it that are mysterious and seemingly inscrutable. This book describes both the known and the unknown: it celebrates the former and puts forth what I hope are plausible explanations for the latter.

Because so much of the charm of this house is in its setting and in its details, and because a picture is worth countless words,

Catherine's photographs are an integral part of the book. They capture the house in context and reveal the simple elegance of its lines and the serene beauty of its location. Although it was never intended to be a grand house, its builder had a grand plan. He did not write down his plan in words on paper but he did realize it with nails in wood. The photographs testify to that.

Previous owners and their children have returned to this place in Maine with all the excitement and fond memories that proud and loyal alumni bring to reunions at their alma mater. Without the stories and recollections of those growing up and living in the house, its story might have been one of architecture and technology devoid of human interest and a soul. By sharing their knowledge and feelings about the place, those who have returned to visit it have populated it with real people with real dreams, hopes, and joys. Without such people and their families, no house could be a home, and no book a story. I am grateful to all who have helped breathe life into both. Those whose names I know and recall are acknowledged at the end of the tale.

Pineledge
Summer 2013

THE
HOUSE
WITH
Sixteen
Handmade
Doors

One

FINDING
OUR
PLACE

PEOPLE HAVE ALWAYS HAD a hard time finding our place in Maine. No matter how precise our driving instructions—even when we give them down to the tenth of a mile between turns—first-time visitors invariably call us from their car within shouting (but not sighting) distance, seeking reassurance that they are on the right track. Those with a GPS device in their car doubt the directions on the screen. We would probably do the same if we were looking for a house on a road that doesn't even look like a road.

The cause of the confusion is that our modest place is reached via a right-of-way through what is the property of our next-door neighbor, whose large and imposing house is as hard to miss as ours is to see from the main road. Visitors looking for us have no trouble following our instructions up to what we have jokingly called our "carriage house" or "gatehouse," but they have second thoughts about making the final turn onto the right fork. It looks like our neighbor's driveway, which it is.

Life's small and large decisions are fraught with anxieties and fears of making the wrong choice. As Robert Frost did, most of us pause at forks in the road, and those who hesitate too long can pay the hefty toll of staying lost. We all want to choose the correct fork, but indecision will freeze us in our tracks and let the trail get cold.

That is where Catherine and I felt we were after several years of looking at real estate on the granite coast of Maine, and that is how we do not want visitors to feel when looking now for our place beyond the fork in the road. Most of them seem to know the perils of indecision, and that is why they give us a ring when they think that they are close by but cannot imagine that the road before them will take them to our place. They are reluctant to head toward a barnlike structure with a green tin roof where the road appears to end.

When we ask our short-distance callers to describe where they are, they invariably say that they are in front of a very big shingled house into whose driveway our instructions are taking them. We tell them that they are on track and should drive straight toward the barn, which has a discreet sign reading "Robert Shultz Builders," and follow the drive that makes a sharp right just in front of it. Even though the improved way ends there, they should continue on the dirt road going down toward the river.

As they execute the turn in front of the barn they see that, although the paved portion does end abruptly, the dirt road continues past stacks of firewood, piles of rocks, loads of underbrush, and lots of trees. Finally it bends out into an opening and heads directly toward an enormous pine tree standing alone in a clearing. But then another fork comes into view, where the lane diverges and loops around the tree. At last the river and our house beside it reveal themselves. We smile when the first-time visitor asks, "How did you ever find this place?"

Finding and buying a retreat in Maine, or anywhere else, is no trivial matter. There are, of course, financial considerations, which include whether the place is affordable and likely to hold its value. But there are also matters of accessibility, livability, and possibility. How far from home must a second one be to qualify? How different must or should the climate be to feel invigorating? Why should

The house beside the river

a retreat be located in one place rather than another? When and where should the die be cast? The decision not taken can be the dream deferred.

Circumstances favor the prepared mind and prompt the ready body. This was certainly the case with Catherine and me. We live most of the year in Durham, North Carolina, which is about midway between Kitty Hawk on the Outer Banks and Asheville in the Smoky Mountains. Many of our neighbors have a house at the beach or in the mountains, either of which can serve for a weekend getaway. Going north or south is a different matter. North Carolina is, via interstate highways, roughly halfway between Florida and Maine; our Durham is midway between Orlando and Orono. For years, we talked about finding a second home, somewhere close enough to the interstates to make it easily accessible but far enough from them so the rushing traffic could not be seen or heard, a place to which we could escape from the hot, humid summers of the Piedmont and maybe get away for a long weekend of rest and relaxation now and then. But which way to go?

When our children were young, we spent our summer vacations on the Carolina coast, renting a house or condominium on the water. The open views were spectacular, but the beaches and roads were often crowded. When there were not thunderstorms or hurricanes, the sun was hot and the air damp, and the salt spray coated our bodies and eyeglasses with a gritty, translucent film. The surf was fun but could be dangerous, even for a strong swimmer like our daughter, Karen. We found ourselves spending more time inside our rented air-conditioned space than walking along the shore and looked only halfheartedly for a beach place to buy.

For a while we entertained the idea of having a retreat in the mountains. We had driven our son, Stephen, to summer camp near Burnsville, North Carolina, in the shadow of Mount Mitchell, the highest peak east of the Mississippi. Though Burnsville is not convenient to much else, on the way to and from it we passed idyllic summer colonies on tranquil mountain lakes. But the narrow, winding roads around them were not conducive to relaxing or to keeping lunch down. We decided that we were not likely to buy or build a log cabin in those woods.

In the meantime, because Catherine was working on a book about the Hathorns, a seafaring family from Maine, we had begun going there for working summer vacations. The folks about whom she was writing lived in Richmond, once a thriving shipbuilding town on the Kennebec River. The Kennebec is one of the six rivers that meet at or flow into the felicitously named Merrymeeting Bay, the others being the Androscoggin, Cathance, Eastern, Abagadasset, and Muddy. In fact, Merrymeeting is not a bay by most geographical understanding, for it is located inland and, although tidal, is mostly fresh water. The Kennebec flows into and out of the bay on its way to the ocean, but it is easy to see why the outlet part, which stretches only about sixteen miles, may have been considered a distinct river and given its own name, the Sagadahoc.

Richmond launched its last wooden ship in the 1850s and its economy has struggled since. For a while, a shoe factory provided jobs for many of the Russian immigrants who settled there, but the town was so small it could not support a motel. At first, we stayed in bed-and-breakfasts downriver in Bath, home of the Maine Maritime Museum, whose archives were crucial to Catherine's research. In subsequent years, we rented houses nearby on the coast. We came to know and like the area, and soon we began to think that it was the place to spend summers. Its waters may be as treacherous as those off Carolina's Outer Banks, but its air was cooler and drier, and its roads were more or less level and straight, at least where we drove.

When Catherine's Hathorn book came out in 1997, she went on an author tour that started in Bar Harbor, the famed resort town located on Mount Desert Island, Maine's largest island. Its name is often pronounced Mount Dessert, as if referring to an after-dinner sweet. No matter how said, it is the location of Acadia National Park, beloved by hikers and bikers, and has been the vacation spot for such notables as David Rockefeller, Brooke Astor, and Martha Stewart. We did not look at real estate there.

The next venue on Catherine's book tour was the expansive Penobscot Marine Museum at Searsport, which put us up for a couple of days in a small guest room above the museum store. This gave us a base of operations and an opportunity to get to know other towns and communities along the northern edge of Maine's Midcoast region, a fuzzily defined stretch between Casco Bay and Penobscot Bay, the former of which harbors Portland and Freeport, and the latter Camden and Searsport. Being based in Searsport, we had the opportunity to look at property in, around, and between nearby towns. The Midcoast's wide variety of lower-key communities both attracted and befuddled us.

Catherine had mentioned in passing to a museum staff member that we were interested in looking at property in the area. The staffer said that she had a small house in Cushing, a nearby farming community, and was thinking of putting it on the market. It was just down the road from a property associated with Andrew Wyeth that had once been the residence of Christina Olson, the polio victim depicted in the painting *Christina's World*, and that can be seen in its background. Wyeth had a three-decades-long association with that house, sometimes using an upstairs room in it as a studio, which gave the staffer's little house nearby a certain cachet. In the early 1990s the Olson House was given to the Farnsworth Art Museum, located in Rockland, and is now a National Historic Landmark. We were given directions to the staffer's place and were told to feel free to go in and look around.

As attractive and storied as the Olson property was, the house we went to look at turned out to be quite a bit less so. In fact, it was tiny, ordinary, and located within just a few feet of the narrow road leading to the Olson place, which we feared meant that on days when the museum property was open to the public, a steady stream of cars and campers would squeeze by, possibly parking on the little house's little lawn. The experience warned us that in seeking a retreat we should focus on property far from celebrity neighbors, far from popular destinations, and far from the road.

The next stop on the author tour was the historic shipbuilding town of Bath, and we were booked for a couple of nights in what had been our favorite bed-and-breakfast before we had started renting houses in the area. It was good to renew our acquaintance with the proprietors, but we were eager to get up to our room, where they had placed the package of listings dropped off by a local realtor. We had outlined beforehand what we were looking for in a piece of property. Chief among the criteria, distilled from our many disappointing treks down driveways marked with for-sale (and private-property and no-trespassing) signs, were seclusion and waterfront, or at least a water view. We were willing to compromise even on those criteria, however, and would happily look at any nice small (but not tiny) house on a nice quiet street in a nice quiet town available for a nice affordable price.

Looking at even a handful of properties along the Maine coast can be an all-day affair, largely because the listings that meet specified criteria are spread among so many small towns and villages, and because those places seem invariably to be separated by unbridged rivers, bays, harbors, and inlets. On the first day of our search we looked generally to the inland side of U.S. Route 1, which hereabouts is known as the Coastal Route. Though U.S. 1 is a north-south highway, along the coast of Maine it is actually oriented more east-west. Following Route 1 North from Bath takes you Down East, which refers to the coast from roughly where the Penobscot River empties into the bay, just north of Searsport, to the Canadian border. The name Down East derives from the sailing term for traveling downwind in northeastern New England and the Maritime Provinces, which carries a vessel to the east. Because the return journey would be against, or upwind, Mainers sometimes speak of going up to Boston, which is of course to the south and west. We looked at a lot of real estate that day and thought we encountered most of the house and land types and combinations thereof available in Midcoast Maine. None seemed right for us.

The next day we were taken to destinations on the seaward side of the Coastal Route, which meant that we would be driving up and down peninsulas and on and off some of Maine's many islands connected to the mainland if at all by a single narrow bridge. To get from one side of a half-mile-wide river or inlet to the other might take twenty miles of driving. It promised to be a long day. One interesting house in Cundys Harbor, the oldest commercial fishing village in Maine, had a wonderful pair of studies in adjacent rooms, each facing the harbor through a wall of windows, but the low ceilings would not let either of us stand up in them.

A category of vacation house that we had to look at, if for no other reason than curiosity and cost, was the so-called camp, a word with an elastic meaning in Maine, but generally designating a small house with hardly any of the comforts of home. The typical camp is built by weekend carpenters who do not even deserve the ameliorating adjective "amateur." The Cundys Harbor house was a camp of sorts, but it was not billed as one. The one true camp we looked at had no hot water, no heat, no insulation, and no boards where they should have been expected in floors and walls. The advantage of a camp is that it is inexpensive to build and not exacting in its construction demands or expectations, so, the reasoning goes, more money can be spent on the land and more time on the water. As a result, many a camp is wonderfully situated with a breathtaking view—as long as you are looking out. Seeing one such camp satisfied our curiosity.

Our itinerary's finale was located on Arrowsic, an island bordering the Kennebec River and connected to the mainland by one bridge and to the next island—Georgetown—by another. Our domestic docent lived on Arrowsic herself, and whether for strategy or convenience, she had chosen to show us this listing last. We ended up there at the perfect time. Sunset was fast approaching, and the house faced west toward a brilliant sky. The living room's large plate-glass windows framed both a spectacular sunset and the wide expanse of water where the Kennebec widens as it exits from a great double dogleg. At slack tide, it was like looking out at an inviting lake beneath a majestic sky.

The house sat on a blunt point of land, bordered by the river on the west and a small cove on the north, with hundreds of feet of the rocky shoreline fronting on deep water. Because the structure was built before setback regulations came into effect, it was uncommonly close to the water, which we liked. The house had only two bedrooms, but they were supplemented by a small guest cabin in the woods behind the garage. What most attracted us to this place was its spacious living room sunlit through the picture windows. The house was modest, but the view was grand.

Since we liked what we saw, we arranged to come back the next morning to see it in a fresh light. We got ourselves there early, ahead of the real-estate agent, who liked to point out features, so we were able to marvel at the silence broken only by an occasional fish jumping clear out of the water and landing with a splat on its side. Without the distraction of the sunset, the view upriver was even more spectacular than we had realized. After the house was opened for us, we walked around, including in the unfinished attic, imagining how it could be turned into a study or two. We also

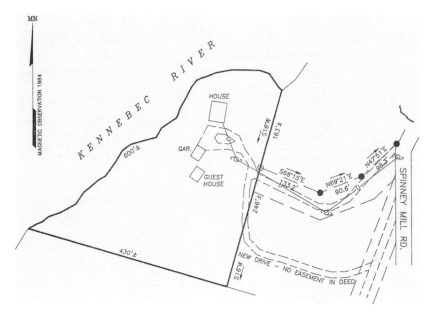

Survey showing disputed drive

inspected the guest cabin, which was furnished to sleep four, and so the modest size of the house really did not matter. The more we saw, the more we liked what we saw.

There were the usual details to be worked out between the lawyer in Maine representing us and the one in Pennsylvania for the sellers, but everything appeared to be on track for a closing in late September—until our attorney called to announce a snag. It seemed that the driveway from the public road to the point property was under dispute between abutting neighbors. To put in the drive, some trees had been cut down, which violated the restrictive covenant that a buffer of trees alongside the road was to be preserved. The area had to be replanted and this would cut off access to the drive.

The only way we would be able to get to the property now would be to use the historical access road, which now included the neighbor's driveway and its continuation, which together would constitute a deeded right-of-way. We had neither seen this approach nor met the neighbor, but on the advice of our attorney we agreed to the change of access. By now we so anticipated having the house beside the river that we probably would have agreed to almost anything. With the necessary paperwork having been received, signed, and returned, it looked to be clear sailing to a closing on what would soon really be our place.

Two

TO THE POINT
OF
BEGINNING

As with virtually every house on which we have made or seriously considered making an offer, I sketched out the floor plan of the place in Maine from memory of the walk-throughs, with some assistance from the realtor's listing sheet. The sketch reminded us that the house we were hoping would be ours was a real home even though it was reachable only via a road we had not yet seen.

By the end of September, we legally had ourselves a retreat, and we were eager to explore it anew and sleep in it for a few fall nights. We expected to discover things that no cursory walk-throughs could have revealed. We made arrangements to fly to Portland—the nearest commercial airport—during my university's fall break.

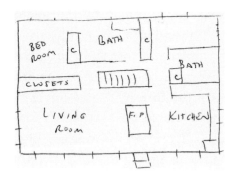

Sketch of floor plan

From our attic, where they had been stored since we acquired wheeled luggage, we retrieved a couple of large old Samsonite hard-sided suitcases and packed them with everything from towels and bed linens to the kinds of odds and ends we had put aside for a second home, without being sure that we would actually use them. We checked luggage at the airport for the first time in years and flew up to Maine on a Friday afternoon in October.

Among the treasures in our overweight luggage was a pair of cast-iron ducks that we always knew would be perfect for a rustic hearth. They were reminders of the mallards we used to visit and feed crusts of bread to in Crystal Lake Park in Urbana, Illinois, where we had met and married as graduate students. While shopping at a nearby mall for first-Christmas presents, each of us had spotted the coal-black iron ducks—one with its head up begging for a treat and the other with its beak to the ground, picking up a morsel. Each of us had debated privately over whether we could afford even a single duck. As I recall, I bought only one of the ducks and Catherine bought the other, one of us thinking frugally and the other thinking that if one of the birds had already been sold, then the remaining one might not be available on the next visit to the store. The ducks could hardly be wrapped, and so we set them out in the dark the night before Christmas, neither of us suspecting that in the morning we would awake to a pair. The ducks had remained beside each other until we packed them into separate suitcases, the more evenly to distribute their considerable weight.

When we left North Carolina it was still summer by the thermometer but approaching autumn by the tree colors; when we arrived in Maine it was well into fall and already approaching winter. Since the fall colors were past their peak, traffic was light. It took about forty-five minutes to drive from the airport to Arrowsic, where we looked for the turn off Maine Route 127 onto Spinney Mill Road, which we found at the bottom of a long hill. Our landmark was a line of mailboxes on the west side of the highway, and we stopped to find ours among them. It was a motley group of black, gray, and rusty-steel rural-mail receptacles in various states of disrepair. Battering them from a passing car, we would learn, was considered great sport by local teenagers. Plastic newspaper receptacles—singular pigeonholes—were haphazardly arranged beneath and between the boxes, signaling that no paperboy went beyond this point. The mailbox that bore the route number of our house was small and black, its door tied shut with a piece of string that we did not bother to untie. We proceeded down the road past the quiet-looking brown-and-white sign warning DEAD END and on past the next one imploring strangers to make a U-turn.

We followed the road through the sprawling marsh. Spinney Mill Road takes its name from what used to be here. This part of Maine was once full of tide mills, powered by in- and outgoing currents driving the waterwheels that turned the gears that revolved the stone that ground grist into meal or drove the saw that cut logs into lumber. The energy of the water was captured behind a dam at high tide and released as the tide receded. A mill was established at this crease in the topography in the early eighteenth century, and for the better part of two centuries a couple of saws operated here. In 1766 the works were acquired by John Potter, and from then through the late nineteenth century, the complex bore his name. Even after the brothers William H. and James L. Spinney acquired the works and operated them, people hereabouts still associated the mill operation—but not the road—with the name Potter. The mill continued to be active until the 1930s.

Its cribwork dam and gates were constructed where the marsh creek meets the river. A 1931 survey drawing showed mill structures still standing, and a building labeled "Potter" located just north of the site. Once, logs were floated down the Kennebec to be retrieved at the mill site, and on a wharf there finished lumber waited to be loaded onto vessels that carried it to market. What is now Spinney Mill Road originally came up through the woods to the south, and terminated on the river side of the marsh creek. In time, culverts were installed in the marsh and a causeway carried the road across it, thus providing a more direct access to the mill and the handful of houses by the river. With this extension of the road in place, the old roundabout way from the south was abandoned. Property that once had been at the end of the old road was now the first encountered on Spinney Mill Road. Places changed places.

The marsh, like the land along the riverbank, is now protected against development, which makes great sense practically, ecologically, and aesthetically. The marsh still floods with the incoming tide, but though the water is no longer impounded to drive any machinery, some of the gears and other parts of it remain submerged near the mouth of the creek. What is left of the mill complex are some low walls of stone where the river meets the marsh and some massive timbers that project from the black soil and can be seen when driving over the culvert at low tide. A nearby section of the road can be under water at very high tide, especially if it coincides with a storm wind blowing up the river, so under certain

Looking north over the marsh creek

conditions even automobile and truck drivers hereabouts have to be aware of the tide schedule. Old-timers who still remember the abandoned road supposedly keep it in the back of their minds as an alternate way in and out when the marsh road might be flooded.

The marsh is a natural treasure, an idyllic setting through which the road taken winds toward our place. Though the marsh grass was brown and the cattails had gone to seed by the time we arrived that first fall, we remembered the waving green fronds of summer and would look forward to their return late each spring with the promise of tall and slender new cattails to come. In summer, the expanse of vegetation would appear thick and impenetrable to humans, but not to deer and other wildlife whose refuge it was. With the green stalks withered to brown, the cover was thinned out, and we could see where great patches of vegetation had been flattened by sleeping animals over the course of the summer.

The oldest house on Spinney Mill Road—which we would soon learn to refer to simply as the Road—sits at the top of a steep rise and close to the mouth of the creek. Every time we drive onto the Road, this is the first man-made structure that we see: the home of George and Milly Stafford. He was born on the island in 1924 and she, born about a year and a half earlier, was "from away," as anyone originating outside Maine is said to be. George's parents were from away, his father having been born in Vermont and his mother in Canada, a place to which many Mainers trace their roots. Milly, née Mildred Baldwin, was born, like her parents, in Connecticut. When she was two years old the family moved to Nobleboro, which is about twenty miles up Route 1. Still, she is as much of a Mainer as one from away can be; she is also as much of an Arrowsican as one born off the island can be. She was teased about all this, especially by George, who would live on Arrowsic—people hereabouts do not say "Arrowsic Island"—for all but about thirteen years of his life. When he was six years old, his family had moved to Woolwich, which is just across the bridge to the mainland, but George moved back to Arrowsic when he and Milly married in 1943. His only other subsequent relocation was to the Philippines, where he served with the Marines and earned a Purple Heart. Before joining the service, George had been a welder in the Bath Iron Works shipyard, but employment in the area was hard to come by after the war, so he

The Stafford house

worked in construction until around 1960, when he got a new job in the shipyard, eventually rising to Night Superintendent. It was only after he had returned to the yard that the Staffords moved from a house on Route 127 to the one on Spinney Mill Road, which is where they have lived ever since. The oldest part of the house dates from perhaps the late eighteenth or early nineteenth century. Milly describes its floor being supported by beams that retain the character of tree trunks, in that they were given a flat surface only on the side on which the floor rests; on other sides the roundness of the log is still visible and covered with bark. The house was once occupied by the mill operator and is thought to be one of the oldest extant on the entire island.

George and Milly were long-standing and outstanding citizens of Arrowsic and its environs. At one time or another he served as Arrowsic's constable, fire chief, civil defense director, town meeting moderator, election clerk, and member of the planning board. Milly was no less giving of her time and energies to the town, serving as an election clerk, town health officer, school committee member, and conservation commissioner. She was long considered the informal town historian and in 1979 became the official Town Historian. Those are some of the roles we know that they played in town life, but given their quiet, modest demeanors, we are sure there were many others.

When we learned, shortly after purchasing our place, that George had taken care of it for the previous owners, Catherine called him one Sunday afternoon and asked if he would continue to watch over it during the winter. At first he demurred, saying he was getting too old and didn't need the headaches anymore, but before the phone call ended the septuagenarian agreed reluctantly to do it, with Milly's help, for one last set of owners. He described how he would close the house down for the winter and open it up before we came in the summer, being sure to have ice cubes ready in the freezer. For this, and for general handyman chores, he explained, he would keep track of his time in a small notebook that he carried in his pocket and bill us by the hour. It was agreed that we would shake on the arrangement when we came up in October.

When we first arrived on Arrowsic that fall, we did not encounter the Staffords or anyone else from the four modest white frame houses that we had to pass on the Road before reaching the fork that led us to our retreat. For the first time, we used the right-of-way through our neighbor's property and continued tentatively along it toward the barn, where what was then a neat gravel drive turned and changed to a narrow dirt way that headed toward the river. Finally, we were on the path we had taken when we first saw the property. First the river, then the roof, then the south side, and then the east side of our house came into view. Had the broad expanse of the river in the background not pulled our eyes to it then, as it still does now, I might have suggested that the realtor turn around without our looking inside. The aspect of the building from the drive was the least attractive to me, something I remembered feeling even when looking at the listing photos. The steeply pitched and unrelieved roof dominated the view, the top of the chimney on the far side being barely visible from the approach road. The attic windows in the south gable were crowded up against the eaves, and those on the lower floor lacked even a hint of symmetry or unity. The arrangement suggested an unsuccessful emoticon. Eventually, when I would figure out more about how the house was built, this funky facade and funny fenestration would be something I would come to view more affectionately each time we drove up to the place.

On that first visit as owners, we parked the car facing the river and sat for a few moments watching it over the low bearberry bushes and through the majestic pine trees that lined it. After a while, we walked up to the front door, which faces the river, and opened it with the keys that had been mailed to us. Stepping inside, we were met with the strong smell of naphthalene, which we soon

Approaching our house

discovered was issuing from caches of mothballs that were distrib-
uted everywhere, not only to fend off moths but also to keep mice
away. As we had correctly remembered, the front part of the house
was open in plan, interrupted only by the great stone fireplace that
stood between the kitchen and the living room. The darkening
shades had been drawn, and as we walked around raising them we
opened the house to the vastness of the view up, down, and across
the river. We had no second thoughts about the die we had cast.

What we had done was buy a nearly completely furnished and
equipped house. This was important to us, because we did not relish
having to spend time outfitting one. The previous owners, Harold
and Gladys Monier, had chosen the house's furniture so thoughtfully
and matched the tones of wood and the colors of fabrics so harmo-
niously that in making any changes we would strive to complement
and not revise the existing decor. Certainly the Moniers would not
have objected to the cast-iron ducks that we placed on the hearth.

When we were settled in for our short autumn visit, we called
the Staffords to thank them for having the house ready for us and
invited them to come over so we could all meet. George was a rough
and weathered man and a master at carpentry in the large. One

Cast-iron ducks reunited on the hearth

of the things he had built for the house was a heavy-duty ramp so Mr. Monier's wheelchair could be rolled in and out. The ramp was disassembled when the house went on the market and its parts were stored in the garage, as I would discover the next summer and thereby solve a little mystery that the realtor could not: the theretofore inexplicable rectangular patch of brown lawn directly in front of the stoop was exactly the place where the bottom of the wheelchair ramp had rested and smothered the grass beneath it.

Milly Stafford was as small and delicate looking as George was big and burly. But she was also a strong and determined woman, and she talked twice as fast as he. Being the town historian, she was the source of arcane knowledge about the ways and byways of the island, and was its living archive. It was she who could tell us when the Road was last paved and who had lived in what house and for how long. Milly was as optimistic as George seemed pessimistic. She was also a local booster and fund-raiser. We would come to expect her to drop by around mid-August each year selling raffle tickets to support the volunteer fire department. We always bought the tickets even though we almost never could stay to hear who won the live lobsters raffled off for Labor Day.

Among the pieces of furniture left by the Moniers was a pair of his-and-hers glider rockers, which were positioned to face toward the sofa and thus away from the river. The "his" one is slightly larger and has wider and thicker armrests and less delicate finials than the "hers." Like the king and queen pieces of a chess set, the chairs at the same time match each other and yet have individual identities. These were the chairs in which George and Milly sat when they came over to meet us. After some small talk, I offered our guests something to drink, and George gladly accepted. He sat in the larger chair, resting his glass of Bombay on the flat top of its right arm, and proceeded to tell a story that he would repeat on future occasions. Years earlier, he recalled, when he was sitting in another chair in that exact position, rainwater dripped from the ceiling right into his drink. He was not telling this story as an amusing anecdote of a chance dilution of a straight-up extra-extra-dry martini, but as a revelation to us that we had bought a twist of lemon in this house with a history of once having had a flat roof that leaked. There did not seem to be too much about our house or our ways of which George approved. But his heart was bigger than his bite.

As they were leaving, Milly asked if we would like them to show us the extent of our property. We welcomed the opportunity to see the boundary to the south, which did not look to us to be easily accessible. With the Staffords leading the way, however, paths opened up in the brush that we by ourselves might never have found. Seasoned trail guides, the couple led us up the hill behind the garage and guest cabin to the top of a ridge, then continued to lead us along a perpendicular ridge onto what they called the Wood-Ho property, which abutted ours. The river was to our right and a small mowed meadow to the left. We walked further south before descending along a gentle slope. Then we changed direction

Glider rockers facing inward

and crossed the meadow, which formed a lawn of sorts in front of the Wood-Ho house, which we could not see from ours. After walking around the house—no one seemed to be home—to where it was accessed from the Road, we returned to our own place via the abandoned driveway, the use of which would have imposed upon the privacy of the house we had just circumambulated. It was an instructive trek, and George and Milly let us know that we should feel free to walk around the property of anyone along the Road, as they felt free to walk around ours.

After the Staffords left, I thought about walking all the boundaries of our land, but that proved to be easier said than done. Land in Maine, it seems, had long been defined by distances given "more or less" precisely between certain old pines and lost iron rods. I learned differently when I was in engineering school and went to mandatory summer camp in the Catskills, where we learned the elements of surveying, mostly under the hot afternoon sun in a rolling clearing, carrying stakes, tapes, chains, rods, transits, and levels over land that had been traversed by countless campers before us. We started at a benchmark, a medallion of cast metal embedded in a rock outcrop, and followed a prescribed course of bearings until we ended up in the vicinity of the starting point. The object, of course, was to finish exactly where we started, but the fact that we seldom did so taught us how the little errors we made in our circumnavigation of the predominant hill did not all cancel each other out. Some errors were cumulative and led us astray. We had been prepared for this in the mornings, when we listened to lectures on topics like the distinction between accuracy and precision. In the evenings we were expected to reconcile the morning theory and afternoon experiment and quantify the shortcomings of the tools of the trade. This humbling experience made a lasting impression on me and prepared me to approach real-estate transactions with a skeptical yet practical eye.

Having previously bought and sold real estate in Texas, Illinois, New York, and North Carolina, where most land is cut into a grid like brownies in a baking pan, I had become accustomed to understanding that whatever we owned had a frontage so many feet wide and extended so many feet back from the street or easement line. I could easily picture the rectangle or near rectangle and calculate its square footage in my head and its fraction of an acre on my calculator. This was not so readily done in Maine. As the mortgage-inspection survey showed, the point of land we bought is shaped like a slice of pizza whose hand-tossed crust defies mathematical description. And the deed to the property reads like an arduous journey through the woods or a scavenger hunt for some of the land's ancestor-owners and abutters:

> Beginning at a point on the westerly side of the Town Road, also known as the Spinney Mill Road, at the northeast corner of that

portion of the property now or formerly of Richard R. Steen and Claire W. Steen, which is now located on the westerly side of said Town Road . . . thence running in a general southwesterly direction along said land of Steen a distance of 137 feet more or less, to an iron pipe; thence running in a general westerly direction along the northerly line of land now or formerly of John Wood and Manli Ho a distance of 235 feet, more or less, to a 24 inch in diameter pine tree (1984) marking the point of beginning of the premises conveyed herein; thence continuing in a general westerly direction along land of said Wood and Ho a distance of 430 feet, more or less, to the base of a large pine tree that hangs over the Kennebec River; thence running in a general northeasterly direction along the Kennebec River a distance of 600 feet, more or less, to an iron rod at the base of a 12 inch in diameter pine tree (1984), which said pine tree stands at the mouth of a small swale; thence running S 16° W (1984 magnetic) along land of William I. Krachy and Roberta S. Krachy . . . a distance of 163 feet, more or less to an iron rod adjacent to the northerly sideline of a gravel driveway which runs from the westerly sideline of the Spinney Mill Road to the premises conveyed herein; then continuing on a bearing of S 16° W a distance of 246 feet, more or less, to the point of beginning.

Reaching that "point of beginning" by strictly following the directions was as difficult in real life beside the Kennebec as it was at surveying camp in the Catskills. The directions were clear, more or less, if one could only tell the relevant from the irrelevant pines. The land was covered with pine trees, and others no doubt had been cut down or uprooted in storms, fallen into the river, or just plain died in the decade or so between 1984 and when we bought the property. How was one to measure hundreds of feet along the crusty river-bank, where the brackish water ebbed and flowed with the tide? And what was one to do when the iron rod that was supposed to be at the base of a twelve-inch pine was nowhere to be found? We took it on faith that what was being conveyed to us was what we understood to be a little over three acres of land with about six hundred feet, more or less, of deep-water frontage. That sounded about right to us.

We had trusted our attorney in Bath when he assured us that we were not buying a pig in a poke. We put the imprecise survey out of our minds, but did hang a framed printout of the quaint narrative in a dark corner of the house, where it catches our eye now and then. Our slice of Midcoast Maine was most prominently defined by the Kennebec River, and for the time being, at least, that was good enough for us. We would take George and Milly at their word and not worry about artificial boundaries based on real or imagined trees.

But not everything would be a walk in the woods, real or otherwise. On one occasion, our water pump stopped operating. We had been warned that wells can run dry hereabouts, and so we had become conscientious about taking short showers and not leaving the water running while brushing our teeth. Catherine prepared typographically discreet water-conservation signs that she placed by the sinks and showers guests would be using. The morning the faucets yielded nothing at all we called George and asked for advice. He said he would come by after lunch; he showed up with little more than a pocketknife. He went down into the basement, I following with a flashlight. I watched him tap this and that valve and pipe. He was taciturn as he put his ear to one of the pipes and appeared to be listening intently for something. After a quiet minute or two, I asked him what he was doing. He said he was listening for a leak, which might have caused the well to be pumped dry and the pump to be damaged. I was impressed.

When there did not appear to be a leak, he returned to the area where the pump and accumulators are. A typical accumulator is a domed steel tank with an inflatable bladder inside. As the tank is filled, the water becomes pressurized against the bladder. When an upstairs faucet is opened, the pressure drives the water against gravity through the pipes and out the tap. The Moniers had installed a second, larger accumulator to supplement the first one, thereby storing more water under pressure and requiring the pump to work longer at a time but less frequently overall. This is desirable, since the noise of the pump is jarring when it starts and stops and is hard to ignore while it is running. Nevertheless, every time George saw the second accumulator he swore it was not doing anything at all, and he wanted to disconnect it. He never provided what I considered a rational defense of his belief, however, and so I would not let him remove it from the system.

After we had gotten past the red-herring accumulator issue, George attacked the pump. With a wrench I provided from my limited toolbox, he first tapped and then unscrewed the pressure gauge, apparently thinking it might be stuck or clogged. Not finding either to be obviously the case, he reinstalled the gauge and focused on the control box on the side of the pump. After tapping it several times with the handle of his knife, he used the screwdriver blade to remove the cover. As he lifted it off, a burst of sparks was released: one of the wires had become loose inside. He turned off the electrical power and worked at reattaching the loose wire, but the thin blade of his pocketknife kept slipping out of the screw's wide slot. Eventually, when all appeared to be ready, he turned the power back on and the pump began working normally, to our great relief. George continued to tinker with the controller, adjusting the screws that set the pressure limits at which the pump starts up and shuts down. When he found it working to his liking, he put the cover back on and talked again about the ineffective accumulator.

The more we got to know George, the more we came to like him. His ways were set in Maine, as was his heart. Standoffish and deliberate as real Mainers can be, they are honest and frugal to a fault. They believe what they believe, even if it is dead wrong, and they will work on a stubborn control box for hours rather than take the easy way out and buy and install a replacement. After his work on our water problem, in our presence George entered his time in his notebook and put it back in his pocket. Like a waiter in a European restaurant, he would bring the bill to us only when we called for it. Or so we thought.

Three

LOOKING
AROUND

THE RIVER VIEW WAS what sold us on our retreat, and for the first couple of visits the water was the main focus of our attention. When there were no visitors expected, we turned the glider rockers away from the sofa to face the picture windows, so that we could look out upon the river as we floated slowly on the waves simulated by our mechanical chairs. The opposite bank of the Kennebec is the eastern shore of the Phippsburg peninsula, which from our view seemed to be almost nothing but trees. In our first years in the house, there was only one building visible across the river, and that was a large three-story structure painted white and sitting high atop a ridge. Except for the clearing around that building, the tree line remained uninterrupted and remarkably uniform in height for as far as we could see. The notch created by the improved land only emphasized this and made the view all the more interesting. The clearing continued down the hill from the large white building and ended at a boat ramp in Morse Cove, which is directly across from us. Before dawn, the line of headlights stretching up the hill told us that boats on trailers were being brought down to the boat-launch ramp. After dawn, we watched these and then other boats move about the river, now and then stopping and casting fishing lines.

We never tired of watching the activity on the water, but in time we began to look about us at our house itself. None other we had owned had the natural distraction of a river or such a panoramic view, but when we turned our backs on the water and looked inward at the house we found it to be equally fascinating. Although our place in Maine is of the same vintage as our home in North Carolina and although both share some fundamental similarities of construction, they could not be more dissimilar. Both houses are wood-framed, but their spindly skeletons are concealed and revealed in very different ways.

Our southern home is faced with brick and its inside walls are finished with drywall and paint, thus leaving the grain of wood

Glider rockers facing river

exposed only in the hardwood floors and shoe molding. Just before we bought it, the house had been thoroughly renovated: walls added and removed, living areas expanded, kitchen and bathrooms redone, floors refinished, and style generally "modernized." The workmanship of that renovation, as we discovered over the course of years, was also modernized, in the sense that it was done more quickly and cheaply than was hinted at in the carefully chosen cosmetic distractions of interior decoration. It all looked good and fresh for a few years, the quick fixes and inferior materials having been covered over with strategically placed rugs and carpeting. Soft and squeaky floors were silenced with shims and shams. Imprecise carpentry had been finished with caulking that has not aged well. That house, like so many newer houses, is an ongoing project of remediation.

By contrast, our Maine house is faced with cedar siding; its interior walls are finished in knotty pine—wood on wood on wood. There is not a piece of drywall anywhere. No caulking was used to hide misfit joints; indeed, in the original structure you have to look long and hard to find a misfit anything. The house was designed and built with care and pride. There were some alterations made about thirty years into its life, but so much of the original fabric was left untouched that some poor decisions in the upgrades can largely be ignored, most of the time.

The living-room wall that we face in our inward-looking gliders is representative of the original house. It is covered with knotty-pine paneling that is strikingly beautiful in color and texture, which change with the position of the sun, minute by minute and hour by hour and day by day. Each vertical board is delineated by the pair of distinct V-shaped grooves that mark junctures with its neighbors, thus allowing a board to retain its individuality among the two dozen or so other boards that make up this wall section. The vast majority of the boards are nominally eight inches wide, but the presence at intervals of a narrower or broader one relieves what might otherwise be too mechanically repetitive or rigidly geometric a pattern. A single eight-inch board of the same knotty pine set horizontally forms an elegant baseboard flush with the wall. The tops of the wall boards meet the ceiling's exposed timber beams in the modern fashion, sans molding. The overall effect is stunning, due in no small part to the impeccable workmanship that went into the house six decades ago. Indeed, the more I looked at all the living-room walls, as well as the others throughout the house, the more I came to realize how much of the house's character was in the subtle details of its design and realization.

I wanted to celebrate this house as a masterpiece, hold it up as an exemplar of careful workmanship, share it as a model of what can be achieved with thoughtful planning, talented labor, and careful

Living-room wall and opening to bedrooms

execution. It soon became my preoccupation to study the house as the product of a creative individual—a designer, a planner, a builder, a carpenter, a craftsman, a finisher, an artist, a carver of poems in wood. Because my career has been one of explaining failures and finding fault with designs, I am not able to restrain myself from being also a critic, even of that which I love. Parts of the house have been altered in ways inferior to the original work. I could not overlook that, but I wanted to see beyond it. I became determined to uncover the elements of the original version and perhaps glimpse the intent of its maker, but I was equally determined to do so without harming the primary structure. I resolved to remove no nail, screw, or board. My deconstruction would be totally nondestructive.

I was confident that the observable facts about the house would provide plenty of basis for informed speculation about how its builder thought and how he acted. Every nailhead is like a data point, representing a bit of information. Collectively, the nails reveal a plot, not necessarily of a graph but of the mystery of a man and his house. The clues are scattered here and there, some more visible than others, some more subtle than others, some more relevant than others. The best mysteries are not open-and-shut cases, but are those that are draped in complex folds in dimly lit settings, with multiple rooms to enter and exit, multiple doors to open and pass through. This house certainly has plenty of doors, especially to closets, and the structures within are very revealing. I have spent much spare time exploring the house's design and construction, coaxing clues out of its fabric.

Difficult as it might have been to walk the precise boundaries of our riverfront property, even aided by walking sticks but unencumbered with surveying instruments, it is easy to circumambulate this rectangular house and grasp its rectilinear layout. But the deceptively simple geometry would prove to have concealed behind its rigid planes of knotty pine the ghosts of its construction. From old-timers on the Road we would hear contradictory explanations of why the house was designed and built the way it was. And the more inconsistent stories and theories I encountered, the more determined I became to find in the house itself—the physical artifact—the logic of its design and the story of its building. I assumed that the house was the result of a rational process and that traces of that process remained embedded in it as secrets of its success and as clues to its construction.

A house first needs a place on which to be built. At one time, all the land around the cove that bounds our property on the north—plus acreage that reached eastward across the marsh, through the woods beyond, and up to and across the shore of a freshwater pond

Inside a closet, showing exposed studs,
furring strips, and back side of paneling

and part of its associated marsh—was owned by a family named Phinney. Edgar Ellsworth Phinney was born in 1876 in St. Martins, New Brunswick, a village on the Bay of Fundy. In 1912, in Lynn, Massachusetts, he married Gertrude Agnes Bradbury. She was born in Boston to parents who both had come from Canada. The following year the Phinneys moved to West Orange, New Jersey, where Thomas Edison lived and had established his "invention factory," facts in which the inventor Edgar Phinney may have found inspiration. The Phinneys had relocated to New Jersey so he could join the newly organized Monroe Calculating Machine Company at the time of its establishment in Orange. He was chief engineer for one of its early high-speed adding machines and later became head of the company's research and development efforts. Many of his inventions for calculating means and mechanisms were patented and the rights assigned to Monroe, whose mechanical and later electromechanical calculators were cutting-edge equipment for engineers in the age before digital computers and electronic calculators.

From the beginning of their married years together, Edgar and Gertrude spent at least part of their summers on Arrowsic. In August 1931, he drew in his best engineer's hand a map that showed properties deeded separately to him, to Gertrude, and to his brother Elton H. Phinney, and also to their abutters and neighbors, along with improvements thereon, including the old Spinney mill and wharf. Edgar owned the property on which those commercial structures stood and additional land around the millpond and creek and along the river and half around the cove. Gertrude's land fronted on the rest of the cove and a stretch of the river and reached across the Road and the marsh and the state road to the pond beyond. Unlike eighteenth-century divisions of the island, her 925-foot-wide slice of Arrowsic no longer reached all the way to the eastern shore.

Edgar and Gertrude moved to the island as year-round residents upon his retirement in the mid-1940s, living in the old Spinney house, which Edgar had previously acquired. They were spending the winter of 1949 in New Jersey with their son Robert when after a brief illness Edgar passed away. A couple of years later, a parcel of land on the south side of the cove and stretching inland from the river was given by Gertrude to Robert and his wife, Wilhelmina, so that they could build a house on it for their family. At first it might have been intended as a camp or summer place, but it would in time become much more than that.

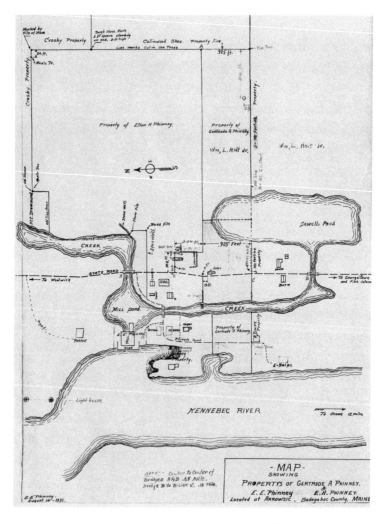

Edgar Phinney's 1931 map

Robert Edgar Phinney had been born to Edgar and Gertrude in West Orange in 1915, and as a boy he demonstrated considerable woodworking skills. When a teenager, he entered a model-building contest known as the Fisher Body Craftsman's Guild competition, which was sponsored by the automobile-body manufacturing division of General Motors. Only boys aged twelve through nineteen were eligible to enter the annual competition, for which they had to construct a one-eighteenth-scale model of the horse-drawn coach that appeared on the "Body by Fisher" emblem, which was affixed to the doorsill plate of GM automobiles into the 1990s. The coach represented the excellence in craftsmanship that General Motors strived for in its car bodies. The design of this Fisher Body trademark carriage was a combination of two used by the Emperor Napoleon—one for his coronation in 1804 and one for his marriage to Marie-Louise, the archduchess of Austria, in 1810.

The Craftsman's Guild competition was established in 1930. In its earliest years, entrants in the contest were provided blueprints of the coach; before long there was a sizable booklet of plans and instructions from which the boys were to work. Contests to build a model Napoleonic coach ran through 1947 and overlapped for the last ten years with model-car competitions, in which boys could build a scale-model automobile of their own devising. The entries were suggestive of futuristic vehicles, and the contest not only served public-relations objectives but also provided GM an opportunity to identify designer talent at an early age and to recruit prospects for its design teams. In 1968, the last year of the model competition, 55 percent of GM's creative design staff had been involved in the Fisher Body Craftsman's Guild.

Making a truly competitive Napoleonic carriage model, which when finished would measure eighteen by eight by ten inches, required the contestant to work on it for about three hours a day for almost an entire year. This amounted to about a thousand hours of work, with some boys spending half again as much time on the project. In extreme cases, a boy might put in about two thousand hours, the equivalent of a full-time job. In the beginning years of the contests, participating boys were expected to secure their own materials and build the coach from scratch. Soon, however, enterprising packagers sold kits containing all the needed materials, including blocks of different kinds of wood (balsa, mahogany, maple, pine) that could be carved into the appropriate parts. One kit contained precast intricate metal parts, such as the filigree trim that bordered the coach roof and the imperial eagles that were mounted on its corners. However, making everything from scratch gave an entrant an advantage in the judging, which at an early stage of each competition was done by General Motors designers and engineers and at a later stage by engineering educators. International awards included four-year college scholarships and a virtual guarantee of a job with GM. In both junior and senior divisions, each national grand prize was a $5,000 college scholarship, which at the end of the Depression was about three times an average worker's annual salary. At that time, the sum could buy eight Chevrolets or Fords, and it was enough money to buy a house.

Posters announcing the new competition and its prizes were displayed in GM automobile showrooms, where interested boys could join the Guild and receive a membership card, official bronze pin, and a set of plans for the model carriage. Advertisements were placed in newspapers and magazines. Newspapers also promoted the Guild and its competitions with stories announcing them, with features about how to proceed in building a model, and with reports of events associated with the judging and awarding of prizes. The Boy Scouts of America became affiliated with the Guild, providing another means for boys to learn of its existence and promise. There were many ways in which a boy like young Bob Phinney, who was a Boy Scout, could have learned about the model-building contest.

In promoting the competition each year, General Motors wished to identify young and promising designers-to-be who had, among other qualities, an artistic sensibility, a good sense of proportion, manual dexterity, and a "propensity for perfection." The house that

Phinney would build as an adult attests to his having had those traits. In the contest's first year, potential model builders were given a booklet on the history and influence of crafts guilds, in which a young boy could read, "The man who can work surely, swiftly and deftly with his hands is always preferable in any employment." In the Guild's official magazine, *The Guildsman,* William A. Fisher, general manager of the Fisher Body Division, wrote that "it is only the fully trained and competent craftsman which can carry this machine civilization to higher levels of efficiency and service to mankind" and that what the world needed most was craftsmen "who are masters of every detail of their jobs." It was at the first Craftsman's Guild awards banquet that GM's president, Alfred P. Sloan Jr., went beyond motivating words; he promised the four top national prizewinners jobs after college. A teenage boy growing up in the Depression could not help but take notice of such an inducement.

Membership in the Guild soon numbered in the hundreds of thousands, but the exacting standards and demands associated with building a competitive model meant that only those boys with the ability and time would submit a completed entry. In the first year of the competition, 1,350 coaches were entered; in the second, 547. (An apprentice class of Guild membership was established in 1934, thus allowing boys to compete by making a model of a simpler design known as a Traveling Coach, thereby gaining experience in model building and encouragement for taking on larger challenges later.) The models of Napoleonic coaches were judged anonymously and rigorously; the time judges spent evaluating just one entry could approach two hours. Only boys with uncommon talent, commitment, and patience survived the ordeal. Young Robert Phinney was one of them.

In 1931, fifteen-year-old New Jerseyan Bob Phinney became a member of the Fisher Body Craftsman's Guild, built a model, and won a prize, though not one of the national prizes. The experience no doubt helped prepare him to build two decades later not just a model house but a real one—the one we now own. His prize money

helped him attend Newark College of Engineering, where he studied mechanical engineering. If he had an opportunity to join General Motors, he declined it, choosing instead to stay close to home.
He took a job as a draftsman, a usual entry-level position, working under his research-engineer father at Monroe, whose products
were symbolically and actually an integral part of the "machine
civilization." The younger Phinney rode to and from work with his
boss, and he would continue to do so for about a decade.

Bob Phinney's future bride, Wilhelmina Straatsma, was born in
1917 to Dutch immigrants living in Roselle Park, New Jersey, which
is only about five miles south of the Oranges. Her mother died in
childbirth, and so her father brought up Billie, as she was called, and
her brother, Theodore, who would die of a ruptured appendix when
he was fourteen years old. The small family lived in a small house in a
small village known as Newark Meadows, where Billie later recalled
that they "had to always watch the cottage and be very careful. The
silverware and linens were often stolen when you turned around."
The area was eventually demolished, and Billie joked that her childhood home was buried under the main runway at Newark Airport.

Billie Straatsma attended the Orange Memorial Hospital School
of Nursing, where one of her classmates was Evelyn Phinney, Bob's
sister. For him, when he showed up one day to give the girls a ride,
it was love at first sight. For her, ever the joker, he was her ride. Bob
and Billie were married on New Year's Eve in 1938 and, according
to census records, lived with his parents for a while before moving
into a "family development" in the Newark suburb of Livingston,
which is within a couple of miles of the Oranges. Livingston was
still Bob's address of record in late 1952, when an application was
filed for his patent on an improvement in two-color ribbon control
devices for printing calculators. But if his activity outside the workplace is any indication, he may have enjoyed inventing mechanisms
somewhat less than he did building models and houses.

After living all their lives so close to their respective birth-
places, Bob and Billie Phinney decided to move to Arrowsic and

live across the cove from where his parents had settled in retirement. The younger Phinneys saw Maine as a "new frontier." To Billie, such an adventure was akin to the one her parents undertook early in the century, when they emigrated from Holland and entered the United States through Ellis Island. It was different in one big regard, however, and that was that unlike her mother and father, who were young and unmarried when they set out on their adventure in America, Bob and Billie moved to Maine as they were approaching middle age—he being thirty-nine and she thirty-seven—and had four children: Sandra, aged fifteen; Robert Jr., ten; Peter, seven; and William, four. To Bob Phinney, the opportunity to move must have promised an escape from working nine-to-five in an office in New Jersey. But first, of course, he and his family had to have a place in which to live. He would begin working on his house beside the Kennebec over summer vacations in the early 1950s, two decades after he crafted his model Napoleonic coach.

Exactly how the house that Catherine and I bought in 1997 was actually conceived, planned, designed, and built remains a mystery, but it all appears to have been thought out by Phinney the engineer with some, if not considerable, deliberation. It was executed by him with uncommon attention to detail and with great care. To me, its position on the land relative to the water, its orientation to the river and the wind that comes down it, the division of its interior space by wood and stone alone, and even the texture and durability of its surfaces all attest to the place being the result of either a great deal of deep thought and calculation or an uncommon amount of good luck. It is as if Phinney had followed the spirit if not the rules of siting a structure that the Roman architect-engineer Vitruvius had laid down two millennia earlier, and been inspired by the genius if not the goals for laying out inner space and fenestration that the Venetian architect Andrea Palladio demonstrated in the sixteenth century.

Vitruvius believed that architecture should imitate nature, and so houses should be built of natural materials. In this way, just as a bird's nest of straw and twigs protects its contents, so a properly built house would give adequate shelter to its inhabitants. Also, according to Vitruvius, a man-built structure should exhibit three qualities: solidity, usefulness, and beauty. Palladio was greatly influenced by his reading of Vitruvius. Although the Italian designed churches and palaces, he became known especially for his villas, in which he employed not grand materials like the stone and marble of city architecture but common ones like brick and stucco, thus making country homes affordable even for less affluent gentry. Palladio's division of interior space was a brilliant integration of rooms of different shape, size, and scale, and his striking fenestration lives on in the Palladian window, consisting of narrower sections flanking a wider, taller, and arched central portion.

But Phinney was neither a classical architect nor even, as far as I know, a student of architecture. His house is not in the least literally Vitruvian or Palladian. What I deduce from his design and construction is that he was a folk architect and a builder in the vernacular, but the house he designed and built was anything but common. It was, in the words of Le Corbusier, *une machine-à-habiter*—a machine for living in—and it was a custom-made machine. It was a structure worthy of an engineer who had worked on precision calculating machines.

Yet the question remains, where did Phinney get his ideas? Did he find some elevations and floor plans to his liking in a book or magazine? Or was he simply self-inspired? What clues, if any, did he leave for us to uncover?

From ancient times, planners, designers, builders, and workers have left evidence of their having been part of a construction project, whether as a leader or a follower. Some simply left their initials or some cryptic autobiographical graffito as testimonial to their contribution. Some have left hints of their involvement in simple drawings or sketches of their plans or worked-out details scratched in stone or penciled on wood. Even modern-era furniture can reveal the hint of a craftsman's hand or thought process by means of rough sketches or precise figures and calculations scrawled on the underside of a tabletop, on the back of a chest, or on the bottom of a drawer. If Phinney did use a pencil to sketch out a floor plan or a construction detail on a sheet of paper or a piece of lumber, perhaps he erased or planed over his thoughts, treating the medium as if it were to be reused as a palimpsest, ready to receive a revised idea. Or, perhaps he burned any plans he had made, feeling that holding his hands over a warm fire in winter was more satisfying and necessary than holding in his hands a rendering of what he already held in his mind. Or, after the house was done, he may have burned any executed plans, the way some homeowners say they burned a paid-off mortgage. Engineers are not known for being sentimental. Once their plans are realized in steel or concrete or stone or wood, unless the structure is monumental they tend not to take the time to reconstruct the thing in another medium. But a certain amount of thinking beforehand is essential, for how else could the kinds and quantities of building materials needed be calculated, ordered, and delivered to a construction site?

One nonverbal medium for thinking through a design beforehand is more difficult to dispose of afterward, and that is a physical model. Christopher Wren created a series of scale models to show his various ideas for a new St. Paul's Cathedral that was to be part of the rebuilding of London after the fire of 1666. One, known as his Great Model, was made out of oak and plaster and stands thirteen feet tall. It is a work of art in itself, and so has survived and has been on display in the cathedral, where visitors could maneuver themselves under it to stand with their head in the space beneath the dome and so gain a 360-degree perspective on the interior design. Unfortunately, the royal commission whose approval was required found it too radical, so the church that was built differs considerably from what the model shows. Wren's ultimate experience with models was in fact not favorable, and he complained that they were time-consuming and, by making the proposed design so easily grasped by everyone, made it subject to the criticism of "incompetent judges." Would Phinney have wanted to risk such judgment?

Catherine and I had lived in our Phinney house for almost fifteen years without finding or being made aware of any model, specification, or blueprint, and we had given up hope of their existence. If there were any evidence of the builder's thinking scrawled anywhere, I figured that it would be found in dark, unfinished places—the basement and the closets. However, only further questions arose out of the basement's shadowy recesses. In the closets, sandwiched between the walls of adjoining rooms, the exposed backs of paneling were as clean as freshly planed wood. I would discover a few pencil marks as my investigations progressed, but they always seemed to refer to a step in the execution rather than a sketch of an overall plan.

Phinney certainly must have used a pencil or point to scribe or scratch a mark on pieces of lumber he measured and cut to size, and he must have followed the wise rule of measuring twice and cutting once. How else could he have achieved the impeccable fits that he did? But for a long time I could find no marks on any cut board. Could he have positioned the saw, and hence the kerf—the slot that the blade makes in progressing through the wood—directly over his mark, effectively obliterating the line by pushing and pulling his saw blade as if it were the sharp edge of an eraser?

Whatever rules he may have followed, Phinney certainly achieved a finished product that attests to the care he took in measuring and sawing every piece of lumber in the house. Had he not, the result of carelessness would be evident where wall-panel board meets windowsill or ceiling rafter or doorpost or lintel—all butt joints that Phinney left exposed as finished work. His careful carpentry meant that there was no need for cosmetic trim to cover sloppy work, no call for molding to conceal gaps, and no use for architectural millwork of any kind to hide rough juxtapositions. None of this would be true had he failed to follow a consistent approach in sawing lumber or failed to take into account the thickness of a saw blade or a pencil line or the angle at which he held the pencil against the edge of the steel framing square or try square that he certainly must have used. In other words, Phinney understood that the seemingly straightforward act of sawing off a piece of lumber of a needed length can be just as affected by the carpenter's equivalent of Heisenberg's Uncertainty Principle and the phenomenon of parallax as an experiment in high-energy physics or an observation in astronomy. The simple acts of the everyday world are embedded in the larger universe by the natural laws and theories of science, the hidebound traditions and formal styles of architecture, the familiar tools and rules-of-thumb of carpentry, and the ubiquitous equations and mysterious heuristics of engineering.

Well into the 1800s, buildings had continued to be framed with posts and beams the way they had been since medieval times. Heavy hand-hewn timbers were connected together largely by means of mortise-and-tenon joints, the kind that can still be found in centuries-old houses and barns. When any kind of nails were used at all, they tended to be treenails—also known as and pronounced *trunnels*—which were effectively wooden pegs or dowels pounded into prebored holes. The practice had long been common in wooden shipbuilding, where metal nails could corrode and tend to promote wood rot. Considerable knowledge and skill were demanded of the boat- or house builder who used only wood, for he had to use a suitable kind and work it with care. A practiced joiner—as a worker in wood who does not use iron nails or metal fasteners of any kind is known—can fashion with saw and chisel the strong framing connections that result from a close-fitting joint. (Recall that Shakespeare chose the name Snug for the joiner in *A Midsummer Night's Dream*.) Joinery was mastered only after a long apprenticeship. Furthermore, the process itself was time-consuming, and the weight of the timbers that had to be lifted into place called for helping hands. It was not practical for an unskilled amateur wishing to build a house for his family to tackle such a task all by himself.

Traditional post-and-beam construction is promoted and taught today at the Shelter Institute, which was established in 1974 in Bath, Maine, and now is based just a few miles up U.S. 1, in Woolwich. A bare structural frame of eastern white pine native to the state stands next to the highway and serves as a landmark for the road leading to Shelter's campus. By pulling off to the side of the road, the curious can inspect the frame and its details. Where not spanned by a truss, the eight-by-eight-inch posts are set about ten feet apart and the tight mortise-and-tenon joints between the posts and beams are inferred rather than seen. The sure giveaway is the round pegs that have been left projecting from the round holes wherever there is a tenon locked in place. Precut timber kits for such a frame can be bought and shipped from the Institute to wherever a building is desired. The frame can be enclosed with a variety of cladding, including prefabricated insulated panels, and a metal roof. I can attest personally to how well nail-less and screw-less construction works. Years ago, from a source other than Shelter, Catherine and I purchased a mail-order kit for a teak bench and assembled it using nothing but glue and pegs to secure its precut mortise-and-tenon joints. The bench remains strong and sturdy today after many summers of sitting outside in the weather.

A couple of things happened in the early nineteenth century that changed the way buildings were erected, at least in the United States and Canada. For one, steam engines began to power sawmills, which meant that they no longer had to be located beside a stream or river or driven by tidal power. Mills also began increasingly to produce lumber in more or less standard sizes. Although a national size standard would not exist until the next century, it became possible at least on a regional basis to obtain lumber with common dimensions smaller than those of the timbers used by house-building joiners. Thus relatively lightweight wooden

Post-and-beam frame beside U.S. 1

structural components could more readily be secured closer to a frontier building site and so transported to it more easily, thereby making construction using the lumber less expensive. Around the same time, the manufacture of iron nails was undergoing change from a handwrought process done at a small forge—producing one nail at a time—to more continuous processes in which nails were formed from iron rods or plates by machine action that cut off the appropriate length and pointed and headed it. This, of course, made nails more uniform in size and shape, and made them more readily available in large quantities at a relatively low price, which with improved machinery continued to drop. Whereas a pound of wrought nails might have cost twenty-five cents around the turn of the nineteenth century, only a few decades later machine-made "cut nails" could be had for five cents a pound.

Out of these developments came a new way of framing houses and other types of buildings. No longer was it necessary to engage a practiced joiner to build the structure; now the job could be done by a carpenter capable of hammering a couple of nails through one piece

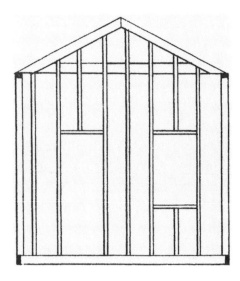

Balloon-framed gable wall

of wood and into another, thereby connecting them without the precision of a snug mortise-and-tenon joint. The resulting lightweight building skeleton came to be known as a "balloon frame," but scholars have debated the exact origins of the revolutionary concept and the curious term used to describe it.

According to the historian and modern-architecture critic Sigfried Giedion, writing in his influential *Space, Time and Architecture,* the first example of a balloon-framed structure was a simple church erected in Chicago in 1833, though later scholars are less certain. In any case, the method was rationalized by William E. Bell in his 1857 book, *Carpentry Made Easy; or, The Science and Art of Framing, on a New and Improved System.* Bell, self-described as a "practical carpenter," argued that a knowledge of geometry was essential to understand why things were done the way they were in the trade. He was thinking, especially, of "the rules for obtaining the bevels of rafters, joists, braces, &c.," which could be learned by rote but which could not easily be extended to new situations without a more fundamental understanding of the geometrical principles upon which they were based.

The defining characteristic of the new system of balloon framing lay in the vertical wooden studs that run from the lower horizontal piece of lumber, or sill plate, set atop the foundation to the upper one, known as a top or upper wall plate, at the level where the wall meets the eaves of the roof, the whole being held in place by nails only. Early writers on the subject both praised and ridiculed the framing concept. On the plus side, it was maintained that neither Chicago nor San Francisco could have grown so quickly from a small village to a significant city had it not been for the balloon frame. There simply were not a sufficient number of experienced joiners among the early settlers to raise so many buildings in so short a time. According to the architectural historian Carl Condit, the balloon frame was "a masterpiece of vernacular building," whose great advantage lay in its simplicity. Furthermore, "an energetic man with moderate skill in carpentry and a saw, hammer, and a bag of nails could build a house or barn in little more than a week. A small crew could build a town."

Generally it was held that, whereas it took a team of men to put up a post-and-beam frame, a man with the help of a boy could erect a balloon frame. Furthermore, even if a carpenter were employed to provide the labor, the cost of a balloon-frame structure was estimated to be 40 percent less than that of a post-and-beam one. And the construction was definitely fast, with some of the early balloon-frame houses in Chicago said to have been lived in within a week of their having been commissioned. The city was rebuilt in no time after the great fire of 1871, thanks to the use of the balloon frame. No wonder the method has also been called "Chicago construction."

As happens with virtually any innovation that threatens to displace an established technology, traditionalists opposed the new method. Joiners who had made a living constructing heavy-timber, mortise-and-tenon buildings naturally criticized the balloon frame. While the term may have been chosen to reflect the ease with which such a frame goes up, like a hot-air balloon, some said the name itself was given in derision. The practical carpenter William Bell seemed to take no offense, however, using it without comment or apology in *Carpentry Made Easy,* suggesting that it was well-established terminology by the mid-1850s. Nevertheless, the term did also suggest that a structure made of the lightweight framing could be, like a balloon, blown away in the wind. An alternative and kinder etymology has the word *balloon* being used jocularly, as a familiar and good-natured nickname for the lightweight construction. The term "basket frame" was suggested as a more descriptive and less derisive name for the structural form, but the more colorful "balloon frame" stuck. In the meantime, nail-making technology continued to advance, and by the end of the nineteenth century nails were being made from steel wire fed into machines that cut, pointed, and headed "wire nails" automatically. No longer were nails typically square or rectangular in cross section; now they were round.

The term balloon frame is often applied to two-story structures, in which studs as long as twenty feet reach from the foundation sill to the wall plate under the roof. The second-floor joists rest on horizontal lengths of wood, known as ribbands, that also tie together and stabilize the long studs. Unfortunately, because the space between the studs can result in an air space connecting the first and second floors, such construction can allow fire to spread from floor to floor, and so a modified system known as platform framing has come to be preferred. In this kind of framing, studs reaching only a story high are used. For a multistory house, each floor rests on a platform built on the walls beneath, thereby introducing fire blocks between the floors. In recognition of the roots of balloon-frame construction originating in the American West, such construction is sometimes referred to as western platform framing; collectively, all stud-based framing is referred to as light-frame or stick construction. By the time Bob Phinney began to contemplate building his house on Arrowsic, light-frame construction was firmly established as the building method requiring the least lumber and the least time, and it was what he would use to build his house.

In the meantime, a new wrinkle had developed in the home-building industry. From Colonial times, house designs had been copied and adapted from pattern books, many loosely based on the model of Palladio's *Four Books of Architecture*, which had in turn been greatly influenced by Vitruvius's *Ten Books on Architecture*. In the mid-nineteenth century, the American horticulturist and landscape designer Andrew Jackson Downing published *Cottage Residences*, which contained not only designs for houses but also plans for laying out their gardens and grounds. Around the turn of the twentieth century, there began to appear mail-order catalogs issued by the likes of Sears, Roebuck; Montgomery Ward; and the Bay City, Michigan–based Aladdin Company, all of which took the concept of a pattern book one stage further. These catalogs presented not only sketches of attractive home styles and drawings of their floor plans but also offered to sell the house so pictured to the prospective customer, even in some cases providing mortgage financing. There were several options, ranging from ordering a turnkey house, which the seller would arrange to have constructed for the buyer, to ordering a kit containing all the lumber, hardware, and other materials needed to build the house yourself, the option that newly married Bob and Billie Phinney chose for Livingston, New Jersey: a small Cape Cod kit house that they purchased from Sears, Roebuck for $5,000, land included.

The idea had been tried on Arrowsic. In the early 1900s, there was located on the east side of the island a tidal sawmill owned by the brothers Charles and Guy Crosby. An earthen dam and tide gates separated the tidal Back River from a pond in which water was impounded to drive the saw. In 1912, for $710 the Crosby Mill supplied Arrowsic resident Ibra Lawrence with all the materials needed to build a house for his family not far from the mill. The mill also catered to "city folk" wishing to build a summer cottage in the area and would prepare all the needed lumber and at the mill store assemble it and additional building materials like nails, shingles, and windows. When everything was ready for delivery, it was loaded onto a scow that a boat towed close to the construction site.

In more populated areas, and where water transport was not practical, larger suppliers like Sears and Wards used the railroad to deliver all the items on a bill of materials. The thousands of pieces of precut lumber needed, along with all the nails for fastening them together, would be brought to the mail-order house buyer's hometown in a railroad car. The advantage of having the lumber ready-cut was one of the selling points of the mail-order home. A catalog touting the Aladdin Readi-Cut System, for example, demonstrated how the builder saved money "by getting 20 feet of lumber from a 16-foot board." Drawings showed how cleverly reorienting the board after each saw cut produced siding pieces for a gable that resulted in no wasted triangles of wood. Such precut lumber not only insured the do-it-yourselfer against waste due to lack of cleverness, mismeasuring, or miscutting, but also saved time, eliminating hours spent with the tape measure, rule, square, pencil, and saw, not to mention not having to handle unnecessarily long, heavy, and unwieldy pieces of lumber. Some kit houses were advertised as capable of being assembled by a single person handy with tools in a matter of weeks or months, or by an industrious couple in about fifteen weekends.

The heyday of the mail-order home began to end with the Great Depression. Montgomery Ward's Wardway Homes ceased doing business in 1931, and Sears Modern Homes closed shop in 1940. In the postwar years, the proliferation of modestly priced tract homes, epitomized by those in Long Island's Levittown, put the final nails in the pine coffin of ready-cut home businesses that had survived the Depression. Aladdin Homes soldiered on until 1981, making it the last of the major old-time players to give up the game.

But the game itself was far from over, as smaller, regional firms began to offer prefabricated roof trusses and wall panels, eventually packaging them with all the necessary additional materials to build a home much faster than one stud at a time. One such company was Pacific Modern Homes, founded in 1968 as a prefabricator of trusses. It began to produce home catalogs reminiscent of those once offered by Sears, Wards, and Aladdin. Lumber companies today advertise "house packages" and "packaged homes" that come in kits with varying degrees of prefabrication. Mostly, however, all the necessary materials—down to nails and drywall mud—are included in a kit. Lindal Cedar Homes, which dates from 1945, continues as an institution in the Pacific Northwest and beyond. Model log houses of all kinds have long been familiar sights beside American highways, and the tradition of home kits lives on in the Shelter Institute and other suppliers.

It is very likely that the Phinneys paged through pattern books and home catalogs as they thought about what kind of house they wanted to build alongside the Kennebec, and they no doubt drew inspiration from them. For example, Sears produced *Homes of Today*, in which "charming interiors" were described in words and pictures. Among the interiors illustrated was one large living room with a "huge stone fireplace" and "knotty pine walls." It also had a "vaulted ceiling" with exposed rafters; another living room had "paneled side walls and hewed oak ceiling beams" framing light-colored ceiling panels. Although the Phinneys' house as built would not have a vaulted or even a very high ceiling, it certainly would have exposed dark-stained beams framing contrasting ceiling panels and, of course, knotty-pine walls. Billie Phinney may have participated in some of the early planning, but the house as built would be more masculine than feminine—more unembellished than frilly—while at the same time having softer rather than harder edges. All things considered, indications are that Bob Phinney was its principal designer.

It was common practice in Maine for boatbuilders to use the skills they learned at the ancient trade to lay out and construct their own homes. Phinney was not a boatbuilder, but he spent much time in Maine with his family and, of course, as a teenager he had been a prize-winning model builder and as a newlywed a kit-house builder. These experiences must have given him confidence that he could design and build his home in Maine from scratch, adapting and expanding features of the Livingston Cape to a growing family.

The Sears design that the Phinneys had chosen for their first home may well have been like the "New England or Stanford type home," which was said to have "a certain softness of design and lasting character." With "monthly payments as low as $28 to $38," it was in the price range that Billie recalled years later. Two floor plans were offered, a four- and a five-room arrangement. The former had the unusual feature of having its kitchen located in the front of the house, and the undesirable one of having a bedroom off the living room, which then had to be passed through to get to the bathroom. The five-room version contained a hall separated from the common rooms, thereby giving "privacy to bedrooms and bath."

For the Maine house, Phinney may very well have noted the pluses and minuses of such layouts, adapting the best and rejecting the worst features of them all. As much thought as he appears to have given to the house's interior arrangement of rooms, Phinney seems not to have worried about distinguishing its exterior. There are no artist's landscaped renderings in any pattern book I know that look anything like the house that Phinney built. He was not an architect of aesthetic facades; he was an engineer of functional interiors—of the guts of machines, of the levers and rods of calculators—which can also be things of beauty. He designed his home from the inside out. But as much as he focused on the interior of the house, he did not forget the glorious setting that would be right outside its windows.

Although Sears had gotten out of the house business long before the Phinneys had acquired their land in Maine, Aladdin continued to issue enticing catalogs full of new ideas. Catalogs from the early 1950s commented on the "recent vogue of installing picture windows," of which the Phinney home would ultimately have six, with the five opening up the northwest corner of the living room separated only by stout mullions made of four-by-eights, thus providing the panoramic view of the river that sold us on the house. These windows are framed on top and bottom simply with two-by-eights set flush with the walls, thereby serving also as trim, and the way they sit so plainly atop the paneling continues to impress me as being one of the most elegant marks of Phinney's compositional genius, which did not end with the structural and architectural. He devised a double-glazed window by separating the two panes of glass with wooden spacers. To avoid trapping condensation between the panes, he would have had to assemble them on days of very low humidity.

Knotty pine was also mentioned in the Aladdin catalogs, but it was available through them only for kitchen walls, and interested readers had to write for a special quote. Phinney used knotty pine not just in the kitchen but throughout his house. Yet in all the elevations and floor plans in all the pattern books and architecture guides through which I have looked—one even containing a Spartan floor plan that had no bathroom!—I found nothing exactly like the house that Phinney built. No type or style name quite captures its essence. It was neither a Cape nor a bungalow nor a ranch house. It was not of the Craftsman or Moderne or International or Wrightian or any other architectural style that emerged in the first half of the twentieth century and, in most cases, went out of style by midcentury. No, Phinney's house was Phinney's house, outside and in.

Thinking about the floor plan of any house evokes for me an image of the whodunit board game of Clue, which I played often with childhood friends and, later, with my own children. The playing board for Clue is a cartoon of the floor plan of the game's fictional venue, said to have been inspired by a residence in Hampshire, England, where the game originated under the name Cluedo. Clue's house has mansion-like features, of course, and our little place in Maine has no long and wide hallways along which game tokens move from square to square, much less a ballroom, conservatory, or billiard room in which murders could take place. But it does have stairs going to a basement corresponding to those leading to the mansion's downstairs and, as I would discover long after I began to scrutinize this handmade structure, a puzzling secret passage, of which the game board has two.

The object of Clue is to guess who committed a murder, with what weapon, and where in the house. (There is no When or Why in Clue.) The answers are printed on the playing cards concealed in an envelope that throughout the game remains on the spot marked X in the center of the board, with the remainder of the deck having been dealt out to the players. They take turns rolling a die, moving their tokens to where they can make suggestions about the murderer, the murder weapon, and the room that was the scene of the crime. If another player has one of the cards named, it must be shown to the player making the suggestion, but only to that player. As the game proceeds, players eliminate suspects, weapons, and the scene of the crime until someone is ready to make an accusation—that is, an educated guess as to what cards the envelope holds. A correct guess wins; an incorrect one renders the accuser a passive player for the remainder of the game. Of course, a declaration such as "Colonel Mustard did it, with the wrench, in the kitchen" could describe a dastardly deed or a constructive act, like fixing a leaky faucet. It is the latter kind of act that builds and maintains houses in the real world. Mr. Phinney did it so, with a plan, on an island.

As in the board game, my quest for clues about our house's design and construction would depend upon the cards the place would deal me and the chance events that would dictate my steps. What room I would land in on any given day and time of day would affect what I would see and what would be hidden in shadows.

Something as ephemeral as a spiderweb might call my attention to a ceiling timber, but then I might not notice something more significant closer to the floor. If I focused on a room's paneling, then I might miss something about its window. If I entered a room through one door and exited through another, then I might move against the grain of the wood, missing its finer texture. If I suspected too early in the game that Mr. Phinney did it with one tool in one room, then I might conclude too easily that he did it with the same tool in other rooms too.

But unlike the board game, it was not what was in the cards but what was in the house that held the answers. Moving from room to room seeking clues and making suggestions was exactly how I spent many an afternoon in Maine with a literal flashlight and a metaphorical magnifying glass looking for the Who, with What, and Where—and also the When and the Why—of this place. Catherine played Mary Russell to my Sherlock Holmes, questioning whether my suggestions were consistent with the gossip, facts, and clues, seeing the house through her own lens and focusing on things I did not or could not see or express clearly. It was to be a game of surmise, surprise, and reprise until some critical and definitive clues would be uncovered. Even then there remained the lingering doubt that what I thought Phinney did was what in fact he did here in Arrowsic.

Four

ARROWSIC
[*SIC*!]

ARROWSIC IS A NATIVE AMERICAN word, but it has nothing to do with bows and arrows. The second syllable, on which the stress falls, is pronounced to rhyme not with the exclamation of surprise, "Oh!" but with that of sudden pain, "Ow!" The last part of the name is pronounced "sick," but is spelled without the *k*. Most people, upon seeing the word for the first time, accent the first syllable and say "*Arrow*-sick." Many insist on spelling it that way too. To be fair, over centuries the island's name has been spelled in a half-dozen different ways, including Rowsick, Arrowseag, Arrowsik, Arowsic, Arowsswick, and Arowsick, and this last is the way it appeared on many old maps. But variations and misspellings are not restricted to the early settlers; I recently received an envelope addressed to me in Arrowski. Was it a typo or a Polish joke? Regardless of its spelling, even some old-time Mainers, especially those from inland parts of the state, if they have heard of the place at all, express surprise when I pronounce Arrowsic as the natives do, making it a shibboleth sibling of Mount Desert, though unlike Mount Desert, Arrowsic is the destination of few tourists.

There is no green exit sign on U.S. 1 North directing travelers to Arrowsic, so it helps to know that it is on the way to Georgetown and Reid State Park. You can look for announcements of those popular destinations, which are reached by taking the first turnoff after crossing the Kennebec on the new bridge, curling off the highway just before the Dairy Queen. At the bottom of the hill, where the street ends in a T, there is a modest sign indicating that Arrowsic is to the left, across a smaller bridge, which carries State Route 127 South onto the island. Arrowsic is one of three "large islands" in the Midcoast region, the other two being nearby Georgetown and Westport.

In the asymmetric manner of highway signage, on U.S. 1 South there is a sign indicating the turnoff to Arrowsic. However, the sign and the exit itself come up so closely together that it is easy to miss until it is too late to get into the right-hand lane for the turn. Over-shooting the ramp means the hapless driver ends up on the new bridge to Bath and, if he or she exits into the city, is confronted with the kind of bewildering traffic pattern that results when a town and its streets are laid out long before the coming of automobiles and highways.

Although some have said that the meaning of the place name Arrowsic "has never been fathomed," others say that the Eastern Abenaki named the island Arrowsic because it was a "place of obstruction." The obstruction referred to was in the water off the northeast portion of the island, where the Sasanoa River was full of shallows and boulders. For centuries, passage in the tidal currents here remained treacherous enough to earn it the name Upper Hell Gate. In the late nineteenth and early twentieth century, the U.S. Army Corps of Engineers cleared the river's course somewhat, but the stretch is still a bottleneck for boat traffic, especially when the tide is low and the boats are many. The west side of the island is bounded by the deepwater Kennebec River, which is navigable and tidal from Maine's capital, Augusta, to the sea, a distance of some forty miles.

Although the area at the mouth of the Kennebec was reached by Europeans as early as 1607, they did not live on Arrowsic until 1625. In 1654, the company founded by prominent Boston merchants Thomas

Clarke and Thomas Lake established a trading post in a fortified settlement at a strategic location on the Sasanoa. A forge, shipyard, and
mills were also established. In 1676, during King Philip's War, the
Clarke and Lake fort was attacked and burned in a battle in which
Lake was killed. In the wake of the violence, the area was deserted by
the Europeans and left to the Indians. It was only after a peace treaty
was signed the following year that European settlers returned.

To the southeast of Arrowsic is the island now called Georgetown but formerly known as Parker's Island. It had been purchased
around 1650 from the Indians by its namesake, John Parker, who
had already owned land and built a house on Arrowsic. Parker is
said to have been his island's first occupant, though settlers from
the Popham Colony across the Kennebec may have lived there at
the beginning of the seventeenth century. Residents of Arrowsic
filed a petition in 1716 to form a township named Georgetown-
on-Arrowsic; in that same year the separate and distinct town of
Georgetown (on Parker's Island) was also incorporated. A 1720 plat
of English land grants on Arrowsic Island shows it to have been
divided up, much the way a loaf of bread is sliced, into parallel lots
that extended all the way from the western to the eastern shore.
(Remnants of that subdivision were clear in Edgar Phinney's survey of land in the vicinity of the marsh and remain visible in some
property lines throughout the island today.) Some nearby areas,
including Parker's Island, became incorporated into the "sprawling" and "scattered" township of Georgetown-on-Arrowsic, which
at one time also included what are now the separate towns of
Arrowsic, Bath, Phippsburg, West Bath, and Woolwich. Through its
own incorporation, Arrowsic became an independent town in 1841.

Distinct geographically and independent governmentally as it
may be, Arrowsic does not appear on all maps, and on some it does
not appear as an island. The AAA *Road Atlas* has shown it as a peninsula jutting south from the mainland near Woolwich. A thin gray
line representing Route 127 was its only feature, passing through the
blank white space as if through a desert. The place would seem to have

had no purpose other than to support the road down to Georgetown and was not listed in the *Atlas*'s index of Maine place names. The map of Midcoast attractions and points of interest in a *Talking Phone Book* for the Brunswick-Bath area did a little better in showing Arrowsic physically separated from the mainland, yet it did not identify the place by name. An early version of Google Maps made Arrowsic and Georgetown appear to be a single island, separated into the respective towns by a political rather than the natural boundary of the Back River. But if Arrowsic had no independent identity, no sign on U.S. 1 North pointing to it, no traffic lights, no advertised attractions or points of interest, no shopping center, no gas station, no convenience store, and no crowds, that made the place all the more attractive to us.

Plat of Arrowsic from 1720

Arrowsic is in fact one of about three thousand large and small islands that dot and otherwise punctuate the coast up here. In shape it resembles perhaps most closely on a small-scale map a modest comma between Phippsburg and Georgetown. To get a good hard-copy representation of Arrowsic in context, it is best to turn to *The Maine Atlas and Gazetteer* published by DeLorme, the map company headquartered in Yarmouth, which is just south of Freeport, the home of L. L. Bean. Mainers refer to the *Atlas* simply as "the DeLorme," but it may as well be called the bible of back roads, back bays, and back rivers. As measured in the DeLorme, the island of Arrowsic is about seven miles long and a couple wide at its broadest, comprising an area of about seven thousand acres, or eleven square miles, three of which are water, at least much of the time. These "wetlands" include a good number of handsome marshes, like the one through which Spinney Mill Road dips and curves. Among the other wet areas is Sewell Pond, which is about six-tenths of a mile long and two-tenths across. This body of freshwater sits right in the middle of the island and is a favorite swimming hole on hot summer days.

The southwesternmost tip of the island, and the Squirrel Point river light located there, is about five miles from the Kennebec's mouth and the open sea. The southeastern side is separated from Georgetown by the Back River, which at low tide is not fully navigable by many boats. When it is navigable, a boat can take the Back River into Hockomock Bay, from which it can follow the Sasanoa through Knubble Bay, past Robinhood Cove and MacMahan Island, through Goose Rock Passage, across the Sheepscot River, and through Townsend Gut to arrive at Boothbay Harbor. If, instead of heading to Boothbay, the boat heads northwest out of Hockomock Bay, up the Sasanoa, and through the Upper Hell Gate, it will enter Hanson Bay, from which it can travel west around the top of the island of Arrowsic to return to the Kennebec River. It is on this leg of a circumnavigation that boaters pass beneath the Arrowsic Bridge, which connects the island to the mainland town of Woolwich.

Early wagon access to Arrowsic was by ferry, and there still is a street in Woolwich called Old Arrowsic Road that leads down to an abandoned ferry ramp. In 1849, a wooden bridge was built at this location, with Arrowsic residents, active military personnel, and people going to or from public worship not having to pay a toll, which at one time was three cents for pedestrians, ten cents for horse and rider, and fifteen cents for horse and wagon or sleigh. The bridge in place in 1913 was not the sturdiest; it was posted with a sign reading, "No Riding or Driving a Beast on the Bridge Faster than a Walk." An

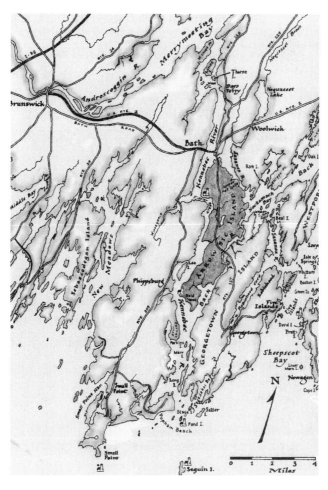

Arrowsic Island and its neighbors

addendum to the sign read, "Automobiles Go Slow." After the bridge collapsed in 1919, perhaps under a galloping beast or a speeding car, the State of Maine rebuilt it as a toll-free crossing with a steel truss span that provided a wider boating channel. The present all-steel bridge was built in 1950. Of the type known technically as a cantilever truss, it is 838 feet in total length, has a main span of 300 feet, and provides high clearance over the water. Although commonly referred to as the Arrowsic Bridge, it was officially named the Sasanoa River Bridge until renamed the Max L. Wilder Memorial Bridge, after the long-time state bridge engineer, who died in 1962. It is a fitting tribute, since the bridge is considered one of Wilder's most successful designs. The main road that it carries across the water is Route 127, which forms the spinal column of the island. Indeed, the Arrowsic Bridge and the one connecting Arrowsic and Georgetown are the only fixed ways on or off these islands. Depending on which island you are on, the state highway is referred to locally as either Arrowsic Road or Five Islands Road, the latter name referring to islands just offshore where the highway ends.

Travelers who do not know or care about Arrowsic typically just drive through it and continue on into Georgetown until the turnoff to Reid State Park and its sandy beach or take 127 all the way to the community of Five Islands, where the eponymous lobster company there cooks to order lobsters to be eaten at picnic tables on the dock. Nearby, boats come and go to MacMahan Island, where many old-timers and their descendants summer in houses dating back a century or more. These structures were often built by local fishermen who, it was said, just had to put a pencil behind their ear to make more money as "summer carpenters."

A boater passing beneath the Arrowsic Bridge heading west will encounter head-on the immense panorama of the Bath Iron Works shipyard stretching along the opposite shore. The fishing is said to

Arrowsic Bridge across the Sasanoa

be good in this vicinity, and so there are often many small boats bobbing up and down in this wide part of the Kennebec, but since September 11, 2001, they have had to stay a prescribed distance—marked by buoys and enforced by patrol boats manned by armed guards—from the shipyard and the high-tech Navy destroyers that are being built and fitted out there.

The Maine Maritime Museum, which is just downriver from the ironworks, has installed on its grounds a striking outdoor sculpture that recalls the largest wooden wind-powered sailing vessel ever built. The *Wyoming,* a 330-foot-long, six-masted schooner, was launched in 1909 from the Percy & Small shipyard, and the virtual *Wyoming,* which is a full-scale skeletal evocation made of steel framing painted white, sits in almost the exact place where the real ship was built. Colorful flags and burgees fly atop the virtual ship's 120-foot masts, and its long slender bowsprit cantilevers out toward the road leading down from the iron works. The towering work of art, a ghost of the ship that represents to many the "apogee of wooden shipbuilding," conveys the massiveness of the vessel without physically or visually obscuring surviving buildings in which components of the ship were designed and fabricated.

Further downriver is the Doubling Point lighthouse, set out in the water and connected to land by a picturesque footbridge.

The light was originally constructed a little to the east of its present location; however, it could be seen easily only by ships going upriver. After being moved to its present location, ships coming down from Bath could also use it as a navigation aid. For a ship heading downriver, the left dogleg at Doubling Point marks the beginning of the short straight stretch of river known as Fiddler's Reach. At the eastern part of the reach, where the river makes a right dogleg, is a fog-signal tower located where a coastal steamer went aground about a century ago. The tower's pyramidal structure housed a clockwork mechanism driven by a weight falling from the height to which it had been hand-cranked by a keeper. The mechanism activated a hammer, which struck a fog bell hung just outside the tower. (The bell and part of the timber cantilever from which it hung were unceremoniously cut down in the 1970s, but efforts are underway to restore the fog-signal tower to working condition.) Further along Fiddler's Reach is a pair of range lights, one positioned upslope from the other. When ships heading upriver toward the double dogleg see the range lights lined up one atop the other, they know they are in the deep navigation channel, which they are advised to follow until they catch a glimpse of Doubling Point light. That is their signal to turn into the reach to continue on their way to Bath. Our house is located just downriver from Fiddler's Reach, and from our living-room windows we can see the white fog-bell tower and range lights.

Arrowsic was where the coastal Maine Wawenocs hunted until the mid-eighteenth century, when they ceased to exist as a distinct tribe of the Abenakis. The island has seen many changes since those times, when it was covered with trees. They were cleared to free land for farming, which was not an especially profitable enterprise in Maine's short growing season. The trees now covering the land are second growth and are cut down to make way not for farms but for a few new houses and to open up views of the water for some existing ones. For the latter purpose, environmental regulations limit the number and size of trees that can be cut, but the guidelines seem to be violated regularly. We can now see houses across the river that a few years ago we did not even suspect were there. Some trees are planted, too, and we are grateful to the prior owner who established the great oaks that now shade our house from the summer afternoon sun.

The island and Town of Arrowsic are coextensive but not populous. In 1850 the town was home to about three hundred people, but, as they did in rural areas throughout the country, industrialization and expansion drew younger people to the cities and the western frontier. Thus the population of Arrowsic recorded by census declined in the closing decades of the nineteenth century, reaching 180 in 1900. An early 1900s scheme to sell land in a development called Rowsic Park to people from the Boston area was intended to make the town "among the leading summer colonies" in the area and give Arrowsic "a new lease on life," but it did not pan out. The 1910 census counted only 140 residents, and the turn-of-the-century population was not exceeded again until the 1970 census, when 188 residents were counted. Counterculture people discovered the island around that time, and groups of them began to live on it in yurts, the circular structures modeled after shelters used by some Asian nomads. It is said that about a dozen or so yurts still exist on the island.

Our neighbor Rob Shultz came to Arrowsic in 1973. He was born, grew up, and went to college in Pennsylvania, after which he served in the Peace Corps in Venezuela. Coincidentally, one of the members of his Peace Corps class was a fellow from Arrowsic, who must have talked about its idyllic ambience and may even have described the marsh, the cove, the river, and Spinney Mill Road, on which Rob would eventually build at least two of its largest houses. He loves to swim in the cove, even when the temperature of the water must be bracing, and he reads *The New Yorker* faithfully, though not always immediately upon publication. (It is because of Rob that I hold onto past issues of the magazine longer than I might otherwise, for on more than one occasion he has brought to my attention an interesting article that I had passed over when the issue was current.)

Whether due to an influx of hippies, builders, or ironworkers, the population grew considerably over the next two decades, reaching 498 in 1990 and then leveling off. The 2000 census counted 477 souls living in 196 households. A decade later the recorded population dropped by 10 percent, to 427. Unlike in neighboring George-town, where as many as two-thirds of its summer population does not spend winter on the island, over 90 percent of people living on Arrowsic in the summer are also here throughout the winter. Today, ours is the only one of the dozen houses on or just off Spinney Mill Road that is not occupied throughout the year.

Back in the early 1950s, when our house was being built and the island was home to about 140 people, Phinneys accounted for more than 5 percent of them. An adult Robert Jr., son of our home's builder and the same fellow whom our neighbor Rob met in the Peace Corps, recalled having moved at ten years old from a New Jersey "housing development" to "the smallest township in Maine," which was an understandable exaggeration. Even today there are Maine townships with a population of a single individual. Nevertheless, Robert Phinney Jr. described his younger self as being a "nature lover/hunter/fisher" who had found Arrowsic to be "a paradise of major rivers and salt marshes full of fish and waterfowl, and big woods with big and small game to be encountered any time—and Art." Compared to New Jersey, where he had seen trees alive with nests of young birds bulldozed and set afire to make room for more housing developments, Arrowsic was a nature preserve and a place of some permanence. He noted that "neighbors didn't commute. They farmed, were woodcutters, lighthouse keepers, and some were even full time Artists! I've never been happier since."

Some Arrowsic neighbors did commute, of course. Before there was a bridge across the Kennebec, they rowed their boats to work. After the bridge was built they took it, often walking rather than driving across, to jobs in the shipyard and elsewhere in Bath, but it was nothing like rush-hour commuting within New Jersey or across the Hudson River to New York City. Ten-year-old Bobby Phinney attended Arrowsic's one-room schoolhouse, which in the 1950s had an enrollment of fewer than thirty pupils, a fifth of what it had been a century earlier. But much of his education must have come from the marsh, in which he watched the movements of water and birds for hours on end. What he observed and learned there would reshape his life from a child of suburban confinement to an artist of rural escape. Bobby attended high school across the river in Bath and spent a year at Bowdoin College in nearby Brunswick, but his heart and soul remained in the open air, woods, and waters of Arrowsic. Although he had carved beetles and Buck Rogers rocket ships when living in New Jersey, in Maine his woodcarving eventually turned to birds. Among his early efforts as a fourteen-year-old was a Canada goose, which he made for his first girlfriend.

Arrowsic neighbors who worked at or close to home encouraged Bobby Phinney's artistic inclinations and helped him develop skills in woodcarving and silversmithing. After school and during vacation time he worked for and became an apprentice to the Woolwich silver artist Clifford Russell, who has been described with geographic imprecision as "an Arts & Crafts era artist from Down East," whose highly collectible jewelry is said elegantly to evoke the rugged coast.

The Phinney boy continued to do woodcraft in his spare time. When he was fifteen, he was featured in the *Bath Independent* newspaper, and a photo showed him with a hand-carved and -painted chickadee, just one example of the many different kinds of birds that he created out of solid blocks of pine. (He found in his grandmother's barn a supply of the well-seasoned, slow-growing, tight-ringed kind that is excellent for woodworking.) According to the paper, "so realistic are the carvings that they are often taken for real mounted birds, even on close examination." His extraordinarily detailed work was introduced to Georgetown summer people, who purchased his art. It soon came to the attention of Frank Herbert Mason, an influential New York painter and teacher, who in turn introduced the seventeen-year-old Arrowsic lad to the well-known Kennedy Galleries that specialized in Phinney's kind of representational art. This helped launch his artistic career nationally and internationally, and he became widely known as a wildlife artist, specifically a bird sculptor whom at least one critic has placed "among the giants of his craft."

Curiously, as idyllic as he had found Arrowsic as a teenager, Phinney would later tell a writer on nature art that the only place he felt "inexplicably at home" was the Annapolis Valley in Nova Scotia, where at about the age of thirty he bought an old farm and settled down, producing there as little as a piece or two of finished original art each year. His low rate of production was in part a consequence of how time-consuming it was for him to create first from carefully prepared drawings an original wooden carving, then a latex mold sheathed in plaster, from which he made a wax duplicate of the original. After the wax replica was encased in plaster, and the wax melted out, the hollow left behind served as a new mold into which liquid metal was poured to create a casting. After much experimenting with different alloys and casting techniques, Phinney mastered this so-called lost-wax process to the point where in his sculptures he achieved delicate feather details that eluded him in painted wood.

One engineer who saw the artist's first all-metal casting of a bird in Toronto's Royal Ontario Museum thought the piece of art belonged also in a museum of metallurgy, "so enormously complex was it in terms of technology and casting." So thin were some of the feather details of Phinney's bird sculptures that he had trouble finding a foundry that would even attempt to replicate them. It was not until he discovered one that produced extremely delicate parts for hardware used on NASA moon missions that success was achieved, but only after seventy-five tries at producing a perfect metal chickadee. The younger Phinney was thus at least as attentive to detail in casting his bird sculptures as his father was in building his Napoleonic coach and, later, his house. According to one nature writer, "Phinney is a man possessed. He must carve, but he must never compromise excellence on the altar of commercialism." With a word change here and there, the assessment might have applied equally as well to his father.

In spite of the junior Phinney's fleeing it for Canada, Arrowsic and its environs remain a low-key haven for artists, and some of those who helped young Phinney in the 1950s are still remembered in the area today. The Lithuanian-American painter and sculptor William Zorach, who lived with his family on a farm near Georgetown's Robinhood Cove, gave the fifteen-year-old Phinney his first carving tools. Zorach's daughter Dahlov Ipcar, a painter, also encouraged the budding artist. Ipcar continued to live in Georgetown, and memories of her father remain strong hereabouts. In 1962, his *Spirit of the Sea* sculpture/fountain was installed in the city park in front of Bath's Patten Free Library, inside of which a fanciful Dahlov Ipcar mural graces the children's room.

Following a typical New England model, the Town of Arrowsic is governed by a board of three elected selectmen, which constitutes the executive branch. The eligible voters of the town collectively and effectively constitute its legislature, convening once a year in the town meeting. As a town, Arrowsic is so small that some of its few elected officials have to wear several hats. Thus, the selectmen are also the town's Assessors and Overseers of the Poor; its Surveyors of Wood, Lumber, and Bark; as well as its Fence Viewers. In many a larger New England town, such historically important positions would have been held by individuals or groups elected at the town meeting or appointed by the select-men, who could then be free to focus on broader issues confront-ing town governance.

One of the pleasures of arriving for the summer on Arrowsic is receiving the town's annual report, a booklet that contains the upcoming fiscal year's "warrant," which is essentially the agenda for the town meeting. The annual report has often been among the first things delivered to our mailbox each June, but of late we have sometimes had to pick it up at the modest Town Hall, when it is open for business on Wednesday afternoons and Friday mornings for two and a half hours each. The Taxpayer's List, which shows the appraised value of every piece of land in the town, along with the assessed value of improvements, the tax paid on them, and the list of delinquent taxpayers, makes for interesting reading. During our first years, the town report was our confirmation of the pace of life across Arrowsic. The document also gave us a sense of demograph-ics. In a busy year, the town's vital statistics will show two births, three deaths, and one marriage.

Arrowsic is too small to support its own modern-day school, library, or professional fire department. For years, the volunteers asked for a new fire truck, the town's old water tanker having been converted from a vehicle that once delivered oil or Coca-Cola, depending on whom you listen to. The fire barn, essentially a garage in which to house the truck, was also in need of upgrading, its ten-by-ten-foot doors allowing just inches of clearance for the old truck and unlikely able to accommodate a modern one. When in 2000 the town's selectmen turned down a request for funds for a new barn, all the volunteer firemen resigned. For ten years, fire protection for the island was contracted out to the Bath Fire Department. It was only when Arrowsic's fire chief secured a federal grant of $190,000 to purchase a new truck that the town's residents, in a specially called meeting, approved an expenditure of $10,000 matching funds for the truck and $150,000 for a new station (with twelve-by-twelve-foot doors) in which to house it. The money got the

Arrowsic's new fire station

town a truck worth $200,000 and a building worth an estimated $220,000, the discount thanks to residents who donated their time and expertise. Our builder neighbor Rob Shultz served as construction supervisor; another neighbor, John Wood, did the preconstruction surveying. Mainers know a good deal when they make it. The new fire station not only houses the new truck with room to spare but also serves as the venue for the annual town meeting, which used to be held under a tent or in the school gymnasium in Georgetown, the Arrowsic town hall being too small to accommodate all the interested citizenry. Early in 2012, Milly Stafford's ninetieth-birthday celebration took place in the new fire station. At the party, Milly, Arrowsic's oldest resident, posed for a picture with six-week-old Stella Kauffunger, the town's youngest, who was being held by her mother, Camille. Milly had been on call to drive her to the hospital for the delivery, but the baby was actually born on the island, making her a true Arrowsican.

Five

DOMESTIC
THERAPY

OUR HOUSE ON ARROWSIC was built as therapy. At least that is what I have heard from neighbors. Though none of them was living on Spinney Mill Road when the place was under construction, they have repeated with an air of certainty what they have heard. According to the hearsay, Bob Phinney had suffered a breakdown and so was going to build this house in rural Maine all by himself, to escape and recover from the suburban rat race. Only after I had had time to study the house in detail did I begin to appreciate how therapeutic the act of planning and building it might actually have been. Whether Phinney really needed rest and recuperation in Maine I cannot say, but I do know that the more closely I looked into his carpentry work, the more I saw a man in full control of his craft and presumably of himself. And before he could wield his hammer and saw, he had to design the house and locate it on the land his mother had provided.

Like most coastal property in Maine, the land is underlain with ledge. Ledge is a catchall term used for an expanse of granite that, if it is not boldly exposed, often lurks just below the surface of the ground. Siting a house, especially one envisioned to have a full basement, on ledge is tricky business. Since the rock is seldom truly flat and never totally predictable in its profile, it can be difficult to find a place that is a ready-made location for a foundation. In some instances the topsoil may be only an inch or two deep, but nearby the underlying ledge may drop off suddenly and quickly reach a depth of several feet. A near tabletop flat surface can be achieved by excavating, chiseling, blasting, jackhammering, and filling, if the builder wants to go to all that trouble.

A less jarring approach for Phinney to establish a place to build might have been to probe the earth with a long iron rod, tapping it gently into the soil until it hit ledge. (Ground-penetrating radar dates from the early twentieth century, but the technology was generally limited to scientific and military applications until affordable equipment for civilian use became available in the 1980s.) Using an iron rod, a virtual profile of the bedrock could be achieved by sounding the land much the same way Henry David Thoreau plumbed the depths of Walden Pond to "recover the long lost bottom." As Thoreau gained insight into human nature and ethics by reflecting on the intersection of orthogonal profiles of the depths of Ralph Waldo Emerson's pond, Phinney may have found himself inspired to a design above ground by what he found below. While larger engineering projects, like skyscrapers and suspension bridges, probe the depths of the soil and sea bottom with devices more sophisticated than an iron rod and a hammer, the principle remains the same. And because the number of probes or borings is necessarily limited, later surprises abound. The Leaning Tower of Pisa exemplifies one such surprise. But Phinney did not want to be surprised.

However he did it, he managed to locate a hollow in the ledge, as is evident within our house today. In the basement there is exposed rock all along the west wall, along much of the east wall, projecting out from the south wall, and massed in the northeast corner. Overall the rock appears untouched by chisel or drill, but from all sides it encroaches like a frozen lava flow into the underground room. The foundation walls are concrete atop a base of brickwork, all conforming to the contours of the underlying and encroaching ledge. Within these bounds lay a concrete floor of irregular outline dictated by the coastline-like ledge and the rectilinear foundation walls. A shallow channel was dredged out of the wet-concrete floor and bounded by a small berm to direct water from the south wall around the perimeter to a drain near the north wall. This system still works rather effectively in conducting water that seeps in after moderate rains and also condensate that drips off the chilled metal surfaces when cold well water is pumped into the accumulators.

According to George Stafford, who did not give Phinney—or many others, for that matter—undue credit for architectural, engineering, or building judgment, the walls of the foundation were first made only to a height just above the prevailing ground level, which would have made for an impossibly shallow basement. George considered this a rank amateur's mistake, a real howler. Not only did it omit a niche on either side in which to seat the ends of a central beam, but also it neglected to include openings for small windows to ventilate the space. Thus, as I understood George's view, an additional pour of concrete was necessary to rectify the error. I cannot find a seam in the concrete to corroborate George's assertion, but regardless of how and why the foundation walls were made the way they were and to the height that they are, today I need only bend my neck rather than my entire back when I walk in the basement to avoid bumping my head on the exposed floor joists.

Phinney's vision for the superstructure style appears to have been something between a fifties ranch and a frontier log cabin, a definite departure from the two-story farmhouse that is ubiquitous in Maine. But choosing a style, even a hybrid one, is not necessarily choosing the scale for a structure, which greatly influences building cost. The size of Phinney's house was most likely determined at least in part by the size of his family and budget. The size of a house is also influenced by the spirit and fashion of the times, and in postwar America something around 1,000 to 1,200 square

Granite ledge and drainage channel in basement

feet may have seemed about the right amount of house for a young middle-class family of six.

But knowing that the approximate floor area should be, say, 1,200 square feet does not fix dimensions, which must be decided upon before any foundation can be laid and building upon it begun. Phinney could have made his house a thirty-five-foot square or a twenty-five-by-fifty- or thirty-by-forty-foot rectangle. For an engineer, functional rather than aesthetic considerations tend to dominate the choice, and in the case of a house the most important functional consideration is arguably how the interior space will be supported and subdivided into rooms. Phinney, no doubt taking into consideration the lay of the ledge, chose to give his structure the overall dimensions of thirty-two feet by forty feet, which results in 1,280 gross square feet of floor area. He may have decided on those dimensions, each divisible by sixteen, because in his judgment they just looked or just felt right. Or, he may have reasoned, with an overall thirty-two-foot span from front to back, he could use for floor joists between a centrally located main beam and the foundation walls lumber that came in standard sixteen-foot lengths, thereby eliminating sawing and waste.

Or perhaps more than anything the number and gender of the persons in Phinney's family inspired his choice of dimensions. Since there were three sons and a daughter, Phinney knew that he needed at least three bedrooms. Probably the most natural, sensible, and efficient arrangement was to make one room for the boys, one for the girl, and one for the parents, and that is what he chose to do. But deciding on the number of bedrooms is different from knowing their measurements and arrangement. With the outline of the house defined, it remained for him to divide up the 1,200-odd square feet of rectangular floor space into rooms and closets, plus a hall and an opening for a stairway leading down to the basement.

How might he have proceeded? He may have started by establishing the dimensions of the rooms necessary to accommodate the beds and other furniture they would hold. He might have drawn, possibly on the quadrille paper that engineers like to use, the outline of the house in plan. A scale of one-quarter inch to the foot would have resulted in a rectangle eight by ten inches, which would fit nicely on a standard-sized sheet. Allowing for the thickness of walls and the size of closets between them, he could have cut pieces of cardboard proportional in scale to the size of the rooms he thought about right and moved the cardboard rooms around within the house's outline, trimming when necessary, until their relative sizes and positions and efficient use of space seemed about right. Or, he might have just eyeballed where the rooms, walls, and closets should go. This would not have been unprecedented: The self-taught architect Addison Mizner, who in the 1920s was responsible for so much of the look that came to define South Florida homes, was said not to have believed in blueprints, and many an amateur builder has surely gotten along without them.

Bob Phinney may not have needed to produce drawings, instead just holding the concept of his house in his mind's eye. Since he was to build it himself, he did not have to communicate his plan to anyone else with the unambiguous precision that fully dimensioned engineering or architectural drawings convey. However, after he had become satisfied with his vision—regardless of how he worked it out—or perhaps to help him arrive at the vision, he did construct a three-dimensional model. The plywood model was not nearly as grand as one for a monumental cathedral nor as detailed as one of a Napoleonic carriage, but it depicted what the house by the river was intended to look like from every angle, and everyone who looked upon it could understand it. But it was also a model of tentativeness, for, like virtually all models, it was not to be realized point-by-point in full scale.

I became aware of the existence of the model only after I had spent several summers of sleuthing around the house as built and musing over its construction. I had contacted Bill Phinney, the youngest of the children, and in the course of our communications he revealed that it had been his mother's wish that her husband's lantern-slide collection of family photos and assorted other snapshots be preserved in digital form. Bill gave me sheets of thumbnail images of the collection and a key to identifying them. Two images labeled "Camp Model" were dated January 1951. An overall view shows a house with a hip roof penetrated by a chimney, and so the model provides clear evidence that the flat roof on the house as built was a feature that evolved from an earlier concept. The image of the model also shows a different fenestration around the living-room corner, in that only three of the windows are of the large picture type. They are flanked on each end by what appear to be windows of about half the width. Whether these were intended to be casement windows is not clear, but Catherine and I are glad that at least one living-room window that opens was actually included in the finished house, for it provides refreshing ventilation when there is a cool breeze coming out of the north down the river.

The model's removable roof was taken off before the second photo was snapped. This one offers a three-dimensional version of a floor plan, showing how at one time Phinney imagined the interior space should be divided. The front part consisted of a good-sized kitchen separated from a large living room by a dominating fireplace. The rear section of the house was depicted down to the placement of model beds and pieces of furniture in the bedrooms—as if in a dollhouse. However, the model was not complete, because it did not show the location or size of the ten closets that the finished house was to contain. Collectively these account for about 10 percent of the gross floor area and reduce the size of rooms accordingly. Thus the model was not definitive, and Phinney would make other changes in his concept as construction progressed. Since design is an evolutionary process, seldom do plans or models anticipate everything that is needed or desired in the completed construction project.

Had the house been built as an exact scaled-up version of the model, it would have measured about twenty-six by thirty-eight feet and contained almost one thousand gross square feet, or about three hundred fewer than the house actually constructed. The house grew by a hundred square feet from model to reality by adding closets between rooms, and by another two hundred square feet or so by making the kitchen larger and the living room longer and deeper. Phinney was evidently driven to these iterations on his design by his family's need for storage space in the form of closets and the structure's need for a central bearing wall to support the ridge of a gabled roof, however shallow it was to be. Even the most thoughtful designers have to rethink things now and then.

One thing seems certain: Phinney did not favor large bedrooms at the expense of space in the rest of the house. In the end, he apportioned 20 percent more floor space to the living room than he did to the floor area of all three bedrooms combined. Neighbors and prior owners had recalled—and Bill Phinney confirmed—that the largest bedroom (measuring approximately twelve by twelve feet) was the one for the three boys, the middle bedroom in both size (nine by eleven) and location was for the parents, and the smallest one (seven by eleven) was for the girl, although hers had the most floor area per occupant. His parents' having the midsize bedroom was consistent with the lifestyle that the model implied. Giving the boys the largest room would also give them ample floor space for play. Furthermore, with the parents' room between those of the brothers and sister, she was effectively separated from the antics of her younger siblings. As with the feel of the beds in the tale of Goldilocks, the size of each Phinney bedroom must have seemed just right for its purpose. A full bathroom was located next to the girl's room; a half bath was accessed only from inside the boys', as if it were a fourth closet in the room—a literal water closet.

For Phinney to arrive at the final layout of rooms and closets, their assignments, and their furnishings, he must have had a plan more detailed than his wooden model. However, that plan may still not have been completely formed in his mind, with the exact final dimensions of the spaces to be negotiated with the lumber he would have on hand. But what building materials he ordered had to have been dictated by what he envisioned using it for. What

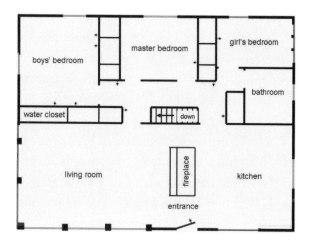

Floor plan of house as built

he did use were a relatively few kinds and sizes of lumber, ranging from one-by-twos to four-by-eights, plus some larger timbers for major beams, their sizes likewise dictated by their intended use. How much of each size and in what lengths he ordered it must have been the result of some calculations, translating the plans from images to numbers. And he appears to have challenged himself to work with a limited palette of materials, to see a two-by-four also as a four-by-two, to see a wall stud also as part of a window framing and casing. In contrast to the thirty-odd different small sizes of pine and maple that a younger Bob Phinney had to deal with in the Fisher Body competition, in Maine the grown man confined his design to using fewer than a dozen different sizes of lumber.

Like most builders and carpenters working on a house-size project, Bob Phinney would likely have ordered his construction lumber more by size than by the kind of tree it came from. Douglas-fir and pine, as well as spruce (collectively referred to as SPF and ordered by the nonspecific acronym) have long been common house-building materials, and, at least now on the Internet, carpenters debate the pros and cons of each. Some say one wood is stronger than the other, and some say the opposite. In fact, given the ranges of strength occurring in natural woods, there can be an overlap, and so each claim can be correct for a specific lot of lumber from a specific part of the country. Some carpenters swear by Douglas-fir, hyphenated because the tree from which it comes is not a true fir, while others say they prefer eastern white pine or southern yellow pine, the former generally being softer than the latter and so generally avoided for use as flooring. Once, when a pair of workers came into our house to give an estimate on some repair work, the younger of them asked the older whether he thought our ceiling beams were made of Doug-fir, using the familiar name for the wood. I don't know if anyone could tell for certain just by seeing the beams' size and looking at their stained surface. To make a positive identification, you have to look closely at the grain and cannot rely entirely on its color. The cross-sectional grain of lumber used in a completed house is usually not available for inspection, and Phinney's house would be no exception. In only a couple of places and usually only temporarily would the insides of any wood be revealed, and for me it would be inconclusive. But my bet is that most if not all of the structural lumber used in our house is common pine.

Phinney may have had the foundation concrete mixed, delivered, and placed by specialists, but likely in forms of his own devising. He certainly must have had some help installing the heavy timbers across the greater dimension of the basement space. (In addition to George Stafford's possible volunteering, there would likely have been jobbers in the area ready to work for a few hours or a day at a time.) Had the six-by-eight-inch, forty-foot-long main beam been all of one piece, it would have weighed about 450 pounds and been expensive to purchase, unwieldy to transport, and difficult to install. The beam in place is actually patched together from three shorter lengths placed end-to-end: two sixteen-foot and one eight-foot long, the longer timbers weighing about 175 pounds each. The composite beam rests at each of its extreme ends in a recess cast into the center of the south and north foundation walls, and it is supported at four intermediate points by five-inch-diameter five-foot-high steel columns bolted onto low concrete footings. Placing a single sixteen-foot-long, 175-pound timber atop the slender columns would tax not only the strength but also the balance of any person, even one working with a helper. Phinney seems to have given the task some forethought, for each timber still bears pencil marks indicating, with the engineering and architectural symbol that looks like a stylized cents sign, the location of the piece's centerline. This no doubt helped in positioning the beam atop its supports. Once all the timbers were in place, on each side two-foot-long one-by-eights were nailed across each of the tight gaps, thereby forming one continuous beam of sorts to help support the floor and walls and roof to be constructed above it.

There is one curiosity about the foundation walls. Four more recesses were formed in the concrete and slathered with the same tarlike protective substance that was applied where elsewhere timber rests on concrete. They must have been intended to receive additional timber beams, but they remain empty. The unused pockets are the same size and shape as the two in which the ends of the main beam rest, suggesting that Phinney had planned to install additional timbers of the same size, in keeping with his apparent penchant for what might be described as structural overdesign.

For whatever reason, Phinney appears to have changed his mind about the house's floor-support structure somewhere between when the foundation notches were tarred and the joists were installed. Perhaps he found the installation of the main beam so difficult that he decided to forgo the use of two parallel ones, realizing

Unused recess in foundation

that this single beam would be sufficient to support the house's floor joists—and more. Adding two additional beams across the forty-foot span would have required additional steel posts, making the basement space resemble a metal-trunked orchard. In any case, he spanned the presumably greater than planned distance from central beam to parallel foundation wall with two-by-eight joists that he doubled and in some cases tripled up on, thereby effectively supporting the floor with four-by-eights and six-by-eights that he could install one manageable two-by-eight at a time. The evidence is that this is what he did, for the double and triple joists are not nailed to each other but just rest side by side beneath the tongue-and-groove subflooring installed on the diagonal.

If the basement suggests that Phinney may have made some false assumptions, caught some false calculations, corrected some false starts, and left some false clues, the upstairs would show him to have learned fast. The workmanship in the cellar does not portend that found upstairs. Although the basement was a proving ground of sorts, from which Phinney would emerge to craft a masterpiece, there was little downstairs that required a light touch with the pencil, saw, or hammer. Thirty-penny nails, at least, had been used to fasten scrap one-by-eights across the joints of tandem timbers to make them into one continuous main beam. These spikes were not driven with much finesse—they were slammed home. In contrast, as we shall see, upstairs finishing nails would be hammered in with such precision and pride that their heads would be left exposed. Phinney may not have had much opportunity in the cellar to practice such fine points, but he must have had plenty of time to think about them. Although the principal beam would have no counterpart upstairs, it provided an opportunity to beat the hell out of any devils in the shadows. And although Phinney needed assistance in the basement, it appears that he built the rest of his house virtually alone.

Family photos labeled July 1952 record the construction milestone of having the subfloor in place. They also show the fireplace built to about ceiling height. One picture shows the four Phinney children sitting on the mantel in a house without walls, rooms, or roof. The front stoop shown in another photo was built up out of smaller stones than in the fireplace, and it provided just a three-step climb up to the next stage of work. But soon fall and winter would intervene, and Phinney's half-built house would hibernate under snow.

The large stone fireplace serves as a partition but not a sharp barrier between the living room and kitchen spaces. Nevertheless, by having located the fireplace where he did, Phinney effectively subdivided the front half of the house in the ratio of approximately 2 to 1, with the spaces spilling around the edifice into each other and creating a fluid kind of keeping room surrounding the hearth. The concept of a keeping room as a multipurpose common space next to the kitchen dates from Colonial times. Such a living area has come back into fashion as a means of opening up and extending the modern kitchen with some space of varying informality that may overlap in decoration and use with a family room. In Phinney's house, the living room and kitchen together can certainly pass for one long keeping room.

Phinney had help collecting the staggeringly wide variety of stones that make up the fireplace: George and Milly Stafford, who still lived on Arrowsic Road at the time, helped gather them from the land around the house. The fireplace sits on a massive concrete pedestal that was most likely poured as soon as the concrete of the basement floor had cured enough to support the vertical formwork and its contents. The fireplace proper is striking in its mass and its variegated colors, but the workmanship of the coarse mortar does leave a little to be desired in stonework that is full of voids. Still, it has lasted for six decades, as has the small stoop and the stone walkway leading up to it. Even though as a younger man he had built a barbecue pit for his home in Livingston, masonry work may not have been Phinney's strong suit, but his sense of proportion was impeccable; the fireplace stands as a monument to that.

The stone fireplace

In a nod to the style of the times, Phinney chose to break up what would otherwise have been a sheer stone back on the fireplace with three large, thick slabs of slate projecting about six inches out from it to form a stair-like arrangement of shelves, probably meant for keepsakes, knickknacks, tchotchkes, and maybe cookie jars. The cantilevered shelves seem almost to have been put there to balance the visual weight of the fireplace's three-piece slate mantel. Otherwise, virtually all of the house's walls, whether made of stone or wood, would remain unadorned by anything but color and texture. Only pairs of abandoned screw holes here and there give a hint that at one time something was mounted on the walls, but not necessarily by Phinney.

In aboveground carpentry Phinney truly did find his métier, and the uniformity of workmanship points to a single hand wielding a single hammer. During construction his family likely stayed across the cove with Grandma Gertrude. Phinney may have found solace in working by himself for himself, alone with the rhythmic sounds of tools in action: the reciprocating tones of saws crosscutting long pieces of lumber into shorter ones and ripping wide boards into narrower ones; the intermittent staccato blows of a hammer driving nails into place; the soothing sounds of planes and rasps and sandpaper softening hard edges; and the hush of cloth rubbing stain into and brush spreading varnish onto smooth wood. Since he alone controlled the tools and the time, he may have found the pounding and other noises therapeutic, he being in complete control of their frequency and intensity. He was free to pound out work tunes as he wished. Mr. Phinney did it with a hammer by the river.

With the long timber beam installed across the basement void, the wooden sills set atop the foundation walls, floor joists laid across the spaces between sill and beam, and subflooring installed over the joists, exterior walls could be erected. It was at this stage that the balloon-frame concept most favored the carpenter. In most cases, the framing for an entire wall, complete with window and door openings, could be laid out on the level open floor and nailed together there—thereby insuring that the wall be flat, straight, and true— and then raised as a unit into place. However, with the standard sixteen-inch spacing of two-by-four studs—which were then much more nearly two inches by four than they are today—the framing for the thirty-two-foot-long south gable wall of Phinney's house would have weighed around five hundred pounds, which would have made it too heavy and unwieldy to be rotated into an upright position by just one man, or perhaps even one with a strong helper. Complete east- and west-wall framing assembled on the floor would naturally have been still heavier and even more unwieldy. Thus, unless Phinney gathered a number of jobbers or strong neighbors to help him in raising the walls up off the floor, he would most likely have built them in shorter sections or, less likely, hammered them together in a vertical position to start with. In fact, for at least the part of the west wall containing the entrance, he had to do this anyway, because the massive, immovable fireplace stood only five feet away, leaving insufficient room on the floor to lay out the framing.

Once the outside walls were framed, Phinney could concentrate on how he would construct the roof. To cross the entire thirty-two-foot distance between front and rear walls in a single span would have required very large and heavy timbers or the use of intermediate supports. He might have employed roof trusses, which may have been what he had in mind when he made his hip-roofed model. In it, the central wall was not continuous, nor was it everywhere over the main beam in the basement (and that may have been why he had made provisions for additional, parallel beams in the basement). In the model, the kitchen was noticeably shallower than the living room. It may have dawned on Phinney, when it came time to put up a real roof, rather than a dollhouse-cover one, that he would have to choose between trusses and intermediate supports. The prefabricated truss, a so-called engineered system, was not yet common in the early 1950s, and so Phinney would likely have had to assemble his own. But the building and raising of each truss into position would have presented the same challenge as raising a complete wall: the truss would have been heavy and unwieldy.

It may have been foreseeing this problem that caused Phinney to change from a hip roof to one so barely peaked that it was considered flat (and from three cellar beams to one, since it was now only above the centrally positioned beam that a major load-bearing wall was to be erected). Thinking of the roof as having just two parts would have required him to span only sixteen feet at a time. But he would have to incorporate into his house's framing a structural ridgepole to provide support for the rafters, which in being almost horizontal could practically be called joists. The need for a central ridge beam more than anything may have caused him to increase the east-west dimension of the kitchen at the expense of the rooms behind it. Doing so meant he could put a single continuous wall directly over the large central beam in the basement, thereby dividing the upstairs space exactly in two. This major load-bearing wall supports one end of each of the sixteen-foot-long, four-by-eight timber rafters that Phinney set on approximately two-foot centers, the imprecision possibly being an artifact of how difficult it was to get the beams into place. The front and rear rafters are offset from each other, indicating that the central wall was not sufficiently thick for them to be butted end-to-end atop it. Nevertheless, the timbers defined both the barely sloping exterior roofline that had a rise of only about one-half inch in every foot of run and the exposed-beam ceiling of the interior space. This resulted in the sloped-ceiling look that today confounds visitors, who often stare at it askance as if wondering whether to ask why it is not on the level.

Phinney may have been able to purchase the rafter timbers in a standard size—a factor that may also have dictated the final east-west dimension of the house—or he may have had them formed at a lumber mill from pine trees he harvested on the land. But it is unlikely that he could have purchased as stock timber the

Braced ceiling timbers

one-inch-thick panel boards or even two-by-eights, the short four-by-seven timbers used as rafter bracing show a gap here and there where either the brace was not cut square or the rafters had warped or twisted. However, because the braces are recessed into the shadows of the rafters, these small imperfections are barely noticeable.

The framing defining bedrooms and closets was complicated by the numerous corners and doors designed into them, but because their walls provide intermediate supports for the rafters, no additional braces were needed. Once the wall framing and most of the rafters were in place, further progress might have had to wait for the massive fireplace chimney to penetrate the roofline, if it had not already done so, and the roof could be framed right up to the chimney. Except maybe for the mortar, Phinney used good materials throughout the house, and he secured everything to stay in place. In the only opening window that appears to be original—an inward swinging casement in the living room—he attached to its bottom rail a piece of metal flashing with a series of precisely spaced nails. The ends of the flashing are bent up into a neat detail that channels rainwater away and out from the corners of the window frame. The window, most likely a standard size that determined the dimensions of the opening, is framed on three sides in common two-by-eights, their narrower face set flush with the paneling inside and providing all by themselves a simple, neat, and finished appearance outside. The fourth side, which abuts a picture window, is framed with one of the four-by-eights that separate the large windows and serve also as posts to support the roof in the northwest corner of the structure. The clever use of so-called dimension (that is, standard-sized) lumber eliminated the need for milled molding anywhere in the house, stock lumber serving nicely not only as the framing but also as the finishing trim for the windows. One exception is the exterior windowsills, which appear to be pieces of clamshell-like molding, used because their sloping profile encourages water to drain away. However, these may have been added later in response to water pooling on a flat windowsill.

Water and its cousins, snow and ice, seem to be the greatest enemies of the house, and the most common remedial work that has had to be done on it has involved the repair and replacement of water-damaged exterior wood. Where unprotected crosscut end-grain sits in water or snow melt, it wicks up the moisture and begins to decay. Unfortunately, the casement window's separate storm window and screen, which have lasted through many decades of seasonal changes, are beginning to show their age. The

Living-room casement window

storm window, which must sit in snow most of the winter, has a bit of rot on its bottom, but it still has left in it some years of useful life. Both storm window and screen are attached to the frame not by the kind of exterior hanging hardware that I remember from my parents' house of the same vintage but by four hook-and-eye pairs that fasten from the inside and so make it easy to change between screen and storm window without having to go outside and use a ladder. Hung on three black H- and L-style hinges, the casement window still fits nicely in its frame and sticks only slightly in damp weather. The modestly fancy latch—an uncharacteristic extravagance—located midway up the window sash is supplemented with a pair of hand-carved wooden turn buttons located near the top and bottom of the frame, just to be sure. (Phinney, apparently a belt-and-suspenders kind of builder, seems to have wanted to make extra-sure about things.) These handmade buttons still function quite effectively, and the window closes tightly in the face of the fierce north wind that Canadian cold fronts bring down the river.

The window proper does not appear originally to have had any hardware capable of holding it full open or at some intermediate position. Thus in the summer, when the screen is in place, the wind can slam the unlatched window fully open against the wall to its right. To keep this from happening, someone (perhaps George) installed some large hook-and-eye hardware on the window and its sill. When engaged with the single eye on the window, one hook keeps it open wide but at a safe distance from the wall. When the other hook is engaged it allows the window to be set in a half-open position. Unfortunately, the hardware is neither elegant nor inconspicuous, and so betrays a slightly heavier hand at work on the house that Phinney built.

In addition to splurging on the four-by-eight rafters, Phinney also did so on the milled tongue-and-groove knotty-pine paneling

Inelegant but functional hooks and eye

with chamfered edges that he used throughout the house. He employed nominal four-, five-, six-, seven-, eight-, and ten-inch widths, with the eight-inch overwhelmingly predominant. The variety in panel width gave him the ability to achieve a sense of randomness in the finished walls. But a sense of randomness is not the same as true randomness, for Phinney seems often to have chosen a particular width of panel board for a particular location to minimize his effort and maximize the aesthetic effect. How did he do this?

The principal interior wall both structurally and architecturally is the high one located directly over the timber beam in the basement. The expanse of this wall is interrupted only by two oversized openings that allow access to the hall connecting to the back rooms. It appears that the exact position and width of these openings may have been determined by the way panel boards fit together to finish the walls. Starting in the northeast corner of the living room, Phinney seems to have chosen board widths to minimize the sawing he had to do to fit the boards around the ceiling timbers. When he approached the point along the wall where the first opening is located, he used a board just wide enough to carry the paneling to the opening. He capped the end of the north section of the wall with a one-by-eight that serves also as a slender post to support a delicate lintel. The length of this lintel was evidently determined by an arrangement of panel boards that would require no rip sawing. This also determined the position of the right-side post and so the width of the opening, which is approximately thirty-nine inches. The physical energy expended would have been minimal, the execution was flawless, and the effect is stunning. These are the kinds of things that captivated us when we turned our glider rockers inward.

Throughout almost the entire house, the knotty-pine boards are installed in the conventional vertical orientation, resting nicely on the single horizontal one used as a baseboard. The effect is architecturally striking in its simplicity, and remarkable in its careful execution. The grooved verticals meeting the chamfered horizontal produce for me a visual effect of outstanding beauty and proportion. The "random-width" boards, with their soft edges, contrast nicely with the single horizontal edge along the baseboard. There is no shoe molding, carrying further the simplicity and cleanness of the design. The fit is impeccable everywhere, even where the tops of the paneling meet the bottom of the sill supporting the living-room picture windows, which are framed top and bottom simply in two-by-eights. The proportions of the ensemble, evocative of those of the base, shaft, and capital of a classical column, are worthy of the modern Vitruvian man that I imagine Phinney must have been.

Each piece of variable-width wall paneling was attached to each furring strip behind it with three finishing nails (except only two were used in the narrowest boards). Nails are neatly spaced and carefully aligned, as if a movable straightedge or ephemeral chalk line were used as a guide. Nailheads are aligned as neatly as the pips of a dotted line marking a coupon to be clipped, and it is difficult to find a nail in a hole that is too big for it. A lesser carpenter than Phinney might have struck a wrongly hit nail sideways to straighten it, leaving an oval wound in the wood, or the

Evocative baseboard, paneling, and windowsill

nail might have been extracted with the claw end of the hammer, and a replacement driven obliquely into a then too-large hole. I have found little evidence that Phinney performed either of these operations. Virtually every nail fully fills the hole it made for itself, and the head of every nail is flush with the surface of the wood. A nail set—the punch used to drive the head of a finishing nail below the surface of a piece of wood—seems not to have been in Phinney's toolbox, or, if it was there, was seldom used. Nail sets are most often employed when there is concern that hammering a nail all the way into a piece of wood might leave an impression of the hammer head. But nowhere have I found a hammer mark on a panel board, which suggests that Phinney had a soft touch with the tool that he must have held and wielded under absolute control. Had he set nails, the hollows left behind would have been susceptible to collecting stain and varnish and dust, calling more attention to themselves than they do. With the nails flush with the surface as they are, neither they nor their holes cast any significant shadows. The stained and varnished nailheads, when they are noticed at all, appear to be just tiny knots in the wood.

Phinney knew the technique of toenailing, in which a nail is driven at an angle to fasten one piece of lumber to another, such as the bottom of a stud to a sill plate. He appears to have toenailed the braces to the rafters, unless he used screws. It is hard to tell because he set or countersunk the fasteners and filled the recesses. But he definitely chose not to use the method on the tongue-and-groove knotty pine, for which it is now considered standard practice to angle-nail through the root of the tongue of each board so that it is pushed tight up against the previously placed one, with the nails used on it being concealed in the process. Hardwood flooring is installed using toenailing; however, unlike flooring boards, which are expected to meet flush with each other—leaving only the color, grain, and texture of the wood to distinguish a board from its neighbors—knotty-pine panel boards, being chamfered along their entire length, form a prominent V-groove where they meet. This distinctive delineation of each board is elegant in itself and also avoids potentially incongruous juxtapositions of incompatible grain patterns and edge knots.

Well-aligned nails

Did Phinney simply not like the idea of toenailing knotty pine, or did he think it unnecessary? Or could he have actually toenailed the wall-panel boards, covering up evidence of the act along the way, then added the lines of two or three exposed nails on the face of the board to be sure the work was secure, as seems to have been his wont? Since I have not tried to take off a board, I have no evidence that wall boards are held in place by anything but the finishing nails whose minimal heads were left in plain view, perhaps reinforcing an argument that Phinney, as adept as he was with his tools, was not the professional carpenter that his father-in-law had been. Billie Phinney remembered Mr. Straatsma as a man who "could pick the right grain of a block of wood at the local fair, hammer a nail in with one blow and win a box of chocolates" for her.

One place where Phinney may have allowed some help was with the entrance. Old pictures of the house show a wooden door with a single small square pane of glass centered in it at eye level. A former owner remembers that it was decorated with the likeness of a deer, perhaps done by Bobby, the budding artist. The front door, like the house's windows, was framed in two-by-eights, which are still in place, even though the original door is not. All interior doorways were, like the ample openings in the main wall, finished in a more delicate post-and-lintel style, the boards used having an actual thickness of three-quarters of an inch, which would have been ordered as nominal "one-by" lumber.

Normally, I would question the use of so slender a piece of wood as a lintel, whose historical structural purpose was to act as a beam spanning the width of the opening—as stone architraves spanning between columns did in Greek temples—and to bear the weight of what was set upon it. As in our basement, beams are supposed to be deeper than they are wide. However, in Phinney's hands the fragile-looking lintel seems to work. With the adjacent walls of knotty-pine paneling evoking stands of trees, a deep and heavy lintel would have created the discordant image of a fallen log high above a forest floor. The one-by-eight scantlings that cap the ends of the walls separating the front from the back areas of the house are set flush with the wall paneling. All edges were softly and carefully rounded, perhaps by means of a well-controlled rasp followed by the use of fine sandpaper but more likely, judging by the uniformity of radius, with the use of a corner rounding plane. The softness of the corners in the over-seven-foot-high doorless openings in the wall between the large, bright front rooms and the hallway leading to the relatively small, dark back rooms make the transition less abrupt. The opening next to the kitchen is forty-seven and a half inches wide, making it easy to maneuver large equipment and appliances—furnace, water heater, accumulator, washing machine—onto the basement stairs located just behind the wall.

All doors to rooms and closets are made by hand out of tongue-and-groove knotty-pine paneling. In virtually all cases, the body of the door is made up of wall-panel boards of uniform width (a nominal six inches) reinforced on their back side with the kind of Z-pattern sway bracing usually found on garden gates and barn doors. In the context of this house they appear to be a natural choice. The doors were constructed and hung so that their joint grooves are offset from those of the surrounding wall, thus giving a visual signal to the door's location. The back, or exposed braced door structure facing the inside of each room or closet, was done with the same care and attention to detail as everything else. The projecting edges of the bracing are chamfered, and the edges formed where the chamfer meets the adjacent faces are all softly rounded. The bracing is attached to the door proper with countersunk screws, which were recessed and the depressions filled, thus leaving no screw heads at all visible on any surface of the door. Only the different way the wood filler has taken the stain, or the way the stain and filler have

A door back with Z-bracing

aged, gives away the location of the screws. The edges of each door are rounded like those of the frame into which it fits neatly, firmly, and softly.

I expect that Phinney's experience as a teenager building a model Napoleonic carriage prepared him well to put the delicate finishing touches that he did on his house. The cutting and carving of the small pieces of pine, maple, and other woods that were recommended for use by the contest plans and instructions no doubt gave him not only the skill but also the confidence that he could work with wood on a full-scale structure. The way he blended hard orthogonal surfaces together across soft rounded edges is masterful and full of respect for the material and its use. He may not have been crafting a carriage for an emperor, but he was doing something more important: making a home for his family.

I deduce from the house's generally adequately wide but uncommonly short (seventy-five-inch-high) doorways leading into rooms

Doors to a bedroom (left) and to a closet (right)

The house in the mid-1950s

and closets that Phinney was not overly tall. I am over six feet tall, and I barely fit beneath the lintels. Our son, Stephen, who is about six-six, has to duck when passing through a bedroom and bathroom doorway. George Stafford was also tall, and Milly once told me how he dealt with short doorways: When entering or exiting a room he stepped deliberately over the threshold, for he had learned that if he placed a foot directly on it his next step would raise his head into the lintel.

All doors that open from the small back hallway into the bedrooms and bathroom are recessed, as would be a typical inward-opening door hung today, thus providing a further visual cue as to their location and function. Outward-opening closet doors were treated differently. They are hung flush with the paneled wall into which they are set, thus providing as much of a uniformly flat wall expanse as possible. There should be no possibility of confusion between a door leading from a room into the hallway and one granting access to a closet, something that cannot necessarily be said about homes whose doors look the same front and back.

The details of Phinney's house suggest a lot about the man: Like Frank Lloyd Wright, he may not have been tall, but he had high aspirations for his art. His saw and hammer skills were superb. He cut each board carefully, leaving ends that were square and full, with none of the missing chips or protruding slivers that mark an impatient carpenter who prematurely thinks he is done sawing and lunges his tool across the finish line. Phinney gave each board his undivided attention. His unerring care is manifest in every detail.

Six

THE RAIN
IN
MAINE

IN MAINE, APRIL SHOWERS bring May mud. The flowers don't arrive till June. July and August can be warm, or hot, or just right. Regardless, few homes have air-conditioning, and ours is no exception. Most summers we never miss it; during those rare others, after a week or so of heat and humidity, we want to take a drive in the car with the cool air blowing across our face. A boat ride is equally refreshing. And four times each summer, we can find relief by attending Maine State Music Theater performances held in the recently renovated and air-conditioned Memorial Hall at nearby Bowdoin College.

On many an occasion we have walked through a warm, gentle rain in Brunswick to reach the theater. Yes, *Singin' in the Rain* has been one of the productions. When it rains in Maine, and when there is no show to attend and little to do but watch the drops pock the river and listen to the arrhythmic tattoos played upon the roof, my mind can be haunted by musical ditties that take it to faraway places and make-believe times and tunes: *The rain in Maine drains Spainly down our lane.*

Our lane in Maine does bring the spring rains down the slope of ground that runs towards the river. When it rains, the lane's two tracks turn into a pair of rushing streams, and anything in the water's path gets swept along. At first, the grade of the lane falls gently and straight from our neighbor's barn, then it gets steeper as it veers to miss the tall old pine tree just before reaching the house. Unlike a car, water has no steering wheel; it wants to continue in a straight line until acted upon by an outside force. The tracks in the lane provide that—until they make a turn sharper than the rushing water can follow. Once upon a time it headed straight for the house, smashing against the foundation wall and seeping into the ground beside it, penetrating the wall, overflowing the basement drainage channel, covering the basement floor, and seeking the drain at the far end to carry it into the cove. If for any reason that drain is clogged, the water has no place to go but up.

The owners before us, the Moniers, must have heard and seen enough of spring rains to understand the ways of the water. One summer, they asked George Stafford to help them with what they thought would be a solution to the lane's rush of water. George implemented the plan by anchoring pressure-treated landscape timbers in a gradually turning line to redirect the water back onto the driveway, thereby marking a division between the lawn beside the house and the gravel drive. As an added benefit, the timber curbing kept the gravel from being washed onto the grass.

But nothing could keep the spring torrents from carrying downhill all the pine needles, pinecones, bird bones, feathers, acorns, leaves, grass clippings, loose pebbles, and other small debris that had accumulated in the lane and its watershed since the previous summer. So when it rained, it poured this residue of seasons past against the wooden curb and left it as a thick and soggy drift to dry in the post-deluge sun. If allowed to stay in place, the hardened ramp of detritus would defeat the purpose of the curb, so it became necessary to remove the traces of fall as a part of spring cleanup.

In winter, snow falls, snow melts, and water freezes—all along our lane. Even though the temperature might not get above freezing, the winter afternoon sun thaws enough ice to coat the road with a fresh slick overnight. This is not a big problem for driving down to the place where the upper lane meets the abandoned driveway. But

Lawn timbers placed to curb runoff

after that the lane's grade begins to increase and what goes down it will not necessarily come up. The greatest incline, the one up into our garage, is totally unmanageable. So, during one winter that we spent in Maine, we soon learned to leave our car parked where the abandoned drive meets the lane and haul our groceries down to the house on foot, taking care to walk on a cushion of snow that gave us some traction over the ice beneath it. Because the snow was regularly refreshed, I did have to shovel a path between the door to our house and the door of our car. Whenever I did, however, I was careful to keep from digging too deep, lest I expose the ice base.

As built, our house had an open stairway leading down to the basement. Perhaps Phinney, who most likely took a course in thermodynamics in college, employed this design feature thinking he could take advantage of the temperature of the underlying rock to keep the house warmer in the winter and cooler in the summer. This concept might have moderated the summer temperature inside the house, but a former owner told us that the open stairway made it very cold in wintertime. Over the course of a long Maine winter, the exposed rock in the basement no doubt gave up its heat before the air of the season gave up its cold.

The house is centrally heated by forced air ducted from an oil burner in the basement. The automatic control device for the furnace was originally located on the wall beside the basement stairway, on the side facing the hall and bedroom area and thus shielded from the rays of the afternoon sun. The thermostat Phinney used was the circular Honeywell model T-86, which was introduced in 1953, when he was probably shopping for finishing touches to his house. The handsome physical appearance of this now-classic instrument was the work of the early industrial designer Henry Dreyfuss, whereas the mechanical and electrical innards were the work of Honeywell engineer Carl Kronmiller, who became known as Mr. Thermostat. He kept dust and dirt from fouling the device by employing a mercury switch, with its electrical leads sealed in a glass bulb partly filled with the liquid metal, which is a conductor. The bulb itself is attached to a bimetallic strip, whose inclination is influenced by changes in the ambient temperature. When it is cooler than the thermostat setting, the mercury comes in contact with both leads, thus completing the circuit and turning on the furnace. As the house heats up, the bimetallic strip responds and reorients the bulb, pooling the mercury at one end and leaving an electrical lead untouched so that the circuit is broken and the furnace shuts off. The iconic circular shape of the device's housing caused the world's most popular thermostat to become known simply as the Round. Its understated simplicity was in keeping with Phinney's design vision.

Winter also causes Maine lakes and rivers to freeze over, which historically brought out the icebreakers, the ice harvesters, and the ice fishermen. Before refrigeration, millions of tons of blocks of crystal-clear ice were cut annually from Maine waters and shipped to Boston, the West Indies, and beyond. The Kennebec alone could yield a million tons of crystal-blue ice a season. On the other side of Arrowsic the frozen Sasanoa supported a colony of fishing shanties anchored over holes in the ice. George Stafford would drive his pickup truck a half mile out onto a frozen lake to reach his shanty, which measured four by five feet in plan and was just tall enough for him to stand up in. The minimal structure was a true balloon frame, a wooden cage over which was stretched sized cloth painted in whatever odd color was found in a can in the workshop. The shanty was furnished with a space heater and a place to sit and wait for the smelt to bite. The small, fat, silvery fish are considered a seasonal treat, and smelt-fishing camps still dot the Kennebec in wintertime.

In the spring, after the ice and snow have melted and the rains have slowed, our driveway, lane, and turnaround are full of the many muddy ruts left by FedEx trucks. These tend to be redistributed and eventually smoothed out by other trucks: the UPS truck, the oil truck, the plumber's truck, the painter's truck, the roofer's truck, the chimney sweep's truck, the furniture truck, the meter reader's truck, the telephone worker's truck, the yardman's truck, the tree surgeon's truck, the handyman's truck, the neighbor's truck. Everyone in Maine seems to drive a truck, or a truck disguised as a sport-utility vehicle. Those who don't drive a truck drive something with four-wheel drive (the state car seems to be the Subaru), not only for the snow but also for the mud and muck. *And where's that muddy lane? In Maine! In Maine!*

When heavy fog rolls across the water, as it often does on a cool morning after a night of steady rain, we cannot see to the edge of the river, let alone across to the other side. We cannot see the cove to the north. We cannot see our guest cabin to the south, or any other house in any direction. We can barely see the garage. We are in the nirvana of retreats, alone with our imaginations and our thoughts and the show tunes like *Mame* that we cannot get out of our mind's ear: *You coax the past right out of the now, Maine.*

I am no more a geologist than I am a lyricist, but I think the river before us must have looked and flowed for thousands of millennia pretty much the way it does now. The granite that defines its banks is so solid and impervious that the fresh water from our well, which is located maybe forty feet from the river, has no hint of brackishness. The river itself is brackish, of course, its current running up and down with the ocean tides.

A soil stack in our basement once took all the house's wastewater directly into the cove and thereby into the Kennebec. The timber, pulp and paper, fishing, and other industries, as well as farms and municipalities, had long discharged waste directly into the river. As recently as the late 1960s, before it had a treatment plant, Bath had thirty-five sewer lines dumping raw, untreated sewage into the river. During a search-and-recovery operation along Fiddler's Reach in 1968, divers described the water as "black," giving them zero visibility. In fact, the granite river bottom itself was quite clean, but the complex and swift currents, occurring in three layers, mixed up the waste-laden water above the bottom into a mucky mess. Public awareness of the problem had begun to grow in the 1950s, the level of pollution peaked in the 1960s, and the great cleanup was sealed by the enactment of environmental-protection legislation in the 1970s. The capping of the soil stack and the installation of a septic system that flushes the pollution under the weedy rug we call our north lawn was the property's small contribution to the cleanup. The river now is clean enough to swim in, as our neighbors on the cove often do.

Savvy Indians and settlers and traders and fishermen and shipbuilders and yachtsmen and recreational boaters and kayakers have long ridden this river with the tides to lessen their effort and speed their journey. We watch vessels pass and imagine a time when there were no steamboats or motorboats, no puff-puff or putt-putt. Then, the only sounds were the push of wind in sails and the pull of oars in water, the near silence that returns when a solitary sailboat tacks along the river.

It seems most quiet when the water is shrouded in fog. Between our place and the river's edge grows a line of oriental-looking black

Black pines against the fog

pines, seemingly stunted in their growth, their branches twisted and drooping toward the ground, as if burdened with life and afflicted with arboreal arthritis. In heavy fog, these pines, being close and dark, are silhouetted against a blank white background, like shadows cast upon a clean sheet. Beyond them, we might hear a lone boat slowly passing or a single fish jumping and slapping down on the water. The modern history of the lower Kennebec (the part once called the Sagadahoc) replays in our minds: the English settlers arrive downriver in the summer of 1607 and establish Popham Colony. They thrive for a single season, harvesting berries to eat and trees to build a ship, the one believed to have been the first ocean-going vessel made by westerners in the New World. The winter is rough, bringing in seven hours' time in the middle of January 1608, "thunder, lightning, raine, frost, snow, all in abundance, the last continuing." Though the Abenaki had quietly made their cedar-framed canoes sheathed in birch bark, the colonists work more audibly, felling great pines, hewing and sawing timber, and shaping and pounding trunnels. But the Maine winter is too much for the Popham pioneers, and before the following winter they give up claim to being the first permanent European settlement in the New World and return to England in their newly built ship, a fifty-one-foot, thirty-ton pinnace they christened the *Virginia of Sagadahoc*. When the *Virginia* next crosses the Atlantic, it will carry supplies to the Jamestown settlement.

Our first visits to our new place had been in the late fall and early spring, when few if any boats were in the water. We had turned our glider chairs to the window and stared out at the river as if it were a wildlife film running sideways. As we sailed our chairs back and forth to tack and ratchet time, we watched the river move to the tick-tick-tock of the tide clock as it hung upon the wall. Ebb and flow, we were as one with the show. As we watched the action on the river, which moved over the course of a day twice in each direction, playing out and winding in, we thought of time, Cole Porter's time—night and day: *Whether near to us or far, it's no matter River where you are, we think of you. . . .*

We watched seals float on the tide up- and downriver, using their energy only to dive for dinner. It became a pastime to watch for where the creatures would reemerge. During an early spring visit, we saw the seals riding ice floes, sunning themselves. We began to understand the drama that the tides brought and anticipated the comings and goings of nature. But nature is also capricious and so can surprise us.

The silence was broken one rainy Sunday morning—one of the first we had spent in our place—by the repeated crack-crack of what we figured were gunshots. We knew there were hunters in the area, and the sounds came from the direction of the marsh. When they stopped and the silence returned, we resumed our river watching through the rain, hoping to see another snout drifting out on the tide, only to erupt suddenly from the water and pull the body of a seal first up and then down in a great arc into a deep dive.

Something was coming downriver that was much too large for a seal's snout and much too irregular in shape for a boat, though our sense of scale and proportion on the river had yet to develop. Could it be a clumsy moose swimming with the tide? Our guesses evolved as the thing approached our point. Perhaps it was some large tree trunk, or a damaged boat with a single outrigger. As it came closer, distinct features emerged. It appeared to be maybe a small rowboat with someone in a yellow slicker struggling with something off the port side. Had a fishing partner fallen overboard? Should we call 911? Did that number apply to water emergencies? Should we try to help? But no one aboard appeared to be calling for help, and we had no boat and we had no line. As we dithered, the boat and its hanger-on moved directly in front of our house.

Since the boat was barely twenty feet from the riverbank—plus the thirty feet down from our perch—we could finally see what was playing out. The person in the slicker was trying to haul a deer into the boat, but the deer was so much larger than the person that all that could be done was to hold it against the side and try to steer the boat toward the shore. We knew that the riverbank was steep and rocky for some distance downriver, and did not know how a boat would access it going in that direction. As quickly as it had appeared, the boat and its occupant and the outrigger deer rushed by on the ebbing tide.

Finally that afternoon the weather cleared up, and we went out for a drive. As we passed the Staffords' house, we saw George and Milly framed in a basement door that we had not seen open before. When we stopped to say hello and tell them what we had seen that morning, we startled them. When we saw what they were doing, they startled us. They were dressing a deer, which they had hung by a hook anchored in a ceiling timber. It was in fact the deer we had seen in the water. The person in the slicker had been Milly, who may be small but is not frail. She and George hastened to assure us that they had not been hunting out of season. Rather, she had spotted a deer limping through the marsh. Evidently an inept driver or illegal hunter had wounded the animal, which had a broken leg. Milly wanted to put the deer out of its misery, and so she had shot at it, hitting it and driving it into the river. When that happened, she ran to their boat and pursued the animal, catching up with it at about the place where we first saw them emerge through the rain. She was not strong enough to haul the carcass aboard, but she was able to hold on to it. In the meantime, George got into his truck and drove to a place where he could catch the boat and pull it and its outrigger cargo to shore. They hauled the boat and the dead animal back home and began to butcher it for their freezer. Mainers do not like to see anything go to waste, including a wounded and drowning deer, and they will go to great lengths to salvage whatever can be salvaged.

Human hunters are not the only ones that we have watched ply and sometimes struggle in the river. Because of all the wildlife around the area, we have worried about the safety of the various house cats we have brought with us to Maine. Bald eagles dive from great heights toward the water and carry large fish away in their talons. We have heard that an eagle will also catch and lift a small cat into the air, taking it to a place from which it will never return. During our first summer or two, there were a couple of domestic cats that walked along our riverbank now and then, but after a while we no longer saw them. We brought our twenty-one-year-old cat to Maine the first summer we had our place but he wisely preferred to stay inside. Now our younger cats, Ted and Leon, who in North Carolina move freely between the indoors and outdoors, upon their arrival in Maine each summer explore the house anew, easily finding the previous year's play routes and napping places, but make no attempt to run out the door whenever it is opened. Perhaps it is the river's expanse or the real-life size of the eagles that regularly sweep past the point that have settled any question of going out.

One June, when temperatures in Maine can range anywhere from late-winter to midsummer ones, we had all the windows in the house closed to keep out the chill. Late one afternoon, with the sun shining brightly and bringing warmth into our living room, and its light illuminating furniture and felines as if they were out-of-season Christmas-window displays, we were startled by a very loud thump. Had one of the cats knocked something to the floor? Or did the water pump gasp its last? We looked out and found a very young eagle sitting stunned in the grass below the window, facing toward the river. Perhaps it had spied one of our young cats sunning himself and had not yet learned that glass is thicker than air. Having hit the windowpane in full dive, the youngster was down, but not out. After a moment, it flew away more gracefully than it had arrived. We and our cats took note. Bird–window collisions can also leave a mess, as we learned one spring when we found evidence of a major impact on one of the north-side windows. The bird must have emerged from the water after a dive and flown directly into the glass at full glide, for there was an oil-and-feather imprint of the side of a head and a sixteen-inch outstretched wing.

I don't know whether cats can tell the difference between bald eagles and other large birds, but I know from experience that some humans have a hard time doing so. Somewhat smaller than eagles, ospreys are often confused with the larger raptors. Seen from far in the distance, they do appear to the untrained eye to soar and dive in a similar way, but ospreys do not do so as gracefully as eagles—or at least those adults that do not crash into window glass. Also, whereas eagles seem to need little human help other than laws protecting them as an endangered species, ospreys often find themselves in positions of need, on occasion becoming causes célèbres and wards of the state.

When the Maine transportation department wanted to paint the rusting Arrowsic Bridge some years ago, there was great public concern over what would happen to the ospreys that nested atop it. Ospreys tend to return to the same nest each spring, raising young to the delight of passersby. A power pole in the median of U.S. 1 just west of Bath is a familiar osprey nest site. When slowed in summer traffic, motorists can watch and study the birds atop the pole. Motorists also drove slowly across the Arrowsic Bridge to see what was happening at the long-established nest atop it. Painting the bridge was put on hold while a solution to the osprey residence was sought. The transportation department finally built new osprey "condos" within sight of the bridge, one in a tree on a point of land just to the east and one still further east, on a high pole in the marsh grass in Hanson Bay. The hope was that once the nest atop the bridge was removed ospreys would relocate to one of these new locations and the bridge could be painted. To prevent the birds from building a new nest on the bridge, it was proposed that metal cones that would shed nesting material be installed atop the

structure, but that prospect was opposed by historic preservationists, who wanted the bridge to remain in its original state.

After a year or two of delay, the ospreys, the preservationists,
and the state cooperated to allow the painting to go forward. One
of the span's two lanes was closed, which required the installation
of a pair of temporary traffic lights—the one at the south end of the
bridge being for the duration the island's only stoplight—to regu-
late alternate-direction one-lane traffic across the bridge while work
was in progress. When the project was finished, the bridge looked
as good as new, with a neat coat of light green, which appears to be
the favorite bridge color of the Maine transportation department.
For years after the painting project, the ospreys did not attempt to
reestablish their nests atop the fresh green bridge. But in the past
two summers we have seen a lone osprey (sometimes with a fish in

Osprey nesting in U.S. 1 median

its claw) perched on a power line that crosses with the bridge. We wonder if it is trying to reestablish its ancestral home. Mainers tend to return to their roots.

Among other hunters and fishers on the river are the cormorants. These large and voracious fish eaters are referred to as "them shag" by the locals, who do not like the birds or their great appetite. Cormorants float low in the water because their feathers absorb rather than shed it, so the only part of the bird that is visible is its small head supported on its long neck, looking somewhat like a raised periscope. When the bird dives, the cormorant shows its clumsiness, but once underwater it is a model of efficiency, catching fish seemingly at will. I have often seen a bird come up from a dive swallowing its catch. The cormorant is the diving bird around whose neck the Chinese have traditionally put a snug ring, so that it cannot eat the fish that it catches, and keep the bird on a leash, so that it can be reeled in like a lure. When free to eat for itself as it sees fit, the cormorant will do so until it decides to move on. However, that is more easily said than done by a well-fed waterlogged bird. The cormorant performs an elaborate Ed Norton–like preparation for flying, which consists of flapping its wings in place to shake the water and then taking off like a loaded bomber on a long runway. The bird's legs are short but its feet still drag for some distance in the water, and it is only after many flaps and much distance that it clears the surface and flies just inches above the water to a rock or other perch to stretch out its wings in the sun and dry itself.

Because the river brings fresh water from inland Maine, there are no lobsters to be trapped off our point, which is a few miles up from the river's mouth and the open sea. The crustaceans need salt water to survive, but whatever seawater makes its way upstream with the tide is soon flushed out by the river current. This means that we have no array of the colorful lobster floats that dot the waters of harbors and bays, marking the location of a line to a proprietary lobster trap. At the mouth of the Kennebec, there is an abundance of these floats, but when the river flows unexpectedly high with spring snow melt or the runoff from heavy rains, they are more likely than not attached to empty pots.

Still, there usually are a few undecorated floats off our point, marking the location of eel traps tended regularly by a chap from upriver whose appearance is heralded by a swarm of seagulls eager for whatever scraps from his traps that the eel man is willing to throw their way. He hauls his catch up into a small outboard motorboat fitted with a winch and a couple of plastic tubs—one for the eels he catches and one for the bait for the traps he sends back down into the deep water.

At the mouth of the river, the lobstermen use a larger, traditional type of boat. The Maine lobster boat is characterized by a high-bowed hull that swoops gracefully toward a low, flat stern. A squarish cabin of sorts, where the lobsterman can steer and haul seemingly without having to move his feet, is set about halfway back from the bow. The restored Maine lobster boat is also a favorite of local recreational boaters, its cabin providing as it does some protection against the wind and rain. It is almost always driven from a standing position, as are virtually all the small working and pleasure boats that run up and down the river. Standing with a spring in the legs provides a cushion against the rough bounce of the boat on the waves and wakes through which it rides and gives the pilot a better view of the water and any potential boat-damaging floating debris.

From our gliding perches we also watch recreational human fishermen—they do seem to be predominantly male—many of whom sit motionless waiting for a bite, standing up only to cast and reel in. The deep and somewhat turbulent water right off our point appears to be a favorite spot of many anglers, but I can't imagine why. Whenever I have watched fishermen at length, I have seen nothing caught of which they might be proud. The semi-diurnal tides both slow down and speed up time. Most of the boats are allowed to drift with the current, so the motor has to be started now and then to keep a boat near the same spot and away from the rocky shore, and this must only scare away what fish might be in the vicinity. Even when there is not a hint of a bite, patient fishermen seem to return again and again to a favorite spot.

Seven

CLOSETED
CLUES

BY MY COUNT, Bob Phinney handmade for his house sixteen Z-braced interior doors, most of them for closets. The place is a maze of closets. Besides those in the bedrooms, there is next to the kitchen a large closet that we use as a pantry, and nearby is a broom and utility closet. At the other end of the hallway is a linen closet, and perpendicular to it an odd closet that in time would present a virtually unsolvable mystery—a knotty-pine mystery. All closet doors are made in the same style as room doors. Every one of them is reinforced on its backside with a Z-brace, though sometimes the brace is a mirror image of the letter. Regardless of which way it is oriented, the bracing always comes up to the very edges of the made door, no doubt to insure its structural strength and stiffness. Those parts of the bracing at a door's edge would normally interfere with the doorstop and so prevent full closure of the door. A lesser carpenter would thus curtail the bracing short of the stop, as was done with two doors added by subsequent owners. However, the resourceful Phinney did not sacrifice strength for shortcuts, and he eliminated the interference by, wherever necessary, carving and chiseling out from the stop a neat recess into which the end or angle of the Z-brace just fits. It is only past the doorjambs in closets that Phinney stopped finishing and detailing. Here, he

Doorstop cut out to accommodate bracing

left the structural skeleton uncovered. Inside the closets, wall studs are exposed, providing an opportunity for the curious to study the structural framing, the construction details, and the otherwise hidden workmanship behind the ubiquitous knotty-pine paneling.

The insides of closets also show that leftover lengths of tongue-and-groove paneling were sometimes used as shelving, brackets, and furring—waste not, want not. Above the door inside nearly every closet is a nicely centered light fixture, which is operated by a switch conveniently located on the outside wall just beside the closet door and next to its pull handle. We are certainly grateful for these lights, but they may not have been a part of Phinney's original plan, perhaps having been added only after someone realized how difficult it was to find something in a dark closet in a dark room. Evidence for this retrofitting was found in an unlikely place: the guest cabin. Some years after we had acquired our place, I found a diagram of the house's floor plan taped inside the cabin's small electrical circuit box. I surmise that this box originally served the main house, until the multiplication of appliances, including an electric stove, water heater, washer and dryer, and wall and baseboard heaters in the bathrooms, demanded an increased number of circuits and circuit breakers. Thus the small box was replaced with a larger one, and the displaced box was repurposed for the cabin.

The drawing taped inside the box's door was likely made by Phinney after the house was all but fully framed—so it was not a structural but rather an electrical plan. It provided a guide for laying out the circuits containing wall outlets and lighting fixtures, and the implied switches and wiring connecting them together and to the main, all of which would surely have been done before the walls were paneled. Outlets and fixtures, with color coding distinguishing those located "upstairs" (red) and in the "cellar" (blue),

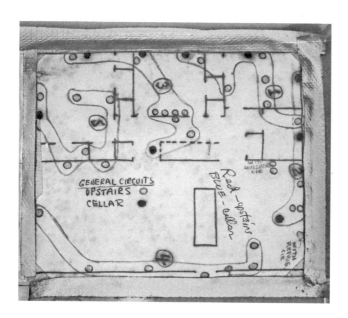

Diagram of original wiring circuits

were grouped into circuits and the circuits numbered in an orderly way to correspond to the numbered circuit breakers housed in the box. The deliberate organization of the drawing argues for its completeness at the time it was created, and the absence of closet lighting fixtures on it surely indicates that they were an added rather than an originally conceived feature.

Throughout the house, original door hardware is black-enameled steel or steel finished to look like antique wrought iron, consistent in style with the hinges and main latch on the living-room casement window. The room doors are hung on strap hinges, with the long part always exposed on the inside, on the arms of the Z-brace. Closet doors are hung on concealed mortise hinges, also known as butt hinges, and in many of them the mortise is of double depth so that it needed only to be cut into the door or into the jamb, thereby leaving the other unblemished. Phinney seems to have arrived at this time-saving strategy after assembling his doors, for in some cases he had to cut through the horizontal braces to reach the proper depth of recess. The artifacts of this afterthought are pairs of exquisite but nonfunctional saw kerfs left behind. Phinney seems to have felt no need to do everything according to convention, but his house shows a determination to be restrained and consistent in his departures.

Doors leading into bed- and bathrooms have outside door handles with an operable thumb plate, which when depressed raises the other end of a simple lever that lifts an exposed latch out of a slot. Opening and closing these doors has a distinctive feel and sound, quite different from that of turning a knob against a spring and hearing a bolt clicking free from or against a latch strike plate. Opening the door to a Phinney room has the feel of pushing down on one lever to lift another lever and the sound of metal sliding against metal and then slipping off the slotted jamb piece in the clutch of gravity. In the installation of the latches, Phinney's workmanship was again impeccable, with each mechanism mounted through and onto a small rectangular one-by block of wood with soft-rounded edges that complement those on the door. The block adds sufficient thickness to the handmade door that the mounted lever mechanism reaches just far enough into the room to engage with the slotted plate fastened to the jamb. On the inside of the room, the end of the lever penetrating through a keyhole-like opening in the door contains a downward bend to give it a crooked end under which a finger or two can be hooked to unlatch the door and pull it open. Closet doors, opening as they do out rather than in, do not have or need such a latch system. Rather, they have a simple pull for

Door hardware mounted on wooden block

opening and are held shut by a roller mounted on the door's inside engaging a spring clip attached to the stop. Virtually all of this original hardware still operates smoothly and reliably.

As can be seen from inside the closets, vertically oriented wall paneling was nailed to one-by-two (or makeshift) furring strips that span between the two-by-four studs, thus pushing the paneling out from the studs by the thickness of the furring. To set them off visually from the rest of the rooms, the kitchen and bathroom were paneled horizontally. Since such paneling could be nailed directly onto the wall studs, it is recessed relative to vertical paneling where the two orientations meet. In the front area of the house, this small detail further differentiates the kitchen space from the rest of the open floor plan. The horizontal paneling used on the east and south kitchen walls also conforms to the horizontal lines of the cabinets and countertops and contrasts with the vertical paneling lines of the cabinet doors. (Had the kitchen been paneled vertically, the unavoidable extended visual offset between the lines of the long

A meeting of vertical and horizontal wall paneling

stretch of cabinet doors and wall might have been discordant, something Phinney evidently anticipated and avoided.)

The kitchen counter along the south wall closely follows traditional architectural specifications, it being about thirty-five inches high and twenty-four deep. However, the above-counter cabinets do not conform, beginning a couple inches lower than the eighteen-inch standard and extending upwards only twenty-eight inches. All kitchen cabinets were handmade. For those above the counter, Phinney used nominal one-by-twelve boards for the body, ripped down to ten and a half inches for the middle shelf, and knotty-pine panel boards for the doors. These cabinets appear to have been designed

Kitchen cabinet with large dinner plates

for dinner plates smaller than the ones conveyed with the house and those we added to them. Unlike lumber, whose actual dimensions over the years have diminished in size, those of at least some table place-setting patterns have increased. When stacked on the shelf, our eleven-inch-diameter Dansk dinner plates project over the edge and prevent the door from being closed flush. But Phinney can hardly be blamed for failing to foresee the trend in supersizing food portions and the china on which they are served. The tops of the shorter-than-traditional upper cabinets provide space for the storage and display of large serving pieces, baskets, vases, and the like, and the ample distance between the south-wall cabinet tops and the slightly sloping ceiling reduces the effect of their divergent lines.

Each of the eighteen handmade kitchen-cabinet doors, depending on its width, consists of either two or three tongue-and-groove panels, the edges of the ensemble rounded at the top, bottom, and sides. The back is reinforced with two nicely chamfered and round-edged one-by-four horizontal braces, there being no need for a full Z-brace on these squat doors. Each one has a number written neatly in the center of the top face of the top brace, indicating the door's position in the kitchen, progressing left to right, beginning with the wall cabinets and continuing along the under-counter cabinets. The neatly formed numbers are curiously oriented, reading right-side-up only when viewed from above and outside the door.

For a long time, the only pieces of plywood that I had found in the house were those that form the backs of the cabinets, through which they are screwed to wall studs. Perhaps Phinney began to run out of time or patience or steam when it came to the cabinetwork, which might explain why the holes over the countersunk screws are not filled the way they are on the braces on room and closet doors. Maybe he let someone else finish this aspect of the work, but whoever did it, it is consistent in design (no doubt imposed by Phinney) and almost in execution with that through the rest of the house. All above-counter cabinet doors are made up of two wide knotty-pine panels; all below-counter ones of three panels, with a narrow

Neatly numbered kitchen-cabinet door

board between two wider ones. For a while I imagined that maybe the screw heads were left exposed as a reminder to close the doors.

After living with these cabinets for more than a dozen years, I thought I knew them inside and out. However, it was only while writing about them that I discovered something that had gone unnoticed. Whether it was the angle of the sun or the focus of my eye, late one afternoon I caught the glint of metal on the face of one of the east-wall-cabinet doors. Upon looking closer, I found what appeared to be the head of a very small nail embedded in the wood. Looking at other cabinet doors, I discovered that there was a pattern of what seemed to be brad heads. But unlike Phinney's straight-line alignment of nails in wall boards, where three brads were used in a cabinet-door panel they are arranged in a neatly stretched-out V or ∧ pattern. Not all cabinet doors showed this treatment, but enough did to make me wonder about it. Did Phinney do this? If so, why? Whoever did it appeared to have nailed through the front of the door panels to tack them to the braces before turning the assembly over to install the screws that provide a more substantial hold than the brads ever could. It is certainly not a technique that Phinney used on room and closet doors—unless he carefully set and filled and varnished over any nail heads, which I doubt that he did—and so it provided further evidence that he may not have made the kitchen-cabinet doors.

But my conclusion about the brad patterns bothered me, in part because it did not explain why not all doors were treated equally and why some of the presumed brads had larger heads than others. After

Kitchen cabinet with mystery brads

a while, I also wondered if the assembler of these doors ever drove a screw into a brad. To check this, I looked at the screw patterns on the backs of the doors, expecting them to be in the shape of a V where the brads on the front formed a ∧, and vice versa, in order to avoid interference. To my surprise, however, the brad and screw patterns matched exactly, which meant that what I thought were nailheads are in fact the pointed ends of screws that had pierced the front of the door panel. The sharp projecting tips had evidently been carefully filed off flush with the door front and so only appeared to be nailheads. I had tricked myself into temporarily believing an explanation that was more complicated than the reality. I misread the data points that form the V and ∧ plots. I had thought of the possibility that the screws had been driven too deep, but they were not that far countersunk to support that idea. In fact, the shallow holes left behind may explain why they were never filled. My new and simpler explanation was that whoever attached the braces to the back of the cabinet doors had used screws that were a bit too long. The projecting tips had been carefully filed down flat, and possibly the screws were backed out a bit, leaving what looked like brad heads set flush with the front of the door. Here, I had used Occam's razor and not made any more assumptions than absolutely necessary.

Not wishing to believe that Phinney himself would use screws that were too long, I continued to think that the cabinet doors were made by someone else. However, the below-counter kitchen drawers, which are also handmade, are surely his. They too have softly rounded edges and mate nicely with the round-edged openings into which they fit. The vertical set of drawers stacked beneath one end of the kitchen counter contains units of five distinctly different

Stack of kitchen drawers

heights, which are graduated in subtly increasing size from top to bottom. The more I look at Phinney's work, the more I see, and the more I see the more I marvel at his attention to detail, proportion, order, and unity.

Whatever their size, all the kitchen drawers move in and out as easily and smoothly as any with a ball-bearing, roller, Teflon, or other modern support mechanism. To see what was responsible for the ease with which I could pull out and push in these almost sixty-year-old wood-on-wood drawers, I removed one and turned it over. To my surprise, the bottom was made of quarter-inch plywood, which was not visible inside the drawers because they are all lined. The plywood is nailed to a frame of one-by boards, some of which are clearly pieces of tongue-and-groove wall paneling cut to size. It was no surprise, however, to find that the numerous nails are neatly and evenly spaced. It seems that Phinney was game to try anything with wood and was not averse to making practical choices. Given the limited palette of lumber with which he worked, his other option—a drawer bottom fashioned out of a one-by board—would have reduced the useful storage capacity of the stack of drawers by a not insignificant amount. It was Phinney's careful planning, measuring, and assembly that made the drawers fit so neatly and slide so easily on their polished wood rails.

The kitchen drawers also indicate that Phinney was indeed more a carpenter than a joiner. The plywood bottoms are nailed in place to a rabbeted back and sides of a drawer rather than held in grooves formed in the front and sides, and the corners of each drawer are nailed together rather than dovetailed. In other words, the body of each drawer is made like an old wooden fruit or vegetable box, its sides, front, and back coming together in butt joints. There is one curious feature to the two bottommost drawers, and that is that their sides are cut lower for a good portion of the length, as if they were the side panels of an open sleigh. I assumed that Phinney had used a coping saw to cut something out to use for another purpose, but for a long time I could not find a piece of wood with a matching profile. It was only when I was double-checking the depth of the cabinet shelves that I noticed their supporting brackets had an end curve that exactly matched that of a drawer-side cutout. Indeed, the length of a bracket is exactly half the length of a cutout: Phinney got two brackets out of each drawer side. And he might have seen an added advantage to the cut-down side: It allows things slightly wider than a drawer still to be stored in it.

The finished face of each drawer is an added one-by board, screwed from the inside of the box to its front, making this part of the drawer two full one-by boards, or one and a half inches, thick. This is all done neatly, of course, and when the drawers are closed the finished faces of the cabinets and drawers are perfectly aligned and completely harmonized. All the kitchen pull handles, whether on door or drawer, are an identical basic-black design popular in the 1950s—a piece of shaped, formed, and painted steel terminating in spearheads where the pull is attached to the wood with exposed matching black screws, their faceted heads making it appear that they, like the pulls themselves, were forged by a blacksmith.

In the original kitchen, there was no countertop along the east wall, where the stove is located. An old photograph shows an easy chair sitting there, next to the cooking stove and near a wood-burning heating stove—and incidentally almost directly over the furnace in the basement—a warm place for one adult to relax and chat with the one preparing dinner. The corner also appears to have served as a message center of some note, for the wall above chair-back height and the cabinet door above it are pockmarked with thumbtack holes. Knotty pine is a soft wood, and the tacks would have been relatively easy to insert and, unlike the holes left behind, remove. There are also larger holes here and there in the kitchen cabinet frames, where screws likely held a can opener or other wall-mounted and hand-operated kitchen tool. One of the cabinets still has a serviceable red-plastic-bodied knife sharpener screwed into the inside of the door. Where something has been removed, the empty screw holes blend inconspicuously into the wood, and only upon close inspection are they recognizable as other than small knots.

One of the house's six large (four-by-six-foot) picture windows is in the kitchen's west wall and provides a view looking out onto the river. The table originally located in front of this window was handmade by Phinney, one of several pieces of white-pine furniture he made for the house. (The basic design was included in his model and did not appear to be significantly changed in the full-scale realization.) The table sat six on benches set perpendicular to the window, so that everyone could look out at something of interest. An old photo of the house shows a child in this window, from which the Phinneys watched birds attracted to the seed left on the shelf once fastened like a flowerbox to the windowsill. Was it here that Bobby Phinney studied the chickadees that as a young sculptor he carved out of wood? Looking outward through the double-glazing might not have distorted such observations, but

Double-glazed picture window framed in two-by-eights

photographing the window from the outside can capture a double image that is in sharp contrast with the distinct lines of the surrounding clapboards.

Elsewhere in the original house Bob Phinney used more-traditional windows with multiple lights, but presumably always framing them in two-by-eights now removed or concealed behind trim around the replacement windows. As the house was built, the larger dimension of the standard pieces of lumber so nicely fit the thickness of the wall, comprising as it does the knotty pine on furring strips on studs faced with sheathing and clapboards, that no trim or other embellishment was necessary to achieve the architecturally consistent and well-proportioned finished look that still exists around both the inside and outside on three sides of the casement window in the living room. The kitchen and bathroom windows in the south wall, which is paneled horizontally in those rooms, would, however, have required a modification to account for the absence of furring strips behind the interior paneling.

The awkward-looking trio of raised windows that had so distracted me upon first driving up to the house took on a different significance after I learned that the small room that they illuminate was originally the girl's room. The relatively high fenestration provided privacy from the headlights and eyes of anyone coming down the driveway and provided more wall surface against which to locate furniture in the tiny room. The three high windows are now fitted with permanent storm windows, in that a second piece of glass is set behind the outside lights and held in place with quarter round. Since such nonflat molding is not present anywhere else inside the house, it may not be an original Phinney installation. By coincidence or by design, the width of the room is almost exactly the span of the trio of windows, their two-by-eight framing butting up against the west wall and coming within three-eighths' inch of the east. But which came first, the windows or the width?

As Phinney's model showed, he also conceived of a trio of high windows on the north wall of the boys' bedroom. Such windows are

Triplet of high windows in girl's room

believed to have been in the house as built, but they are no longer there, that wall now containing a double casement window. Before we knew of the model, Catherine and I had speculated on whether the casement replaced a triplet like that in the girl's room, but any evidence of that having been done was hidden behind the retrofitted-window trim and abutting wall-mounted bookshelves inside and the clapboards outside. In keeping with my desire to remove no nail or screw in my deconstruction, I have not attempted to look behind the bookshelves. However, their position and size are consistent with them masking the scars left from removing a triplet of windows.

One summer, we asked a number of local painters to give us estimates on repainting the exterior of the house, and one from elsewhere on the island informed us that he also lived in a house made by Phinney. The painter told us that the triple high windows were a dead giveaway about who had built the structure. (For a while after this encounter I wondered whether Phinney became a professional builder or just derived pleasure and, hopefully, profit from something he did so well.) The painter also told us that when he was putting on an addition to his own Phinney house the trio of windows was carefully preserved as part of the original structure, out of respect for the idiosyncratic carpenter. But the painter further told me that when he had to remove some other window frames during the expansion he cursed Phinney's penchant for using three nails where one or two would have done. The frame was so firmly held in place that it took the strength of a couple of men handling a crowbar to do a job that normally should have been easy for one.

The middle bedroom was shallow—just under nine feet deep—and even less spacious than what the closet-less camp model showed. For some reason, Phinney extravagantly gave this modest-sized room in the finished house not one but two entrances from the hall. One possible explanation for this may have had to do with privacy. With the south door open, people in the kitchen could have had a direct view into the northeast corner of the room, where in the camp model Phinney placed the bed. By adding a second doorway, Phinney provided an alternate way into and out of the room. While this doorway was in direct line with the opening in the living room wall, relocating the bed from the corner position to one between the doors would have made the bed less fully visible when the second door was open. With the head of a double bed against the west wall, it would have jutted out into the narrow room and left little space between the footboard and the window, especially if some other piece of furniture were located there. The second door would have facilitated access to the left side of the bed without disturbing a sleeping spouse.

That the second doorway is about three inches narrower than all other bedroom doorways in the house suggests that Phinney may have wished to gain some wall space for placing furniture between the bedroom's two doorframes. A bed with a full-size mattress facing the window would likely have left no more than about six inches on either side. However, since he made all of the house's original pine furniture himself, he could have made everything to fit. If Phinney did alter his plans to gain wall space, it would confirm that he designed some of the house, at least, around certain room arrangements and modified his design as the building progressed. Otherwise, following his penchant for consistency, he should have provided the room with a single doorway of a width equal to that of all the others in the house.

The diagram of the house's original wiring circuits shows the second doorway, indicating that it was framed in before the walls were paneled. The wiring schematic further shows that the west wall of the bedroom was fitted with four electrical boxes, which could have represented a baseboard outlet for each side of a double bed and, higher up on the wall, provisions for separate fixtures for sconces or reading lights, thus obviating the need for bedside tables on which to place lamps. The fact that this bedroom was the only one that seems never to have had a centrally located ceiling fixture reinforces this supposition. However, it cannot be verified nondestructively because the areas where the sconces might have been installed are located behind renovation work done in the 1980s.

Another possible explanation for the second doorway into the middle bedroom has to do with accessibility. The standard-size door, which we can assume was the first to be framed in, was located directly across the hall from the stairs down to the basement. While the stairway was open in the original floor plan, it did have a banister that might have gotten in the way when moving certain large pieces of furniture—such as a double mattress and box spring—into the room. Since it is likely that the banister was put in place as a safety feature even before the walls began to be framed in, Phinney could have discovered the interference before the bedroom wall was complete. If he did, he might have opted to frame the second doorway in line with the opening from the living room in order to have unobstructed access to the bedroom. Recognizing the importance of maintaining a minimum wall distance between the two doors, he might have been forced to make the second door narrow.

Except for the fixed high windows in the girl's bedroom, now Catherine's study, the picture windows, and the inward-swinging casement window in the corner of the living room, all the conventional original windows were replaced by previous owners with modern thermal-pane, crank-operated, outward-opening casements. Unfortunately, the new windows were trimmed inside not with the two-by-eights that Phinney used to both frame and trim the originals but with one-by-four boards overlapping the wall paneling and butt-jointed at the corners. Such woodwork can be more forgiving of slips of the saw and gaps in the fabric beneath, but here it detracts from the of-a-piece original design, especially since the matte stained finish and unrelieved hard edges of the newer woodwork do not match those of the varnished and soft-edged two-by-eights favored by Phinney. Fortunately, when the glass in the picture windows was replaced with thermal pane, the proportions and frames were left as Phinney appears to have designed and built them.

It was also some previous owners who directly in front of the kitchen window had hung what looks like a craft-kit stained-glass lamp from a retrofitted and disharmonious panel-board box set between two ceiling timbers. This suggests that they, like the Phinneys, had their kitchen/dining table here. Catherine and I have tried this location, sometimes sitting across the table from each other, one of us looking up and one down the river, each on the lookout for something interesting coming our way. We have also sat side by side at the table, both of us looking out across the river. Unfortunately, having the table by the window restricts access to the refrigerator. In recent years, we have moved the table to the middle of the kitchen, positioning it directly behind but not up against the back of the fireplace. This has worked nicely for us, and we have found it to be the preferred location when there are more than two of us for a meal.

Bob Phinney's attention to detail led him thoughtfully to locate the house's full bathroom next to the girl's room. Since the hallway is offset at that end by about half a door width, she would have easy and relatively private access to the bathroom. In the boys' room, Phinney located the half bath, complete with a small door for ventilation through a louvered opening to the outside. The otherwise windowless half bath, like the central hallway, had originally been illuminated by a skylight set into the flat roof.

The half bath—later converted into a vanity-closet—contains a uniquely curious feature in its door latching mechanism: it is installed in the opposite way from all other similar door latches. On all doors leading from the hall into a bed- or bathroom, the thumb lever is on the outside, unbraced side of the door. For the water closet, where there is no hall involved, the thumb lever is on the inside, where the Z-bracing is. The door to this tight space necessarily had to open into the boys' room, as do all its other doors, but why was this hardware seemingly installed backwards? My guess is that Phinney wished to be consistent in a situation that tested consistency, and this seeming inconsistency was in fact deliberate. All other closet doors have simple pull handles, thus distinguishing them by touch alone from doors leading into rooms. Those have the thumb-lever mechanism. But from inside the room, a closed door is unlatched not by depressing a thumb plate and pushing but by raising a crooked lever and pulling. Had Phinney installed the water closet's door hardware consistent with that on the bedroom door, then it would have been inconsistent with the way the WC door opened. By installing the unconventional door's hardware unconventionally, he provided a tactile cue—what human-factors engineers term a haptic device—to the direction in which the door opened. This would certainly be a welcome aid to someone feeling around in the dark of night for the door to the bathroom.

The structural design of the basement stairway feels to the legs to have been common, but to the eye it is anything but. Instead of conventional stringers, with the incised cutouts that give rise to the familiar saw-tooth profile of the sides of functional stairways, Phinney's descent into darkness and ascent into light has two-by-eight stringers that the saw touched only at their ends, that is, the stringers have parallel long sides. To the insides of these are fastened rounded-edged triangles of wood on which the stair treads rest. Screw holes are filled and stained over, providing a degree of finish seldom found in cellar stairs. There are no riser boards, allowing air to move freely through the open structure. The balusters that once ran around the opening in the floor were evidently made out of two-by-fours finished with Phinney's signature softly rounded edges.

About thirty years into the life of the house, an alteration enclosed both the old stairway to the basement and a new stairway to newly created attic space. The balusters were unceremoniously sawn off at floor level, leaving their unstained pale insides exposed. Each stump remains where Phinney anchored it firmly to the floor structure, showing the thoughtful sculpting and the careful craftsmanship that he expended on even this small detail. The treads on the steps leading down to the basement, as well as on the narrow portion of the floor beside them that was enclosed with the stairs, are covered with what appears to be the house's original floor covering—what as kids we called inlaid linoleum. It has a multicolored, almost abstract pattern that on closer inspection appears to be a representation of crushed rock, perhaps meant to simulate terrazzo. The predominant colors are dark green and black, and the overall effect is to date the flooring's installation in the 1950s. Whatever original flooring may remain in the house, it likely rests beneath the lighter-colored brick-pattern sheet vinyl installed thirty years later by the Moniers in the kitchen and bathrooms (and guest cabin). The living room, bedrooms, closets, and hall are carpeted in a harmonizing neutral tan color bearing the signature of Mrs. Monier's good taste in furnishings.

Throughout the house, the knotty pine appears to have been finished with a varnish that has held up exceedingly well. The wood has darkened underneath, which gives it a rich, warm look. When we first viewed the house, the real-estate agent remarked that the place was perhaps rather dark but could easily be brightened up by painting the paneling an off-white. We didn't say anything but have many times thought to ourselves, thank goodness that nobody ever did paint the paneling—except in the bathroom, where it serves the purpose of making the walls look more like they are tiled, and perhaps less like those of an outhouse. That a half dozen or so owners have left so much of the cottage as close as they did to the way it was built is a testament to their appreciation of the rightness of how it was designed and made. The house, in turn, has been fortunate in having been passed along a line of owners approving of Phinney's plan, taste, and execution.

Phinney may or may not have been consciously influenced by the Arts and Crafts movement, which originated in late-Victorian England and prized fine handcrafted work in decorative design over products of increasing mechanization and uniformity, but his design sensibilities certainly seem to have been consistent with it in spirit. In that so much of the movement's philosophy stressed organic relationships between the various elements of a design, Phinney might have qualified as a naïve, late disciple. Throughout his house there is a true amateur's attention to detail, the work of a man who thought in his own individualistic way about how board crosses board and timber meets timber. In this regard the house's interior does evoke an arts-and-crafts tradition, but does so mainly in the softness of its edges, the darkness of its wood, and the soundness of its builder's design decisions.

Bob Phinney certainly must have found some peace of mind and a great deal of satisfaction in working on this house. There is no sign that he ever tired of measuring every board probably twice or thrice before cutting it once, or of carefully rounding the edges of pieces of pine to a perfect radius. Even the difficult task of fitting the tops of the knotty-pine boards around the exposed ceiling beams was done with forethought, care, and precision, which was important because he never used a piece of molding or finishing strip (or caulking) to hide sloppy work. Where the use of a wider board would have necessitated making it fit fork-like around a timber, which in turn would have necessitated using a coping saw to negotiate a tight turn to cut across the grain, Phinney chose a narrower board, into which he could cut straight inward from the end and the side, thereby insuring true right interior corners. He did not butcher wood, he filleted it. The precision of his work is most readily seen in the front room in the late afternoon sun.

He must have always been looking ahead to the next step. The fact that the sawing, fitting, and nail spacing is so uniformly done with such precision throughout the house strongly supports the assumption that one man did it all alone: the measuring, the sawing, the sanding, and the hammering. That we have found throughout the house only a couple of popped nails and that none of the close-fitting boards around the ceiling beams has cracked or split or separated provides incontrovertible evidence of the care and attention that Phinney gave every detail of his carpentry, which more properly deserves to be called craftsmanship.

In a rare use of something other than wood, Phinney fitted the recessed spaces between the exposed timber rafters with a substance similar to that used in 1950s acoustic ceiling tiles. But instead of consisting of squares, these panels are for the most part one continuous piece for the width and length of the space defined by the timbers and braces, an expanse that can be of the order of two by eight feet. Although it is a bit faded now, the color that all of the original panels were painted was a fifties' pastel light green.

Each of the large panels is held in place by nails whose largish heads look almost like but are not exactly the kind used by roofers. They are uniformly spaced à la Phinney, and the nailheads appear to have been lightly covered over with the same thin green wash as the panels themselves. This nicely reduces what otherwise might have been a stark contrast in color and texture between the hard nailhead and the soft acoustic panel. The nails are set so close to the timbers that I continue to wonder how anyone could drive them without leaving a scrape from the hammerhead on a single timber in the house. This must have been especially difficult because the nails had to be driven nearly vertically upward. Furthermore, in only one case have I found the timbers adjacent to the panels to bear a stray brush mark, even though the nails certainly must have been painted after being installed, since nowhere have I found the paint on a nailhead chipped. Did the artist Phinney do this exacting work lying on his back on a scaffold, like a Renaissance fresco painter?

The purpose of the panels may have been not only to cover the underside of the roof boards but also to provide some acoustic relief to the hard surfaces throughout the house. All but a few of the panels appear to be original. One glaring replacement, which was never painted, is bright white in color. It appears to have been nailed right over the original, because the retrofitted panel is noticeably lower

Ceiling panel neatly nailed in place

(by about a panel's thickness) than those in adjacent recesses. It is unlikely that Phinney made this quick and dirty repair himself, for the panel bears the impressions of a hammerhead and, while the nails are more or less spaced evenly from each other, they are not as close to the bordering timbers and so do not display Phinney precision.

The reason for this odd replacement panel may have been that the original was ruined by smoke or heat from the wood-burning stove that once sat beneath it. (The back of the fireplace still holds a fixture for connecting a wood stove's flue.) Or the original panel may have been ruined by water from a leak in the roof at this location. There is some evidence of water damage on one of the original panels still in place in the living room, but it is slight and hardly noticeable. Only the bare nailheads at the low end of the ceiling, which show a touch of rust, call attention to it. Drawn by this subtle clue, at the right light of day a careful inspector can also detect some faint water stains on the panel itself. So perhaps George Stafford's recollection of water dripping into his drink was quite accurate regarding its location.

But who can fault a builder for a leak here and there? Even peaked roofs can leak. Overall, Phinney's wooden house is as solid and safe as the third little pig's brick one. When tropical storm Irene blew through New England in 2011 and caused extensive damage, the house that Phinney built held tight and made no sound of straining against the wind. The house was built to last with a minimum of maintenance. The wood paneling has kept its freshness. The cedar siding has held up well, in spite of the insult of its having been patched and painted. That the structure has remained totally sound and certainly square and sturdy after six decades of standing up to winter winds, spring rains, summer heat, and fall chills is a tribute to Phinney and his execution of the design he saw in his mind's eye.

A Mainer might say he made a wicked good house, Mr. Phinney did. Mr. Phinney did it with aplomb, even if in solitude. It is as if he recalled decades later what he had read about the rewards of craftsmanship contained in the booklet of plans and instructions for the General Motors model-building competition in which he participated as a teenager:

> It takes men who know how to work with their hands as well as with their brains to suggest and perfect better ways to do things. As a member of the Fisher Body Craftsman's Guild, you are doing more than building a strong, handsome, craftsmanlike model coach. You are learning a lesson in honest, sincere workmanship. You are learning to carry on for yourself, to depend on your own efforts, and to finish the job in every detail.
>
> May every success attend you. Whatever your work in the future may be, may you be rewarded by achieving high rank as an able master of your craft—a man who has learned to work honestly and well.

Phinney did exactly that.

According to his son Bill, Bob Phinney spent about $17,000 building his house, not skimping on the quality of materials that he used. But in time he may have wished to realize some return on the sweat equity he had put into the project. The Phinney family lived in the house by the river for only three years before it was sold in 1957 for $23,000 to Peter Woodbury, a federal appeals–court judge from New Hampshire.

Judge Woodbury had been looking for a place to which he could retreat. His ideal was to go to remote, rustic Matinicus, described in *Yankee* magazine as "the most remote inhabited island on the Atlantic seaboard." It was a good ferry ride out into the Gulf of Maine from Rockland, which itself is another hour's drive up the coast from Bath. This would have meant that it was at least a three-hour drive from his home in the Manchester area just to get the ferry. However, the judge's mother wished him to be no more than about two hours' drive from home, should he need to return in an emergency. The house on Arrowsic, being located roughly midway between Manchester and Matinicus, fit the bill nicely, and so the judge bought it from the Phinneys. The following year he bought also some adjoining land from Phinney, but this was considerably more property than came with the place that we purchased four decades later.

Billie Phinney was not happy with the sale of the place she had come to love, but Bob the engineer must have had something else in mind. As much as Catherine and I think it ideally situated for summer living, Phinney may have been disappointed that in winter he had to fight the frigid north wind to get into the front door, and once inside he may have still felt the cold. After the sale to Judge Woodbury was completed, Bob Phinney and his family moved back into his mother's house across the cove. It was also around this time that Phinney began to be identified as a carpenter in the Bath city directory, which included entries for Arrowsic residents, and began to build a new house more inland on the island, but still on what was historically Gertrude Phinney's land. The new homestead fronted on Arrowsic Road and bordered on the northern reaches of Sewell Pond and the adjoining marsh. To distinguish it from what had come to be called the River House, the Phinneys referred to the new one as the Pond House. Bob Phinney began making pine furniture for sale, but the carpentry business must not have been enough to support his family. In the 1963 city directory, his occupation was listed as clerk, and in subsequent years he was identified as working at Yankee Lanes in Brunswick, a bowling establishment whose automatic pin-setting apparatus may have reminded him of the guts of calculating machines. At the time of his retirement in 1975, Phinney was manager of Yankee Lanes.

Years earlier, Bill Phinney, the youngest child, built a prefabricated house of his own across Arrowsic Road from the Pond House, on another portion of his grandmother's land. On the same property, Bob Phinney constructed a barn for his son, but the workmanship was not quite up to that in the River House—or even to that of its garage. Where he had once used countersunk screws, he now used large nails and left their heads protruding from the wood. Instead of solid timbers, he built up principal beams from side-by-side two-by-eights and joined them in tandem over posts of the same composition, all of which he could have done with little if any help. Phinney appears to have demonstrated once again that a carpenter, no matter how accomplished, is no joiner. Although some neighbors have claimed that the entire barn is a post-and-beam structure, it is in fact basically a balloon frame, with posts and beams providing needed intermediate support for the upper floors because of the structure's wide expanse. Windows were, as was to be expected, framed in the Phinney manner, though not nearly as neatly as in the River House. This was, after all, a barn. But Phinney appears to have learned his lesson about flat roofs and put a steeply pitched one on the three-story outbuilding. However, he provided little overhang to the gable, and so over the years water ran down the sides of the structure, leading to cracking and warping of the vertical siding and rotting of the windowsills. Nevertheless, the repaired barn still stands solidly, while the prefabricated house was torn down to the foundation and replaced by something larger.

Eight

COAST
LINES

THE MAINE COASTLINE IS a ragged collection of desolate beaches, curving shorelines, long peninsulas, narrow inlets, granite ledges, and more, including islands near and far. On the navigation chart that hangs on our living-room wall, our stretch of Midcoast is laced with a labyrinthine collection of water routes, some of whose navigability ebbs and flows with the tides. If we squint at the chart we can imagine all sorts of shapes running into and retreating from the sea, like the footprints of children testing the surf at the beach. The Boothbay Harbor region is especially evocative, its outlines suggesting a swimmer towing the whole of the state of Maine toward the Atlantic. The harbor proper is nestled in his right shoulder; Southport Island is his muscular right arm outstretched for the pull stroke; East Boothbay is his left armpit; and Linekin Neck is his left arm, just emerging from the water to reach for the next pull stroke. The snouted peninsula containing Spruce Point is his head.

It is from coastline extremities fanciful and plain that ferries large and small carry passengers, supplies, and hopeful escapes to and resigned returns from the distant islands that dot the Gulf of Maine. A century ago, ferries of all kinds were the lifeblood of the state, and for the boatless they were usually necessary to reach islands even within a stone's throw. Something can be so close

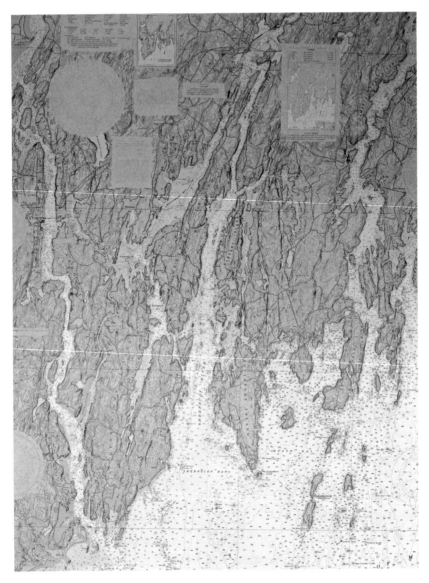

Navigation chart including Boothbay Harbor region

and yet so far up here. It is about 225 miles as the crow flies from Kittery, the state's southernmost town, to Lubec, the last town encountered on the U.S. mainland before crossing the water to the historic Roosevelt family retreat on Campobello Island, which is in Canada. But walking around every inlet and cove to get there would make it a 3,500-mile journey. When the maritime islands are included, the coastline of Maine measures some 5,000 miles. Negotiating the coastline and the roads that hug it can be at the same time an experience of scenic beauty and peptic upset.

One summer when we had rented a house on Georgetown's Indian Point, we experienced in practice what the maps had only laid out before us in theory. The drive from the house to the nearest supermarket was a good half hour; it was a bad half hour back. This may be fine for those on a leisurely vacation schedule with an unerring knack for making up a complete grocery list. However, I tend to be in a hurry and neither Catherine nor I can seem to remember everything we needed until we unpack the groceries at home. There was a small village store in Georgetown, about ten minutes away, but its stock was limited. When we became determined to find a place of our own, we kept in mind the regular need to shop for fresh food, especially seafood. We would not want to take a ferry back and forth to the fish market.

For shopping, one option is to go up the Coastal Route toward Wiscasset, whose welcome sign promotes it as the "prettiest village" in Maine. It is quaint and has some fine specialty shops, but it is an enormous traffic bottleneck during tourist season. (A groaner that some native Mainers repeat every summer goes, "If it's tourist season, why can't we shoot 'em?") Pedestrians cross and recross Route 1 in downtown Wiscasset going to and from Red's Eats, which *The New York Times* once declared to serve the state's best lobster roll. Traffic can be stop-and-go for many miles on either side of the town—northbound backs up all the way beyond the small shopping center to the southwest and, coming the other way, toward the bridge over the Sheepscot River, well beyond the turnoff for Boothbay Harbor.

Since the late 1950s, there had been talk about a bypass highway to carry traffic around Wiscasset. There were, of course, proponents and opponents, and possible routes were identified and studied by the Maine Department of Transportation and praised and criticized by interested parties. After about, literally, a half century of debate, one bypass option seemed to be a real possibility. It had received the approval of the Army Corps of Engineers, which oversees waterway resources, but then the Fish and Wildlife Service determined that a protected eagle's nest in the path of the planned route could not be moved. In summer 2011, the state's transportation commissioner finally decided to abandon all plans for a bypass of any kind, arguing that projected costs outweighed any possible benefits. The decision was a harbinger of others sure to come across the nation in a time of tight money and growing competition for it among infrastructure projects. Route 1 through Wiscasset will remain perhaps the prettiest traffic bottleneck in Maine.

Because of the uncertainty of traffic in Wiscasset, years ago we only occasionally shopped at the small independent market, Yellowfront, just this side of the village. Yellowfront was where we first found fiddlehead-fern crosiers during their very brief season from late May to early June. (Sautéed fern crosiers accompanying pan-fried freshly caught Atlantic grey sole became a combination our mouths watered for throughout the winter.) Until it closed, which occurred about the same time that a large Shaw's supermarket opened across the road, Yellowfront was one of the most popular of the last-chance grocery stores before the turnoff to the Boothbay region. It was frequented by locals and regular summer people who had become accustomed to stocking up there before going on to their cottages and cabins in such long-established seasonal communities as Capitol Island, where everyone knows or is related to everyone else, and the rare unrelated visitor who chances upon it has to wonder how its residents get along with just its single narrow one-way loop road. Those same visitors may also wonder why Route 1 is only one lane each way in so many places. Mainers seem to like one-lane roads—and one-lane bridges—perhaps because one lane is obviously all that's needed for nine or ten months of the year, and two would be an extravagance.

So the traffic is endured, and on sunny summer weekends it can seem to take as long for a station wagon laden with trail bikes and kayaks to get from Boothbay to the Kennebec as it did for the river's waters to flow down to Bath from the river's headwaters in Moosehead Lake, which has a shape suggestive of its name. From its origin there in the Maine woods about which Thoreau wrote, the Kennebec—the state's longest river—flows south for 150 miles before it passes our house and empties into the sea. For over a century and a half there was a dam across the river at Augusta, but in 1999 the modest structure was breached to reopen the upper Kennebec to kayakers, canoers, and, most importantly, spawning fish.

In the late nineteenth century, the Kennebec was crossed by several bridges at Augusta, but as recently as the mid-1920s there was no fixed crossing south of Gardiner, which is about thirty-five miles from the mouth of the river. Bath is the most prominent city on the lower Kennebec and one of the most historic on the road—now U.S. 1—that has long bisected it. That road and the Maine Central Railroad were the principal means of travel along the coast to such summer destinations as Rockland, Bar Harbor, and, for a young Franklin D. Roosevelt, Campobello. But the river introduced an unpredictable delay in the journey as travelers waited for the ferry. The railroad-car ferry *Hercules*, which was in service in the late nineteenth and early twentieth century, could accommodate up to six passenger cars on each crossing. The Bath State Ferry did not operate around the clock, even during busy summer months, and in winter it stopped its crossings near dusk. Bad ice conditions on the river could halt service for both ferries completely. Even when they were operating, lines of automobiles could experience seemingly interminable delays waiting for their turn to drive onto the boat in order to be carried across the river and proceed to their final destination, perhaps after waiting for other ferries along the route.

Such was the situation in the early 1920s, when talk about a bridge over the Kennebec at Bath began to be accompanied by action. Local boosters worked on gaining statewide support for the project, which was championed by State Senator Frank W. Carlton, whose hometown was Woolwich, located directly across the river from Bath.

Although Carlton sought legislation authorizing a free bridge over the Kennebec, he and his supporters compromised on a toll bridge, and it was the subject of a $3-million bond referendum in September 1925. The authorization led immediately to the selection of a consulting engineer and to the beginning of construction the next summer.

The principal engineers for the bridge were John Alexander Low Waddell, a flamboyant world-class consultant who had begun his practice in Kansas City, and his assistant engineer at the time, Shortridge Hardesty. The bridge design that they settled on involved a series of fixed truss spans sitting low over the water. Railroad tracks occupied the lower level of steel, roadway and sidewalks the upper. Little clearance was left for boats near the shores but plenty was provided near midstream by a movable span consisting of a 150-foot-long steel truss that could be raised like an elevator car as much as 135 feet into the air. This kind of vertical-lift bridge had been introduced by Waddell in 1895 with the structure he designed to cross the Chicago River at Halsted Street. The bridge type—often considered ugly and ungainly by all but the engineers who appreciate the difficult constraints it must satisfy—is at least as much machine as structure. Its most prominent features are the two tall steelwork towers, which have been described by a historian of the Bath bridge as "two praying mantises squaring off for combat," an especially apt description when the towers were painted Maine-bridge green. In time the structure grew so badly rusted, however, that it looked as though the insects were molting. The towers, which reach a height of 220 feet above the water and loom over the river and city, are essentially stationary cranes at the ready to hoist the movable section up and let it down on demand. The only structures of comparable height in the vicinity are the giant mobile cranes of Bath Iron Works and the cupola of the Sagadahoc County courthouse perched upon a hill overlooking the city's downtown.

Named for the senator who championed it, the Carlton Bridge was opened to traffic in 1927. Tolls ranged from five cents for pushcarts and wheelbarrows to $1.50 for a ten-ton truck. Pedestrians crossed free, but passengers in vehicles were charged a nickel. (A lot of cars must have discharged their riders before the tollbooth and met them at a prearranged place across the bridge.) A toll of ten cents a head was charged for small livestock "on hoof"; larger livestock cost fifteen cents. The tolls were a particular annoyance to local residents, who were eventually made exempt in 1935 when their towns agreed to pay some of their automobile tax to the bridge authority. In 1941, under the administration of a governor who was also a resident of Bath, the bridge was made toll-free for all.

As is the case with any narrow bridge, traffic on the span could be slow going. At the right time of day, it was less than a ten-minute drive from our place on Arrowsic to the Shaw's supermarket in Bath, but at the wrong time of day it could easily stretch into three or four times that. For many years, the wrong time of day occurred at the changing of the shift at Bath Iron Works, which is located just south of the bridge. The bottleneck was caused by seemingly all of the ship-yard's thousands of employees wanting to join the traffic stream at three-thirty in the afternoon. As early as 1981, engineering studies looked at alternatives to the Carlton Bridge, but it didn't take any kind of study to know that there was a great need for a new bridge with more traffic lanes. A crossing that did not open for ships would also be very welcome. At peak periods in 1995, the number of vehicles crossing the old bridge each day exceeded 30,000, and predictions were that the number would increase to 45,000 by 2015.

In the mid-1990s, when a bridge project in Portland came in $38 million under budget, the Maine Department of Transportation saw an opportunity to use the excess federal funds for a new bridge at Bath. Federal regulations required that the money be obligated quickly, which did not allow time for the conventional process of serially designing a bridge, inviting construction bids, reviewing the bids, and letting a contract to build it. To accelerate the overall process, special legislation allowed for Maine's first design-build contract, an arrangement whereby the same engineering/construction team or joint venture is chosen at the outset to handle both ends of

Bath's new and old bridges over the Kennebec

the process, often enabling final design and construction to proceed simultaneously.

When completed, the fixed crossing provided a seventy-five-foot clearance for water traffic. Though this is much less than the Carlton Bridge could provide in its lift span's fully raised position, it was considered adequate in a new age of recreational sailing. Tall-masted commercial ships no longer sailed past Bath, the way they had done in earlier times, and only a few relatively low fishing boats each day left from and returned to the Stinson Seafood Company upriver, where sardines were canned. Taller ships just had to dock a bit further downriver, at the Maine Maritime Museum. With the new maximum clearance, the old movable bridge span could be parked at the seventy-five-foot level and be lowered only when a train needed to pass over it. Rail traffic on the Maine Central line had become very limited, with only one or two freight trains using the tracks daily. During the summer and into early fall, for a time the Maine Eastern Railroad ran three scenic excursion trains each way daily, five days a week, between Brunswick and Rockland, with stops in Bath and Wiscasset, though recently the service was cut back. The railroad, like the Coastal Route, does not exactly follow the coastline; they each take slightly inland shortcuts between harbors and bays, connecting the bridges that span the rivers, seldom touching an island like Arrowsic.

Nine

RAISING
THE
ROOF

CONVENTIONAL WISDOM MIGHT HAVE it that a house should be constructed before a companion garage, but I wonder what Phinney thought. If he completed the garage first, not only would he have gained practice with his tools but also he would have had a sheltered space in which to store and prepare the lumber used on the house. He could have done all the necessary measuring, marking, sawing, sanding, staining, and additional preparation of lumber indoors and so out of the heat of the summer sun and also out of the wind, rain, and snow, if not the cold, of Maine winters, should he have chosen to work during them. Extant building permits in the town records go back only to 1982, so to determine whether the garage or house came first, I would have to let the structures do the talking.

Normally, if something works, the tendency among engineers is to make derivative things less conservatively, but I would not expect Phinney necessarily to have behaved in that way. Had he built the garage first and the garage's roof design worked as expected, then the conservatively inclined Phinney should not likely have wanted to change it for the house. But if the garage roof did not perform as designed (say, it leaked in the rain or under melting snow), then Phinney would likely have wanted to adjust the plans for the house accordingly, giving it a roof with a greater pitch. But in fact, the original garage roof was constructed with a greater slope (about one and a quarter inches rise per foot of run) than the original one on the house (about a half inch per foot), strongly suggesting that the outbuilding was built second. Nevertheless, either of these slopes puts a roof into the category of "flat."

Much of the lumber used in constructing the garage was clearly reclaimed from an earlier use. The visible wood is full of empty nail holes, juxtaposes unusual nonrectangular shapes, and has some boards covered with a grayish-white gritty substance, a sign that those boards had previously been used as formwork for a structure's concrete foundation and then reused as "barn boards" to clad the balloon frame. As can be seen easily from the garage's unfinished interior, the exposed boards show them to have been nailed diagonally across the two-by-four studs comprising the vertical framing, thereby serving as bracing against the structure's racking, and so producing a stiff building. The garage is indeed a very stiff structure, one that shows not the slightest movement in the fiercest wind.

Over these boards, on the garage's exterior, uniformly neat cedar clapboards were installed, in the conventional horizontal orientation. Nailing the horizontal boards over the diagonal cladding minimized the chance of inner and outer joints coinciding and letting in drafts. This may not matter much in a garage, but it does in a house, where I expect that Phinney used the same technique. The only drafts in the house that I notice come though the replacement casement windows on the house's south side that cannot easily be shut tightly without someone pushing on them from the outside. In any case, the similar clapboard exteriors and original window framing of the house and garage made them match architecturally.

Whenever it was done, I am certain that the garage was built by Phinney, for it clearly exhibits his signature touches. The workmanship on display in the smaller building demonstrates that as much attention was given to its structural details

Recycled lumber used in garage

and strength as was given to them in the house. However, he seems to have grossly overbuilt in this instance, using an eight-by-twelve-inch ridge beam, which is certainly larger than was necessary. Perhaps it was a recycled piece of timber that he got for a very good price. Still, the timber had only to support the garage's roof, whereas the six-by-eight main beam in the basement of the house had to support floors, walls, and roof too. When my brother, an experienced structural engineer, first saw the garage, his immediate reaction was that it was way overdesigned. But overdesign is what Phinney did, and it is why his work has remained solid.

Recall that in the basement of his house Phinney used for the main beam a number of timbers joined in series and supported on steel posts. In the garage he used the single large timber that runs the entire length of the twenty-six-foot-deep structure. This beam must weigh in excess of five hundred pounds, and it certainly could not have been raised into position by a lone man, unless perhaps he used some kind of mechanical jack or hoisting device. The weight of the beam plus the load of the roof resting on it is supported by the front and back walls of the garage and at an intermediary point by a steel post. At the rear, the load had to be directed around the center window, and this was accomplished by using a four-by-six header resting on posts made up of multiple two-by-fours. This arrangement could have been avoided by eliminating the window entirely or by locating it off-center, but that option would surely have offended a perfectionist's sense of symmetry. Except for this one window, all others are simply framed and trimmed in two-by-eights, just as in the house. And whereas most garages have few if any windows, Phinney's has a total of ten, which means that the interior is nicely

Massive main beam in garage

lit by natural light, even when the doors are closed. Of course, framing all those windows made for a much more expensive and time-consuming carpentry job, but obviously that did not deter Phinney. Furthermore, leaving the inside of the garage unfinished to reveal the secrets of its recycled lumber and the details of its construction was consistent with Phinney's treatment of the clothes closets in the house. A garage is, after all, but a large closet for machinery and hardware. Neither kind of closet needs to be finished internally.

Although the garage windows let in plenty of light, they do not open and so do not let in air. Phinney seems to have compensated for this by incorporating a doorway into the southwest corner of the structure to facilitate ventilating it with the breeze that comes along the river. Like all the doors inside the house, the side access door to the garage was hand-fashioned. Its outside face consisted of just three nominally ten-inch-wide tongue-and-groove panel boards, making for a twenty-eight-inch-wide door fifty-eight inches high. The fit between the boards was good and tight, something that would have been important to keep out the wind, rain, and snow, which may on occasion have drifted up against the structure and over its eaves that where the door is located are barely five feet off the sloping ground (hence the short door). On its face, the door was unremarkably plain and simple: a flat surface broken only by the two top-to-bottom V-grooves along the paneling joints. The look took no special imagination. On the inside, however, the door showed distinctive manifestations of the Phinney style. The door was strengthened and stiffened by backing it on all four sides with one-by-fours and filling in the rectangle so formed with one-by-four diagonal bracing. However, unlike the Z-braced doors in the house, this garage door is diagonally braced in a symmetrically executed X that nicely fills the box—the vote on an election ballot cast by a stickler for detail. All the one-by-fours were attached to the back of the panel boards with screws that I estimate to be of the same size as those used on the doors inside the house. The edges of the boards were rounded, but not nearly to so great a degree as those in the house. A detached garage is not a home and so its doors no more needed such refined finishing touches than did its windows need curtains. Still, fastidious Phinney countersunk and filled the screw holes in the door bracing.

The low-headroom door remained closed and padlocked for at least fifteen winters before the ravages of the seasons could no

Back of original side door in garage

longer be ignored. Each year while we were away, wet leaves piled up against the door and became covered over with snow and ice, which repeatedly melted and refroze. This took a toll on the doorsill, the lower portions of the doorjambs, and the outside bottom of the door itself. Even if from inside the garage the door looked perfectly fine, from the outside it did not look like its support structure would last another winter. We asked Rob Shultz for advice, and he reasoned that because the door was not functioning as one, we might consider just removing it and its frame, covering over the opening, and facing it with clapboards. If we did not like that idea, he said he could install a window where the door was, thereby matching the opposite side of the garage. That would be true as far as the exterior look was concerned, but in the interior the brick steps leading up to a phantom door or to a window would be a dead giveaway of the change.

In the end, we decided to have just the rotten wood of the doorjamb and sill replaced, thus leaving most of the original doorframe as built. We decided to have a faux door fabricated out of tongue-and-groove boards and affixed to the frame, thereby giving, from the exterior, the appearance of a door. The view from the interior would be of the back of an unfinished door that did not function as one. The carpentry work was done in conjunction with a repainting of the house, garage, and cabin, and it stands in stark contrast to our memory of the original. Not only do the new pieces of door frame show how the size of dimension lumber has changed over a half century but also the casual workmanship of the Z-brace on the new door emphasizes by contrast Phinney's careful way with lumber and the tools with which he worked it. Before the remedial work began, we took the old door off its hinges and have been talking of making it into a coffee table, putting Phinney's X-in-a-box under glass as a testimonial and conversation piece. Until then, it rests on some blocks of wood in the garage.

The original front garage doors no longer hang at the entrance to the two bays, having long ago been replaced by weather-tolerant fiberglass overheads, but I can imagine how nicely the originals must have been made.

I had long thought that what we call our guest cabin was not built by Phinney, at least not at the time or in the frame of mind that he built the house and garage. Although the exterior of the eighteen-by-twenty-four-foot cabin followed that of the other two buildings with clapboard siding and asphalt-paper-covered flat roof, it had several structural features that suggested a different designer and builder. First, the windows are trimmed in a narrow millwork molding rather than in Phinney's signature two-by-eights. Second, the roof, while being flat, is supported by a twenty-four-foot-long, ten-inch-deep steel beam under its ridge rather than a timber one like those Phinney used for the main structural support in the house and garage. And finally, the cabin does not appear on a survey of the property when the Phinneys first put it on the market, in the mid-1950s.

My best guess was that the cabin was built sometime between 1957, when Judge Woodbury acquired the real estate, and 1970, when he died. That it was built closer to the earlier than the later date was confirmed by his daughter, Grace Woodbury Stone, whom we got to know as a friend and source of much information about the Road, its people, and its properties—especially the River House. Grace, who was to acquire the land and its improvements not long after her father's death, often told us that he had referred to the small building as "the shop," suggesting the purpose for which he had it built. The judge was an avid woodworker, and the building housed his tools, which included a treadle lathe of the kind that enthusiasts covet.

The shop itself does not appear in a striking bird's-eye-view photograph of the land and its improvements. We first saw the black-and-white photo when Grace gave us an 11 x 14 glossy print of it. She did not know for sure who took the picture or when or how, but she thought it might have been the Portland real-estate agent handling the 1950s listing. The photo became the subject of much speculation. There is a small municipal airport located in Wiscasset, and on occasion small airplanes do fly over the house. Perhaps the aerial view was taken by someone riding in such a plane. I have also wondered if the photo could have been taken by someone standing on the roof of the shop, which would have meant that just because it did not appear in the shot did not mean the structure had not yet been built. On closer inspection, I ruled this out, however, because the vantage point is too far back from the garage. Furthermore, the view is over the top of the leafless tree in the foreground, which would put the camera a good deal higher than the cabin roof. Years later, when Bill Phinney visited us, he brought with him a copy of the same photo and told us that his father had taken it from atop a tall pine tree. It would have had to be a very tall pine growing atop the ridge beyond the garage for Bob Phinney to have gained this

Bird's-eye-view of River House and garage, about 1955

high-angle bird's-eye perspective. In any case, with all the trees that have grown up between the garage and the ridge in the meantime, the view could not be captured today.

When I showed the photo to Milly Stafford, she proposed another possibility for its provenance. In 1968 a small plane crashed into the Kennebec at Fiddler's Reach. Other aircraft came to search the accident site and to photograph it for newspaper stories. Small boats dragged the river for days before finding the plane and the bodies of its two occupants. An aerial photo that Milly has of the search-and-recovery effort shows only houses, like hers, that are much closer than ours to Fiddler's Reach and from a much higher altitude than the photo of the house and garage on our property, which does not appear at all in the published newspaper photo. Furthermore, the shop was surely standing at the time of the airplane incident, and so it is very unlikely that the bird's-eye-view showing the house and garage only would have been taken at that time. Although I still wonder about exactly how the photo was shot, I am very happy to have a print of it, showing as clearly as it does the house and garage as Phinney built them.

As for the house itself, the judge and his family soon became so closely associated with it that the Phinneys took to calling it Woodbury's Place. The judge's son David and his bride, Candy, spent their honeymoon in it. But the Phinneys were not to be through with the place. Their daughter, Sandra, and her husband also spent their honeymoon in the house by the river, and in 1972 and 1973 Bill Phinney and his family rented it when the judge's widow, Margaret Woodbury, was not using it. Bill's mother, Billie, had elicited a promise from the widow that should she ever wish to sell the property outside her family, the Phinneys would have first option to buy it back. In 1973, Mrs. Woodbury sold it to her daughter Grace for $40,000. Four years later, when she and her husband, Al, were relocating to Iowa and wanting to sell the house in Maine, he felt strongly that they should honor the promise made to Billie Phinney. The Stones subdivided the property and sold the part on which the River House stood back to the Phinneys for $60,000. Billie, who had wished the house had never been sold in the first place, was happy at the prospect of moving back beside the river. Bob, perhaps for the sake of domestic tranquility, signed the papers reluctantly and continued to express his disappointment in the house's winter-worthiness. The place may have been to his liking in July, but not so in January. His view of it as too cold for comfort, whether real or imagined, prevailed. As fine a house as he had built, the engineer still found fault with it.

The Phinneys never did move back in. Barely seven months after reacquiring the property, they again sold it, this time to Alan Robinson, a helicopter pilot stationed at the Naval Air Station in nearby Brunswick, and his wife, Lauren. After a year or so in the house, during which time they heated it with a wood stove, Robinson was reassigned. He and Lauren considered keeping the place in absentia, but among the factors weighing against that was the leaky roof. The property was sold to Robert Lawrence, president of a California company called L-W International, and to his son-in-law and daughter, William and Roberta Krachy. Within months, Lawrence sold half interest in the property we now own to his company and half to the Krachys, who at the time already held an adjacent parcel fronting on Spinney Mill Road. It is likely that the Krachys also had been or became involved in the Lawrence enterprise, for after a few years that part of the property in which they were half owners was sold to L-W International "in consideration of one dollar," as so many of the real-estate transactions were characterized.

I understand from neighbors that for a while the shop building served as the place in which movie projectors or some other small appliances were assembled. A business named Mill Road Manufacturing was listed in the city directory for 1981. Like the garage, after which it was most likely modeled, the shop was built on a concrete slab and left unfinished inside. I suspect that much if not all of the wall space might have supported long workbenches along which projector-like products could be passed assembly-line-style, in stop-frame action, from station to station, from worker to worker, until they reached the end. The open center of the cabin might have had some additional worktables set up there and may have served as a packing station, alongside of which stood sealed cartons of finished goods ready for shipment. At some point, the workbenches would be removed, but the many chest-high electrical outlets that remain in place are the giveaway for what this building once was.

What appears to have been a cottage industry off Spinney Mill Road may or may not have been a success. Whatever exactly L-W International did, less than a year after the corporation acquired full title to the property it sold it to Harold and Gladys Monier, who at the time (1985) were living in Jupiter Island, Florida, an exclusive enclave located on a barrier island about midway between Miami and Cape Canaveral. Jupiter Island has a population comparable in numbers to that of Arrowsic, and like it has no post office of its own. Who knows how many people winter in Florida and summer in Maine? Since Florida has no state income tax, it is the much-preferred place to have a primary residence; Maine is a relatively high-tax domicile, to which the property-tax list in the Arrowsic annual report attests. Gladys Monier, who grew up on Philadelphia's Main Line and maintained a third residence there, traveled as a child to her family's vacation homes in both Florida and Maine.

So, in the course of about three decades of its existence, the house that is now ours had changed hands eight times, or on average once every four years. Of its prior owners, Judge Woodbury and his wife Margaret had held and presumably enjoyed it for the longest time (he for thirteen and she for fifteen years), but the Moniers came in a close second at twelve years. Now, as I write this in the summer of 2013, our sixteenth year here, Catherine and I have held the property the longest of all. But no matter how long we may continue to hold, enjoy, and scrutinize it, I doubt that all of its mysteries will be resolved.

We have been told that it was while the Moniers owned the place that the interior of the shop was finished into a guest cabin, but there have been conflicting reports as to whether it was a grown son or a local carpenter who did the actual work. Whoever did it was not Phinney's equal as a carpenter. He put up walls to divide the interior space into a front sitting room and a back bedroom, and he finished these walls in pine panel boards, thus evoking the interior of the main house, but in name only. The latter-day, lesser-grade boards used in the cabin retain the fuzzy surfaces and hard edges with which they came from the lumber yard and do not have nearly the number of interesting knots that mark the boards used by Phinney, nor the finishing, softening touches that he conferred. The paneling boards in the cabin were installed horizontally directly onto the wall studs and were never finished. Needless to say, there is no distinct baseboard. The sun has darkened the wall wherever a picture or mirror had not been hung, leaving those locations that were once covered marked by ghostly empty rectangles.

In the front room, two large picture windows were installed, one looking down the hill onto the driveway loop and, beyond it, to the main house, and the second looking out over bushes and through trees onto the river. Each of these large compound windows likely replaced two smaller ones, but the cabin still has eight of the originals, trimmed inside and out with narrow stock molding. The newer and larger windows are trimmed on the inside in one-by-fours that overlap the wall surface, just like the trimming on the replacement windows in the main house. The corners are not mitered but rather are butt-jointed to mimic a post-and-lintel arrangement. Indeed, the style and execution of the work in the cabin strongly suggests that it was done by the same hand that did the wood framing of the kitchen window in the main house. The off-level positioning and splintered ends of its framing boards are dead giveaways of a post-Phinney carpenter.

The renovator also incorporated a closet and small bathroom into the dividing-wall structure. In order to accommodate the plumbing beneath it, the bathroom floor was raised about ten inches above the cabin floor—necessitating a large step up. Because of the difficulty of reaching the pipes for repairs, this arrangement

Sitting room of shop-turned-guest-cabin

has proven to be troublesome when they are not drained thoroughly for the winter. But after a couple of spring lessons, I learned how to be sure that all of the water is out of the pipes before we close down the cabin for the year. I drain the system as much as a week ahead of when we will depart and leave it open to the air, allowing any last water to evaporate from low spots before I close up the plumbing.

As built, the cabin's floor consisted of plywood set on sleepers resting directly on the concrete slab, leaving a compartmentalized plenum in which moisture, if not water, collected during the spring thaw and after heavy rains. The persistent dampness and the cycling of the seasons led to a delamination of the plywood and its consequent structural softening. Walking on the floor came to feel like walking on a mattress with randomly spaced springs. Only the pliant vinyl flooring that had covered the plywood kept my foot and the feet of the furniture from punching through. At first I dealt with this by placing squares of newer plywood here and there stepping-stone-like over the flooring and under some braided area rugs, but after a while there was nowhere left to hide the problem. We finally had the failing floor of the front room torn out and replaced with thicker plywood resting on pressure-treated lumber. After a few years, the back-room floor began to deteriorate.

We asked Rob what he thought we could do to achieve a more permanent fix, and his suggestion was to tear down the whole structure and rebuild it from scratch. The problem, he felt, was that water was entering from the east, where it was channeled down the wooded slope and against the low foundation wall there, which itself may have been cracked and so was pervious. His fix was a little too drastic and costly for us to consider, and so we opted to repeat in the back room of the cabin what had been done to the front. As long as we were having the back of the cabin floor replaced, we had the exposed water heater relocated into one end of the closet, which still leaves plenty of room for guests to hang their clothes. This made for a cleaner-looking and more easily navigated space in the bedroom. But the persistent problem of water infiltrating under the floor is likely to present us with more decisions in the future. Quick fixes are usually just postponements of the inevitable.

When we bought our place, the garage and guest cabin still had their flat roofs, but the house had a steeply pitched one. There was more than one reason for this. The water that once had dripped into George Stafford's glass of gin had given him a lifetime license to rail against the designer of the house. Everyone agreed that it was foolish to have a flat roof in this climate, where one with a pronounced pitch was obviously so much better able to shed water, snow, and ice, and not accumulate them. One year Grace Stone watched about a foot of snow pile up on the roof overnight. Rather than wait for her husband, Al, to return from an out-of-town meeting, she went up and cleared it off before ice dams could form and cause leaking.

Even if it did not leak, when a typical flat roof was under too much snow, it had to be shoveled off lest the added weight be more than the structure could support.

Another year, the then-current owner called upon the place's caretakers to do something about the couple of feet of accumulated drifted and compacted snow, an amount that might bear down on the roof with as much as fifty pounds per square foot of pressure, or more than sixty thousand pounds—thirty tons—of total force. That would be like a few hundred people standing atop the structure. One Christmas, Milly Stafford recalled the year she and George climbed up a ladder to get onto the roof and begin clearing it. They shoveled the snow down the shallow grade and off the sides, and the mound of snow that they had created on the ground reached up to the eaves. According to Milly, when finished shoveling they simply stepped off onto the pile and slid down its slope.

Milly recalls that there was an urgency to clear off the roof because there had been some splitting of the wall structure in the northeast corner of the house. I can find no trace of structural

Snow and ice on the flat roof

damage or repair there, but the nails holding a ceiling panel in place show significant rusting from a one-time leak. Needless to say, the roof did not collapse, nor was that ever likely to happen to a Phinney roof, whether pitched or flat, given his penchant for overbuilding. Where two-by-eights might have served for rafters, he had used four-by-eights; where two nails would have done to attach a board, he had used three or four; where two screws might have done to fasten a brace to a section of a door, he had put in more. Engineers call this kind of structural insurance a factor of safety. In the case of the Arrowsic house it was a factor of Phinney. He was clearly not economy-minded when it came to lumber or screws and nails, or his sweat equity in driving them home.

But neither Phinney nor a conservative building philosophy alone changed the house's roof from flat to pitched. That was done in the early 1980s, probably when the property was owned equally by the Krachys and L-W International, and it was evidently done in anticipation of a restrictive ordinance limiting how much interior space could be added to a building located near the water. The Maine Mandatory Shoreland Zoning Act, passed in 1971, required the state's Board of Environmental Protection to establish minimum guidelines, and these would become effective in 1990. There was thus an almost twenty-year window of opportunity to build expansions that were expected to be grandfathered in when the new rules took effect.

If our house were still in the flat-roof configuration as Phinney built it, and if we wanted to expand it today, we could not increase the floor area or volume by more than 30 percent. That would mean that the peak of the old flat roof could be raised by only about five feet, which would not be enough for a stand-up attic. But the house was grandfathered where and as it stood when we bought it, and its proximity to the river and the spacious if unfinished attic with a new ridgepole about a dozen feet above the old roof's peak were among the notable features that drew us to it. The house with its peaked roof is now classified as a nonconforming structure by the legislation, but we are able to maintain and improve it as part of normal upkeep.

Since the roof was peaked to circumvent an impending new rule rather than to meet immediate needs, there was no great interest at the time in spending any more money than was necessary. The carpentry work was done well structurally, but it had accomplished only the bare minimum, namely erecting a peaked roof over the so-called flat one and providing an access stairway to the newly created interior space. The house thus had an attic in name only. Its floor was just the top surface of the house's old roof, still covered with its weathered, gritty asphalt roofing material. In other words, the attic floor sloped away in two directions from the old roof's low ridge. The attic was accessible but barely usable.

The stairs leading up were constructed directly above those leading down to the basement. Eventually, an enclosure was built around the new stairway, thus concealing not only it but also the way to the basement. This produced an improvement in the quality of life inside the house, for the dampness and mustiness that used to rise up from the cellar when it took on water in the spring were now somewhat contained behind walls and a door. The basement stairway enclosure must also have provided a reduction in anxiety for parents and grandparents of very small children living in or visiting the house.

But building the new and enclosing the old stairways also meant that the Honeywell Round thermostat that had been on the wall facing the back hallway was now closed off from that living space. Rather than sensing the temperature of the bedroom area, the device would sense that of the unheated and uninsulated attic void. It must have been this that led to the relocation of the thermostat to the other side of the wall, thus putting it in the living room and exposing it to the late afternoon sun. The relocation should have been an easy job, for the most obvious place to install the thermostat on the front wall would be directly opposite its original location on the back. However, whoever did the relocating evidently realized that that would have put the thermostat over a groove in the paneling, which would not only look awkward but also allow more dust to get in from behind the mounting. So, the

Iconic thermostat, relocated

Honeywell Round was located just to the right of the groove, which placed it off center on the panel board. Although Phinney would likely have centered the mounting on the board, as he did in the original installation, the thermostat does not look terribly out of place where it is. The Round now sits in plain view of visitors, a period piece serving as a plaque of sorts attesting to the authenticity of the period structure. On the other side of the wall, the unvarnished circular patch, pockmarked by abandoned screw and wire holes but perfectly centered on its board, remains as an evocation of a plaque to Bob Phinney, Builder.

For whatever reason—perhaps it was a building code requirement or perhaps it was just common sense—the stairway to the attic was made several inches wider than the one to the basement, and this plus the five-inch thickness of the enclosing wall structure caused it to encroach on the back hallway, leaving it an uncommonly narrow passageway only twenty-eight-inches wide. (The stairway-enclosing wall is the thickness of a two-by-four faced directly on either side with knotty-pine boards. Had furring been used, this would have added another inch and a half to the wall thickness, thereby further reducing the width of the hallway.) But everything has its plusses and minuses. The wider stairs to the attic have proved to be a blessing when it comes to moving bulky things like furniture up and down. And my elbows appreciate the extra width when transferring bankers boxes full of books and files for my current writing project every time we move between North Carolina and Maine.

In enclosing the stairways, there appears to have been a vague intention to use wood paneling and construction methods somewhat similar to those Phinney had used in the original work. However, whether for reasons of availability, taste, cost, convenience, or

Hallway narrowed by stairway enclosure

competence, the effort fell short. It may be that the knotty pine used by Phinney was no longer readily available three decades later—at least at an affordable price—but that alone would not explain why the new woodwork did not follow the original design more closely. The new boards appear to have been toenailed through the now-concealed tongue-and-groove detail, because no nailheads show on their surface. (I confirmed this when I stood on a step stool and shined a flashlight near the tops of the boards, revealing some ill-fitted joints that showed a nailhead at the root of the tongue.)

It is likely that a baseboard was omitted because, with no furring across the studs, the bottoms of the vertical boards had to be toenailed to the horizontal two-by-four used as a sole plate at floor level. When I push against the wall about midway between floor and ceiling, the give under my palm suggests that few if any intermediate nails were used, except perhaps where the tongue fortuitously fell over a stud or the stairway stringer. In any case, the absence of a baseboard means that the vertical paneling, whose finished width (five inches) is monotonously uni-form rather than somewhat random, goes unrelieved from floor to ceiling, from end to end. Furthermore, whereas Phinney had employed boards with chamfered and rounded edges—"eased," a lumberman or carpenter might say—the newer ones were left with relatively harder, sharper, and more harsh edges, emphasiz-ing the sterility of the wall's appearance. (At least the boards used in the house are of better quality than those in the cabin.) The ample half-inch-wide exposed V-groove that is emphatically but gracefully defined wherever Phinney wall boards were mated is opposed by the sharper-edged and narrower, three-eighths-inch-wide groove in the newer ones. While ostensibly the toenailing is an improvement on Phinney's method of installing panel boards, the absence of visible nailheads just adds to the monotonous and antiseptic appearance of the newer wall. Finally, the dissimilar-ity in style from one side of the narrow hallway to the other is disconcerting.

This contrast between the original and added vertical paneling is especially striking within the attic stairwell, which under certain conditions is better lighted than the hallway. To the left of the ascending stairs is the new and to the right the original paneling. When we bought the house, the stairwell was not fully finished, for the raw ends of the timber rafters that had been amputated to open up access to the attic had been left exposed. The glaring reminder of the insult done to Phinney's careful and respectful work was disturbing, and we eventually would have the line of gaping wounds covered with horizontal paneling that at least gives the remains a decent burial in knotty pine.

The added doorways to the attic and basement are framed in one-by boards, but they also were left with hard, sharp edges, which highlight any irregularities of straightness, cut, or fit. The doors themselves are made up of the same constant-width tongue-and-groove panel boards used in the wall. The alignment of the grooves on a door and the wall section above it reinforces an impression of mechanical rather than manual construction. The backside Z-bracing on the newer doors does not have its hard edges chamfered and softened, nor are there neat recesses chiseled and finished into the doorstop to receive an end or corner of the Z. Rather, where the brace on the attic door met its stop, the interfering part of the brace was simply—and not at all neatly—cut off, leaving a gouge in the door from a hastily wielded saw blade and a brace with a beard of wood fibers disheveling its end. All this makes for a disordered rather than a rustic look.

Even the door hinges depart from the kind Phinney used. The new ones are of the bright brass mortise type rather than black strap hinges. Certainly it should have been possible to find something inexpensive resembling the latter, or at least black mortise hinges could have been used. There does appear to have been an attempt to match the original lever-operated door hardware. Wrought-iron-style door handles with thumb plates were used on the newer doors, but the latching mechanism does not work as smoothly as that on

Poor workmanship on non-Phinney door

the original doors. The newer basement and attic doors do not close readily, and one has to be sure to seat the lever properly lest the door open too easily for small children or curious cats. To prevent unauthorized entry and a dangerous fall into the basement, some-one installed a supplementary slide-bolt latch on that door, but over time this has come out of alignment, perhaps as a result of the structural insults of having had first the continuity of the floor joists interrupted and then that of the rafters. In order to engage the bolt, the somewhat warped basement door itself has to be lifted up forcibly. Of the house's original doors (and their latches), all but one still work perfectly, even though they could tolerate a mismatch with the doorframe of no more than about a sixteenth of an inch.

The original door that does stick, especially in humid weather, is the one that once opened into what was a clothes closet in the boys' bedroom. The back wall of the closet was removed to create a pass-through or passageway into what was the central (the original parents') bedroom, and no doubt the removal of the wall section has produced a structural imbalance that led to the door's sticking. Severing the tongue-and-groove boards, the furring strips, and the studs compromised the structure's continuity between the house's east wall and the room's north one, allowing movement in the frame. The old middle bedroom was converted into a large bathroom, thus forming a new and more commodious master suite of sorts. The oversize bathroom houses a shower and a washer and dryer, a great improvement over having laundry facilities in the basement. The opening from the bathroom into the master bedroom is framed in a mode consistent with that around the double-glazed replacement casement windows but inconsistent with Phinney's vision and style of simply using one-by-eights to frame a doorway.

Phinney seems to have made conscious decisions about the relative appearance of different areas of the house. The nicest and most interesting pieces of knotty pine appear to have been

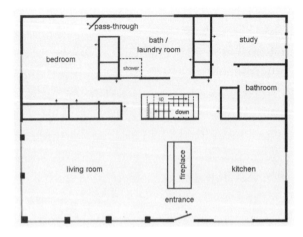

Floor plan of house as modified

used in the front rooms, especially in the living room. Also, whereas these common areas have their knotty pine well varnished, as is that comprising the walls of the hallway and the boys' bedroom, the girl's bedroom has a less glossy finish and the original parents' bedroom a still more matte finish. Perhaps he ran out of varnish, but a more plausible explanation might be that the walls of those rooms were finished by a different person or to a different person's preference. Or maybe Phinney himself wished to break the monotony, or his arms simply got tired of applying varnish.

The creation of the passageway, the installation of a shower stall, and the enclosure of the stairways were all most likely done at the same time, judging by the design, workmanship, and finish. Furthermore, there is a clear departure from the original in the stain and finish used on the newer woodwork. Whereas the original generally has more depth to it and is usually more glossy, the newer wood looks flat. Even the color is slightly off, the newer being more red or cherry than the original's golden brown. Most annoying to me, though, is the lack of a baseboard for either the bathroom shower-stall or stairway enclosures, clashing with the style of the rest of the house. These are details that are not so noticeable at first—we certainly did not notice them when we originally viewed the house or even when we first occupied it—but once you do notice them, the effect is jarring.

But perhaps I should be more understanding of how and why any given thing was done the way it was. I have certainly given Bob Phinney the benefit of the doubt and rationalized his empty foundation pockets, his notorious flat roof, and his exposed nailheads. Different people do things differently at different times and under different circumstances. Unless we understand all the differences, we probably should not pass judgment. Nevertheless, we still have the right to like or dislike the choices made and the ensuing results. I like the overall Phinney look and tolerate the rest. I guess we could redo some of the later alterations to make them more to our liking, but this place is supposed to be a retreat for relaxing, reflecting, writing, and rewriting—not for tearing out walls and redoing them. Besides, I doubt that I could match Phinney's materials and I know I could not match his workmanship closely enough to ever fully satisfy the critic in me.

Ten

DOWN
THE
WAYS

LIVING ON A RIVER naturally draws the eye and mind to the vessels that ply it—and to thoughts of their origins and destinations. A great deal of the river traffic that passes before our place either comes from or is heading toward Bath, just a few miles upriver. Endowed with perfect topography for shipbuilding, Bath became a center for that industry. The "City of Ships," as a highway welcome sign advertises it, is located on the west bank of an extensive straight stretch of the Kennebec known as Long Reach, where the granite-based shore slopes gently into the water and then drops off sharply beneath it. The river is wide at Bath, but it is also deep. A ship being launched here not only can plunge violently yet safely into the river before the buoyant force stabilizes it, but also by its momentum can coast a good distance across the water before needing to be brought under the control of lines played out from shore or attached to tugboats. Thus Bath was an ideal location to build and launch large ships using the natural force of gravity and the primitive machine of the inclined plane, just as the Phoenicians are believed to have done in the ancient world.

However, ships meant to slide down the ways into the water necessarily have to be built on the incline. This means that plumb lines, levels, and customary surveying tools that exploit gravity to identify the vertical have to be supplemented by shims, wedges, jigs, templates, and the like, all calibrated to the angle of the ways. Shipwrights, being highly adaptable human beings, long ago learned to work on the slope just as ceiling painters learned to work on their backs.

For much of the nineteenth century, ships were built largely of wood, and the abundant forests in Maine provided tall, straight pines for excellent masts and hemlocks for solid trunnels. Bath and its environs provided an ideal location to build ships that engaged in profitable world trade, with the vessels in many cases operated by the same family that built them. Wooden ships still needed metal fittings, however, for their anchors, chains, hauling machinery, and, with the rise of the steamship, for their boilers, engines, and stacks. These needs naturally provided opportunities for blacksmiths and, eventually, an ironworks at Bath.

Thomas W. Hyde, a local Civil War hero who had returned to his hometown a brigadier general, in 1864 started an iron foundry to make commercial castings and ship parts. By 1870 he was producing a patented windlass, and in 1884 he incorporated Bath Iron Works. The works did not remain for long just an adjunct to shipbuilders. By the early 1890s it was operating as a shipyard in its own right, having laid the keel of a 205-foot schooner-rigged gunboat, capable of running under steam and sail. Launched in 1891, the *Machias* was the first in a long but not uninterrupted line of U.S. Navy ships that have been the mainstay of the business of BIW, as the shipyard is commonly known and referred to hereabouts. Today, on the grounds of the Hyde School, a boarding institution located not far from the site of Hyde's industrial establishment, a stately family mansion stands as a reminder of the success of the patriarch's endeavor. Before the school occupied the location, the mansion served as the headquarters for the Pine Tree Society for Crippled Children and Adults, for which Billie Phinney worked for two decades. Small world.

Though Navy contracts played a major role in the growth of the Bath shipyard, it also built its share of luxury steam yachts and passenger steamers. During slow times it launched wooden sail-boats as small as twenty-four feet. By the mid-1920s the company had gone bankrupt, but it was revitalized by 1930 with the launch-ing of the 343-foot, 3,000-ton, black-and-gold steel-hulled yacht *Corsair IV,* built for the financier J. P. Morgan. At the time, it was the largest yacht built in the United States. Soon, BIW began again to build destroyers, under contracts that carried severe penalties imposed by the Navy for failure to meet fuel-consumption goals or weight limits. The Bath shipyard did meet the requirements of the contracts and launched sixteen destroyers before World War II. At the peak of the conflict it was launching a destroyer every eighteen days, with a total of eighty-two ships built by V-J Day. All of these ships, the large and the small, passed by our point of land on their way down the river to the sea.

The postwar era brought lean years for BIW, and the yard once again resorted to subcontract work. Some Navy ships were built in the Korean War era, but the real turnaround for the firm came in the 1970s, when new shipbuilding techniques were introduced at Bath. Prior to this time, the harsh Maine winters would hamper progress. With the introduction of modular construction methods, in which whole sections or units of a ship were built indoors, sched-ules became more dependable. There was, of course, a limit to how large a module could be welded together and prepared for electrical and communications systems, and this limit was set by the capac-ity of the yard's No. 11 crane, which can lift up to 220 tons of steel. (For a while, lighter aluminum had been preferred over steel in the construction of Navy ships, but after a 1975 collision between the aircraft carrier *John F. Kennedy* and the cruiser *Belknap* left it with casualties and a severely damaged aluminum superstructure, all future "surface combatants" were ordered made of steel.)

For a long time, it was the distinctively painted red-and-white tapered box boom of No. 11 crane, its jib towering as high as four hundred feet in the air, that first caught the eye of people in cars approaching Bath on Route 1. Along with the Carlton Bridge, No. 11

was the virtual symbol of the city. The movable crane was often visible from downtown, and when viewed from there it looked like a Godzilla walking among the buildings that it dwarfed. But this was a benevolent monster that fed the economy rather than terrorized the community.

Bath Iron Works, especially having as it does so visible a presence, can give the city a distinctly blue-collar image, unlike the country-club gentility of summering towns further up the coast. But Bath, in addition to shipbuilding, has a long history of banking, commerce, and trade, as attested to by the dignified gray granite

Bath Iron Works' No. 11 crane

customs house building on Front Street, now converted into various other kinds of offices but still looking out over the Kennebec. North on Front Street—and also two blocks over, on Washington—the grand old houses built by ship captains evoke a different time, as does the great clock at the corner of Front and Centre streets.

Among the things that most attracted an engineer and a maritime historian to this area are its living industry and the associated technology, no matter how déclassé some may consider it. Washington Street south of Route 1 is dominated, if not encroached upon, by the long side of the corrugated-iron-clad assembly building of the shipyard. This rear end of the yard is not a pretty sight. On raised land across the street sits a more presentable red-brick structure that is suggestive of a colonial outpost of civilization. This is the headquarters of the Supervisor of Shipbuilding, Conversion and Repair—the SupShip (pronounced "soup ship")—who oversees the Navy's billion-dollar contracts with BIW. There are only four SupShips in the Navy, the other three being located at Groton, Connecticut, which has responsibility for nuclear-powered submarines; at Newport News, Virginia, which deals with nuclear-powered aircraft carriers as well as submarines; and at Pascagoula, Mississippi, which oversees surface-ship building and repair work along the Gulf Coast. The Navy captains who serve as SupShips are fully aware of the power and influence they wield in the community, and they act accordingly. When we once visited the Bath SupShip in his large office overlooking the hulking iron works, he asked immediately if we would like tea or coffee, and our choice was promptly brought in by an enlisted man with all the deference and efficiency of a billionaire's butler. September 11, 2001 introduced a good number of hastily erected barriers, fences, and guard booths around the SupShip's castle, but his view across the street was never blocked.

In 1987, the works unveiled Crane No. 15, painted all white and sporting a three-hundred-foot-tall trussed boom. It provided an additional 330 tons of lift capacity in the yard and thus increased the size of ship modules that could be handled. When the booms of the cranes were up, they dwarfed every other structure in Bath. But unlike the rest of a static cityscape, the stance of the BIW cranes was ever-changing, as they moved up and down the rails beside the shipbuilding ways and constantly altered the direction and angle of their jibs and booms in response to the lifting tasks requiring them to dip into the yard and haul something up from below. Like a pair of giant mechanical dancers performing a pas de deux, the BIW cranes could so distract those drivers crossing the nearby bridge that most got only a fleeting view of the city's collage of brick-and-wood-frame buildings or the expansive yard itself, where ship units as large as forty-eight feet long and a full deck high were being put together in its Brobdingnagian thousand-foot-long, hundred-foot-high assembly building.

Up until the early part of this century, there were usually three ship hulls in varying stages of completion resting on the ways. The most nearly finished of the ships was naturally the most easily spotted, with the angle of its raked conning tower and communications mast exaggerated by the roughly one-in-twelve incline of the construction ways. The ways themselves were usually obscured not only by the ship hulls taking shape on them but also by the ships already launched and tied up at the docks at the river bank. Around the turn of the century, these battleship-gray destroyers had the numbers 81, 83, and 85 painted in twenty-five-foot high white numerals on the bows of the 480-foot, 8,000-ton ships. (At the time, BIW built the odd-numbered hulls; the even-numbered ones were built in Pascagoula, by Ingalls Shipbuilding, Bath's competitor for contracts.)

The sleek ships at Bath were classified by the Navy as "DDG-51 Arleigh Burke-class Aegis guided-missile destroyers." Aegis, which is Latin for shield, designates what the Navy described as an "advanced, automatic detect and track, multi-function phased-array radar" system that was "capable of performing search, track, and missile-guidance functions simultaneously." If Navy ships were multifunctional, their classification scheme was somewhat multiredundant. The DD in DDG stood for the particular class of destroyer, with the G indicating that it carried guided missiles as its principal armament. The number 51 was the one painted on the bow of the first hull of the class, and the ship commissioned in 1991 was christened *Arleigh Burke,* after a World War II admiral and three-time Chief of Naval Operations who advocated using the speed and stealth of destroyers to play a more aggressive role in the naval fleet. As was customary, all subsequent ships in the series were designated Arleigh Burke- or DDG-51- or Aegis-class destroyers, even though each would bear its own distinctive name and number.

On July 2, 2000, the *McCampbell* (DDG-85) was launched at Bath. The cloudless and windless Sunday afternoon provided near-perfect weather for a launch, and the usually restricted grounds of the shipyard were thrown open to all who wished to witness this Independence Day holiday-weekend event from ground level. Some guests had seats in the hot sun, but thousands of shipyard workers, their families, local residents, tourists, and the curious stood shoulder-to-shoulder on the hot concrete. The more fortunate spectators huddled in the rim of shade cast by the roof overhang of the assembly building. Regardless of their place or station, they had all come to listen to speeches by local, state, and national politicians; shipyard-owner General Dynamics officials; and Navy brass; and to see Secretary of State Madeleine Albright crack a bottle of champagne over the bow of the *McCampbell,* which towered eighty feet above the covered launch stand. But mostly they came to see what happened after the launch trigger was pulled. Then, gravity took over and dragged the six thousand tons of yet-to-be-outfitted ship down the ways. All through the program that day, Crane No. 15 traveled up and down the incline beside the ship, like a nervous father-to-be pacing outside the delivery room.

Timing was crucial, and it was important that the speakers limit their remarks and stick to a strict timetable, so that the launch itself could occur exactly at slack high tide. This ideal condition exists when there are no currents to carry the ship up or down the tidal river. Tug-boats were at the ready to secure lines to the newly launched vessel and slow its powerless progress toward the opposite bank, but there were still many things that could go wrong at a ship launching. For one, the vessel could get stuck on the ways, not only disappointing the assembled crowd but also presenting an enormous challenge to the launch crew. Anticipating this complication, hydraulic rams were at the ready to exert pressure on the wooden cradle supporting the bow of the *McCampbell*. They were not needed this time.

But not every ship had slid down the ways on cue. Before the Aegis-class destroyers, Bath Iron Works built guided-missile frig-ates, and the first to be launched was the *Oliver Hazard Perry*. According to local lore, when it did not respond to the launch trig-ger, the actor John Wayne, who was on the launching platform that day, responded to a call from the audience to push on the ship's bow. Unbeknownst to the crowd, the hydraulic ram had already begun exerting its great force against the cradle, and the ship began to move just as the actor leaned against it, gaining him his fans' credit for the accomplishment.

One of the chief hazards of a launch down the ways was the presence of the Carlton Bridge just a few hundred yards upriver, and Murphy's Law could make it effectively even closer. In 1975, the cargo ship *Maine* left the ways at twice the normal launching speed and continued to move at a good clip toward the opposite river bank. Tugboats were at the ready to slow the ship, but several unfavorable things happened simultaneously. A stiff wind suddenly began blowing upriver, driving the ship toward the bridge, which was crowded with spectators who thought it the best vantage point from which to witness a launch. One of the tugs, whose role it was to help keep a second tug in position downriver from the ship, had its engine fail. This left the second tug drifting upriver into a posi-tion from which it could not take in its towline, lest it pull the ship closer to the bridge. The tug recovered its position when the ship was only a hundred yards from the bridge and towed it to safety beside the dock. In the process, however, another tug had struck a rock and was sinking.

Even when flawed, the spectacle of an enormous ship sliding into the water, leaving behind a pair of launching rails overhung with the orange-colored grease and wax extruded by the four-foot-wide timber supports carrying the vessel down the ways, was an encounter with the physics of inclined planes and the conquest of friction on a grand scale. The acceleration of a massive ship from zero to eighteen feet per second over the five-hundred-foot length of the ways provided a display of dynamics seldom experienced by humans. The *McCampbell* was the next-to-last Navy ship to slide down the ways at Bath (or anywhere else in the United States, for that matter). The last one to do so was the U.S.S. *Mason,* in the summer of 2001, marking the end of an ancient tradition and the beginning of a new era at the shipyard.

For years BIW had been planning to replace its traditional launching ways with a more efficient and economical "land-level transfer facility," in which ship modules would be assembled in a horizontal position on railroad carriages. Center stage for the operation would be a floating dry dock, into which a completed ship could be rolled and giant doors closed behind it. With the fully assembled ship inside, the dry dock would be moved out into the center of the river and flooded, so it would sink, allowing the ship to rise off the carriages. With the sinking dock's doors opened, the new ship could emerge as if from a disappearing gift box. In a telling example of the decline of American superiority in shipbuilding and other heavy industry, the new 750-foot-long floating dry dock itself was manufactured in China. Even with the added cost of having to tow the completed facility half way around the world, there was no American bid that was competitive. Today, cranes painted to match the blue dry dock dominate the landscape at the south end of the shipyard, competing with old Crane No. 11 in their ever-changing configurations for yard's tallest.

We were not in Maine when the Chinese dry dock was brought up the Kennebec, but we have been in residence when a number of

Aegis-class destroyer on its way to sea

Aegis-class destroyers passed our place, filling the picture-window frames with a massive gray presence. No matter how many times we have seen one of these enormous ships pass, it is always an awe-inspiring sight. We got so familiar with the process that we began to know when such an opportunity was coming even before the ship was in sight. The approach was signaled by the deep-throated sound of diesel engines and, if the wind was right, the distinct aroma of diesel exhaust. On other occasions, our first indication of a destroyer coming down from Bath was the incongruous sight of a conning tower floating above the trees along Fiddler's Reach.

After September 11, 2001, there were new signals that the ships were coming. During the twenty-four hours preceding a destroyer's transit, helicopters flew up and down the river, some passing right over our house. Bright-yellow patrol boats and Zodiacs ran beside the banks, their armed guards eyeing the houses on the ledges and in the hills beyond. Finally, the great ship itself would come, moving majestically and proudly, whether going out to sea for trials or coming in for repairs. Catherine used to rush out onto the point to photograph the ships as they approached and passed, but after being scrutinized by the guards she no longer does it so overtly.

Eleven

PHINNEY'S PHOLLY

UPON OUR FIRST MOVING into the house, Catherine and I divided up the closets in our—the original boys'—bedroom as follows: Since she always sleeps on the right side of the bed (or in the right-hand bed when there are two), she used the vanity-closet on that side of the room to store her open suitcase and bulky clothes, such as sweatpants and -shirts. The closet next to it, which is fitted with deep shelves top to bottom, we reserved for blankets, board games, and boxes of photographs brought up to Maine from North Carolina finally to be sorted and albumized. I took the closet near the foot of the bed on my side of the room. Since the adjacent boy's closet had been given over to making a passageway to the bathroom, there was no closet left in the bedroom for Catherine to hang dresses, the vanity-closet having no clothes pole. So she put the dresses in the odd hall closet, located between the door to the boys' bedroom and the narrow door that once led into the middle bedroom.

The small hall closet is odd not only because of its location, but also because it is one of only two without a light inside it (the other being the utility closet), and this just enhances its aura of mystery. Furthermore, rather than its clothes pole being parallel to the back wall of the closet, it is oriented the other way, perpendicular to the back wall with its end sticking out beyond the bracket holding it in place. When I saw this during our first fall visit, I immediately thought it to be a hazard. As was common in the 1950s, the pole is a piece of what we then (and as one of the Clue weapons is still) called a lead pipe, cut to the appropriate length with a hacksaw, so that its exposed open end was encircled with burrs. In a typical Phinney closet, the clothes pole was painted black and its burred ends butted up against the sides. In the odd closet the pole's rough and unprotected end was at about eye-level, and it was not difficult to imagine that one evening Catherine might hit it while reaching into the dark space to get something in the back. So, I capped off the bare pipe end with an old yellow tennis ball into which I had cut a small x with a utility knife. The snug fit has kept the ball in place ever since. Perhaps it was my satisfaction with having averted disaster that kept me from peering further into the small, shallow closet at the time to look for clues as to why it was configured the way it is.

Since the odd closet in the hall was not mine, I did not look into it again for years. However, as I started thinking more about the house, I began to examine all its closets more closely, systematically searching for any clues about Phinney's intent and method. One

Tennis ball capping end of clothes pole

afternoon, I took a flashlight to the odd closet and pushed Catherine's things back and to the right. The left wall looked very much like one inside any of the other closets, in that it was unfinished, showing the studs, the furring, and the backs of the knotty-pine wall paneling boards of the adjacent room. It also revealed the exposed electric cables and boxes for a light switch and a baseboard outlet. When the flashlight beam reached about eye level, I saw attached to a shelf support what I surmised to be hardware to hold the left end of a pole oriented in the conventional way—parallel to the back wall. I double-checked this hypothesis-in-waiting by pushing the clothes to the left and looking at the right side of the closet. Sure enough, there was a matching piece of clothes-pole hardware there. So why was the lead pipe not supported by it?

There was also something that looked odd about the right inside wall of the closet. It appeared to be finished like a wall outside a closet, complete with nicely varnished vertical boards. But these were tightly butted up against each other, showing no groove along their seam the way the finished side of knotty-pine wall panels does. When I put my head into the closet to get a better look and ran my eyes up and down the height of the wall, I discovered that it has a one-by-four running diagonally across it, connecting upper and lower horizontal braces. Collectively, these form a Z-brace, and one executed as neatly and completely as those on all the original doors in the house. Unmistakably the back of a door, this one had for one final time been engaged by a clip latch, just like all the other closet doors in the house. This one was not visible from the other side because that area was hidden behind the fiberglass shower stall added during the Moniers' renovation. The discovery also explained the odd closet door handle I had found in the kitchen drawer full of assorted hardware and electrical parts. The handle obviously had been removed so the shower stall could be slid into place.

For years, the protective tennis ball had distracted me from looking more deeply into Phinney's pholly, the odd closet with the redundant door. Now I saw that the ball had also obscured my

view of how the pipe was supported from the shelf above. Someone had shaped and smoothed two blocks of wood on which to
mount the hardware that positioned the pipe at the proper distance below the shelf. The piece of wood in the back of the closet
is distinctly trapezoidal; the one in the front more rectangular in
shape. Neither has its edges rounded in the uniformly neat Phinney way. Each block is attached by screws, with the trapezoidal
one being fastened neatly to the back wall of the closet. However,
the top edge of the more rectangular one is improperly aligned
with the front edge of the shelf to which it is attached. In addition, the screw heads are not uniformly countersunk, some being
left flush with the face of the wood spacer and others projecting a
bit above it. This meant, of course, that the screw heads could not
be concealed behind wood filler. These details, like those of the
braces inside the kitchen-cabinet doors, are missing Phinney's
exacting finishing touches.

The odd closet had become even odder: who would have thought
that such an apparently straightforward house could have had an
abandoned secret passage of sorts, one that for almost fifteen years
we had not suspected even existed? Judged by what looks sure to
be unmodified Phinney framing and finishing, both the still-used
hallway door and the former bedroom door to the closet must have
been made and hung when the house was built. Judging from the
shelves above the clothes pole, the original intended access to the
closet seems definitely to have been from the hallway. I imagined
that the pole (but not the shelves) was reoriented to its present
position to give it the conventional clothes closet configuration
when accessed from the parents' bedroom. Perhaps someone felt
the need for more closet space in that room. In any case, when the
shower stall was added years later, the closet door opening into the
parents' bedroom had been for some inexplicable reason unceremoniously nailed through. A galvanized nail pierces the center of
the door and extends about an inch beyond it, a hazard to any hand
reaching in the dark for something on the shelf. Why the closet's

pole was not re-reoriented at that time, using the hardware already in place, remains a puzzle.

Could Phinney have made a mistake? Could it be that originally he framed the closet door to open into the hallway only, forgetting that it should have been framed to open into the parents' bedroom? Or vice versa? Or did he create the hall doorway to maintain symmetry in the hallway? His wiring-circuit diagram, most likely made before wall studs were covered with paneling, shows only a hallway door to the closet. Reframing the bedroom wall to add another closet door should not have been difficult. Rather than redoing the hall side of the closet, he seems to have just added the second door, leaving the first in place. Phinney could also have added a door to open into the boys' bedroom, thereby giving them another closet, but he obviously had chosen not to do that. I had certainly uncovered a new clue, but to what? I felt farther than ever from understanding Phinney's plan in full.

One Saturday in the course of working on this book, Catherine and I revisited the odd closet. In preparation for photographing it, she had emptied it of all its contents, which enabled me to squeeze into the tight space and scrutinize it. Among the first things that I noticed was a hook dangling from inside the doorstop, which made me seek an eye with which it might pair. Sure enough, on the top brace of the hall door is an empty eye, and together the parts comprise a hook-and-eye latch that could prevent that door from being opened from the outside. Obviously, this latch could only be engaged from the inside, and this provided strong evidence that at one time the odd closet had been accessible only from the bedroom. Fortunately someone thought to unlatch the hall door when the shower stall was put in place, or we might have had a mystery closet whose door we could not even open.

While the closet was empty, I made another discovery. Projecting out of the floor in the very back is what appears to be the stump of a wastewater pipe with a rubber membrane clamped over its end. Aha! This was once a second water closet, accessible from both the hall and bedroom, I thought, and the hook-and-eye latch ensured privacy to a user. Although I could not imagine wrangling a commode into this space tighter than an airplane's toilet, I ran with the hypothesis that added a still odder layer of mystery to the odd closet. But if the closet did contain a commode, there also should have been signs of an abandoned water-fill pipe. Perhaps that had been cut off below the carpeting that now covered the floor, but then why was the waste pipe not cut off the same way? I went into the basement to look at the underside of the closet space. I found the waste pipe easily enough, but I could find no sign in the vicinity of a supply-water pipe or any hole through the floor to signal that one had once been there. Only then it became obvious that the capped pipe had not led from a commode but provided emergency access to the waste pipe for dealing with any blockages that might develop in it. Too easily can we be misled by clues and base upon them improbable hypotheses.

A variety of things having to do with owning a remote place are always more pressing than games of Clue. One year when we were back in North Carolina, we received a telephone call from our neighbor Rob Shultz. Although he is not a native Mainer, Rob can be as taciturn as one, but in this case he was voluble. A freak windstorm had come up the river suddenly, knocking down the great pine tree that stood at the end of our driveway. We had admired its majestic size every time we drove up to the house. Unfortunately, the uprooted tree had fallen across a corner of the garage, destroying that section of the roof. The Stones, our neighbors across Spinney Mill Road, sent pictures of the damage that made us wince. So this is what went along with having a place in Maine.

Since just restoring the structure to what it had been would be a major repair job, Rob suggested that we might consider at this time replacing the garage's essentially flat roof with a more steeply pitched one. We could use the insurance money to cover at least part of the cost. This all made sense to us: the old roof would soon have been in need of resurfacing anyway, and replacing it with one with a more pronounced pitch would be an aesthetic improvement to the compound, bringing the garage stylistically more in harmony with the house. We told Rob to go ahead with the improvement, matching the slope of the garage roof and the color of the shingles that would cover it to those of the house.

When he sought the building permit, Rob was reminded—and then he reminded us—that the roof could not have such a steep slope, since that would increase the volume of the structure by more than what was allowed by the Mandatory Shoreland Zoning regulations that had prompted the peaking of the house's roof and were now fully in effect. He told us what the maximum pitch could be, and we told him we would have to think about it. Our hopes of bringing the house and garage into geometric harmony were suddenly dashed. We found ourselves in the position of many a property owner who was trying to do the right thing aesthetically, but found that goal was incompatible with the environmental rules.

I made paper triangles with the eight-over-twelve slope that we had hoped to achieve and the approximately five-over-twelve that we were told was allowed. There was naturally quite a difference, the latter resulting in a much lower peak—one too low to allow standing up under. When we had agreed to the steeper roof, the thought had crossed my mind that one day we might finish the space above the garage for use as a study or an additional guest room. It was a long-range plan, since at the time I was happily using the cabin beyond the garage as a study, albeit one I had to vacate when we had guests. It was also clear that if we finished the attic in the main house I could use that as a study.

In the end, we decided that we would peak the garage roof to the extent allowed by law and rationalized it like this: There were three buildings on our property, not exactly aligned but with the ridges of their roofs all more or less set in a roughly north-south direction, like the course of the river here. The house already had its steeply pitched roof, which had contrasted greatly with the essentially flat roofs of the garage and guest cabin. If we had been allowed to peak the garage roof to the extent that the house's was, then the guest cabin would have been the odd structure. Making the garage roof's pitch intermediate would result in a nice progression of profiles, while at the same time preserving the virtually flat roof on the guest cabin to remind ourselves and to show visitors how it all used to look.

In the course of having talked to various painters and carpenters over the years, I had learned that painters prefer to install the rougher surface of clapboards out because paint adheres to it better; some carpenters, it seems, install clapboards with the smoother side out because this gives a more uniform look. Thus arises a classic confrontation between form and function. Rob assured us that he would use new cedar for the clapboards under the eaves of the garage and would match in size and texture the siding that was already in place. Furthermore, he would have everything finished by the time we arrived the next spring. There was a great advantage to having such work done in our absence. We did not have to listen to the noise or deal with the mess. But perhaps more importantly we also were not tempted to micromanage, involving ourselves in every little detail that we thought might be verging off the track to perfection. Trusting Rob's judgment and craftsmanship, we returned to Maine in the late spring to find that he had done an excellent job on the roof, even to the color of the shingles. Neighbor Deirdre Barton, who owned a boutique in Damariscotta and whose horticultural talents brightened the

Cabin with flat roof behind garage with newly peaked roof

right-of-way with flowers, had served as color consultant and had made the perfect choice.

But it's funny how some transitions are unintended. Over the years, a red oak growing close to the southwest corner of the garage had sought more and more sunlight and so had spread its canopy out over the new roof. Just as the tree cover that arches over Spinney Mill Road keeps moisture on the asphalt much longer than the dew remains on the grass in the meadows, so the spreading oak trapped moisture on surfaces beneath its leafy boughs. This not only had exacerbated the problem of the rotting garage-door sill and jambs but also encouraged moss to take over some of the lawn along the west side of the garage and to cover some of the west slope of the roof, changing its color from brown to green and threatening the integrity of the shingles. The only solution, we were told, was to get rid of the tree, and so we did. But cutting down a tree means transforming its trunk, boughs, and branches from being off the ground to being on it, choking the grass on which it lay. Once again, solving one problem presented a new problem, a situation familiar to anyone who owns a house and property. Since we used our place almost exclusively during summers, we had no need for additional firewood, and the new problem was how to move the heavy remnants of the oak off our property and onto someone's who desired it. Fortunately, most people on the Road do burn wood during the winter, and Spinney Mill neighbor Doug Ware volunteered to transport the oak to nonagenarian Milly Stafford for her use.

The cedar clapboard siding that clad the exterior of the house that Phinney built had in its early years not been painted but stained a natural brown. The photographs given to us by our friend and neighbor Grace Stone show that after the peaked roof was added the house was painted yellow with brown trim. When we bought the place, it was blue with brown trim—as were the garage and cabin—in keeping, we were told without further specifics, with

The house from the river

Mr. Monier's Canadian roots. When it was clear that a new coat of paint was in order, our choice was to burn off all the old down to the bare cedar, which appeared to be in generally excellent condition. Unfortunately, it was very poorly matched in places, and so we decided to paint the house a gray-beige with brown trim, the latter chosen to obviate changing or painting the gutters or the garage's overhead doors, all of which were in fine shape. When the work was done, we drove over to Morse Cove to look at the paint job from across the river. When we had done so on previous occasions, we had found the predominantly blue structure to clash with the green trees surrounding it. Our hope was that the new, more neutral color would bring the house better into harmony with the woods, and we were pleased to see that it did.

Twelve

GRAVEL
AND
STONES

GEORGE STAFFORD TOOK CARE of our place through our first winter and into our first summer of ownership, during which time we wondered whether the things he told us were his sense of humor or were meant to indicate that without him we might be helpless. I was not without manual skills, having repaired bicycles and cars as a teenager and, as an adult, worked on many do-it-yourself projects in the various houses we had owned. Now with less free time for such projects, it was easier to pay others to do the work, and in Maine that seemed to mean having George do it. But the more he told us, the more I worried. He once gleefully described opening up the guest cabin one summer and forgetting to close the water-heater drain valve before turning on the cabin's water supply at the master valve in the basement of the main house. By the time he climbed the basement stairs, walked up the hill, and entered the cabin, its floor was flooded. He also described fixing leaks in the cabin by using a blowtorch to solder copper tubing in the cramped space beneath the bathroom floor, once almost setting the cabin on fire.

The driveway leading down from our right-of-way was mostly dirt over long-buried gravel, but the loop around the tree and in front of the garage was crushed stone. During our first summer we noticed that our driveway didn't look as nice as the expanse of small, light-colored pea gravel that we drove over every time we took the right-of-way and thought it would be a great improvement to have something similar to Rob's gravel on our driveway loop. We mentioned this to George one day, and he said to leave it to him.

Early one morning we heard a truck pull up and begin to dump something on our driveway. Rushing out to see what was happening, we encountered George and his truck. He had deposited part of the load in one corner of the drive, but there was a problem: What George had brought looked to us more like rocks and dirt than gravel. It was brown and sandy and what pieces of stone there were in it appeared to be angular and dark rather than rounded and light. We asked him why he had brought this kind of gravel rather than the lighter-colored pebbles, and he told us this was good river gravel and didn't cost as much. He said it would dry out to a nice light color. We reluctantly let him finish what he had started, hoping that the gravel would change as he said.

Milly had followed the truck in their tractor, the small snowplow blade of which George used to push the gravel around. (George's motor pool, kept in and behind the various outbuildings on his property, included just about every kind of wheeled and powered vehicle.) Mounds of gravel were spread in gritty silence into a level surface. The final smoothing and compacting would occur after we drove our car over it in the course of coming and going, George said, but it seemed to us that that might take years, since we only drove in and out once a day, at most, and only for a couple or three months a year. For several days we considered the driveway. This was not what we had envisioned it looking like for the guests we expected later that summer. It seemed no lighter or smoother and, in fact, it was developing ruts from our occasional driving over it.

One day, as the wrong gravel sat on our driveway, Catherine came back from the mailbox in an agitated state. I would not believe what had happened, she said, as she dropped a bulging white envelope onto the kitchen table. Inside was a set of house keys and a note from George. Since it did not seem that his tastes and ours were compatible, we had come to a parting of the ways; he enclosed his final bill, which did not include the cost of the gravel. We did not know George that well but knew him well enough to know there was no point in trying to change his mind. We paid the bill promptly, contacted a gravel supplier, and within a few days had a new smooth, hard driveway that did not yield under our car's tires. Unfortunately, in the process we had lost our custodian and handyman.

George was not without sympathy for us, however, and he suggested to a young boy who lived up the Road that he come down and ask us if we needed any help. The boy showed up a few days later and offered to cut our grass, move dirt, and otherwise do the heavy lifting. We welcomed him and put him to work adding topsoil to the flower beds surrounding the house. He drove his stepfather's riding mower down the Road and cut our grass in a fraction of the time it had taken me with a regular power mower. When we ordered a cord of split wood in anticipation of using the fireplace in the cool evenings, he stacked it neatly in the garage according to the way his father had taught him: with tall cribs buttressing each end of a more conventional arrangement of stacked wood. Two of those cribs are still standing today on either end of a void, and two others are still holding back a half cord of wood that we have yet to use up during our summer sojourns.

No account of our place in Maine is complete without saying more about the Stones. After George and Milly Stafford, Al and Grace Stone were the first residents of Spinney Mill Road that we met, when they appeared at our door one evening to welcome us to the Road. On a subsequent early evening get-together, Grace brought a large envelope full of pictures, including the print of the aerial photo of the house and garage with their near-matching flat roofs. These photos and the stories accompanying them have been central to reconstructing the provenance of the place.

When Al and Grace had sold the River House back to the Phinneys, they kept for themselves a parcel across the Road and a separate strip on our side of it to give them access to the cove. Al and Grace loved Arrowsic, and it was here that they established their own summer home on a four-acre piece of land. Rather than fronting on the river, it looked out onto the marsh, and in their retirement they expanded the house with a handsome addition with a high-ceilinged great room separated from a small dining area by a large brick fireplace. A study was located in an alcove; books and artwork lined the walls.

Al and Grace had retired to Spinney Mill Road in 1991; he enjoyed golf and she horses, but they also spent much of their time doing truly good works in Bath and around the area. I once came upon Al—who in his career had been chairman of the English department at Emory University and of the American Studies department at the University of Iowa—at a corner table in the library patiently teaching a grown man to read. Al also volunteered as a docent at the Maine Maritime Museum and taught extension and adult education courses for the Maine university system. Grace kept two horses up Route 1, near Montsweag, where she went regularly to keep them schooled in dressage. She also worked with adult literacy programs and counseled abused women, coming to be described as a "social activist and equestrian." The Stones both worked unstintingly on fund-raisers for the Episcopal Church in Wiscasset, their place of worship.

We spent many an enjoyable evening with Al and Grace, roughly alternating between their coming down to our place beside the river and our going up to theirs overlooking the marsh. We enjoyed drinks before, wine during, and Irish whiskey (Tullamore Dew) after dinner, with animated conversation throughout. Al and Grace introduced us to neighbors and islanders and newly discovered books. It was always a pleasure to return the Stones' hospitality. We soon noticed that when they came to our place they invariably occupied the same seats: Grace sat at the far right end of the sofa, looking out at the river; Al took one of the glider chairs facing the sofa, thus sitting with his back to the view. To Grace the house would always be remembered as the River House.

Eventually the winters got too difficult for Al to negotiate the ice with his orthopedic shoe and artificial hip, and the Stones decided to move to Atlanta, where their children and grandchildren lived. Their last summer in Maine was a bittersweet one, busy with packing and making arrangements to drive down to Georgia in their

Grace's favorite seat

new Prius. Catherine and neighbor Lucy Pieh planned a going-away party, and Catherine made the Stones an album of neighborhood photos and memories of Maine. After drinks and hors d'oeuvres at our place, the party moved across the cove for a potluck supper. The evening ended up with just about everyone on the Road sitting around the Piehs' large living room telling stories about themselves and the Stones, an impromptu communal roast.

One tale involved an incident that occurred long before we even knew Spinney Mill Road existed, and the tale had probably undergone many embellishments in its telling and retelling. As we heard it, one evening at dusk a large animal was walking slowly down the middle of the Road, bothering no one. The nearsighted Al Stone, who was out with his dog, spotted the stray animal from afar and thought a horse had escaped again from a nearby pasture. After taking the dog back home, Al pursued the loose animal, seeing as he approached it that it did not have any bridle or lead to catch on to. Thinking that he needed something to cinch around the steed's neck, Al took off his belt and tried to loop it over the animal, at which point the moose let Al know that it was no horse and left Spinney Mill Road behind, though its story remained.

Among the things we anticipated most warmly while driving back to Maine each year was the time we would spend with the Stones, having cocktails with them, engaging in academic gossip, and going to Portland for lunch and the art museum or dinner and the theater. They always knew of a new restaurant they wanted to try. We did not see them as much as we would have liked their last busy summer in Maine, but we did meet their children and reminisced briefly with them about their having lived in the house that was now ours. The last time we saw Al and Grace, they and their son, in town to help with the final packing and long drive south, came over for dinner. We were leaving town ourselves for a few days in New York, to celebrate my mother's ninetieth birthday and for me to give a talk at a meeting on bridge engineering. We told the Stones to feel free to come down by the river and spend some time at the house while we were away. The tonic water and half-empty bottle of their brand of gin left behind told us that they had indeed come down and said their goodbyes to the River House.

 *Thirteen*

HEAVY
LIFTING

AMONG THE THINGS THAT kept puzzling me about how our house was built by the solitary carpenter Bob Phinney was exactly how he had raised the roof beams. The sixteen-foot-long, four-by-eight rafters must weigh in excess of a hundred pounds each. Their weight, plus their unwieldy size, must have made them difficult to put in place across the open space between an outside wall and the one that divides the kitchen and living room from the bedrooms in the back. Since the timbers obviously had to be longer than the inside distance between the walls, they would have had to be maneuvered into place with some jockeying within the balloon framing. Perhaps Phinney lifted one end at a time, something that was probably well within his capability, and carried it on his shoulder up a ladder to place atop the wall frame. But was that effort humanly achievable without mistake or injury the several dozen times that he would have had to repeat it? Should I, like the enthusiasts who, in order to demonstrate how the Egyptians might have raised their monolithic obelisks, build a mockup on the lawn and try it for myself?

Another puzzle was how he finished the stone fireplace, whose chimney core reached high above the floor even before the house was enclosed with solid walls and a roof. It must have presented a striking contrast when seen through the wood framing, like a caged gorilla reaching for freedom. Today, the gorilla in the finished house is a source of solace, but it still presents some questions. The fireplace's more-than-seven-foot-long, one-foot-wide mantel is made of two-and-a-half-inch-thick slate. If it were all of one piece, the slab would weigh about 250 pounds, and this may explain why the mantel is not all of one piece. Phinney assembled it out of three nearly equal sections, each of which weighs less than a hundred pounds. Not only might the three shorter sections together cost less than a single long piece of slate, but also they would have been less likely to be damaged during the process of hoisting and setting them in place. Phinney may well have had to ask someone to help him lift and install each dense and compact part. His son Bobby would have been about twelve years old at the time, an age when a boy can be stronger than he may appear. Whoever might have helped with the mantel, when I look at the finished product, I admire how the sections meet and present an even, if interrupted top surface. I also wonder if the way I imagine Phinney and a possible helper to have achieved these feats of strength with such precision is realistic. Or are carpentry and stonemasonry necessarily occupations full of mechanical aids?

The individual stones in the fireplace are not so large or heavy that they could not have been lifted from the surrounding land and hauled to the construction site by a man or woman of no special strength. George and Milly were certainly up to the task of helping Phinney do this. I have always marveled at the effort expended in clearing a field of boulders and building a neat wall around it out of the same stones that once littered it, bringing order to disorder,

Mantel in three sections

making useful the useless. Dry-stacked stone walls vary greatly in style and execution, both of which depend a lot on the size and shape of the stones, as well as local custom. Wide, flat stones can be piled bricklike, but without using any defining mortar, to produce something of remarkably sophisticated beauty and delicacy. Such a wall, with a gentle outward curve that gives it an arch-like strength against being pushed over, borders the Shultz front yard. I admire it every time we pass by upon entering or leaving our right-of-way. Other stone walls, such as one out on Five Islands Road, have become little more than piles of rubble, but they still define a space and locate a place that otherwise would be unrecognizable as such. Some stonework comes about by chance: on entering Georgetown there is a large rock sitting atop other rocks; it is painted green to call attention to its resemblance to a giant turtle. But not all rocks and stones can be easily moved or can be simply used where they are found.

The problem of moving and removing, usually at tortoise-like speed, large rocks and boulders is one that is prehistoric. Think of the thousands-of-years-old post-and-lintel Stonehenge on England's Salisbury Plain and the even older corbelled Newgrange passage tomb located north of Dublin. In fact, in one form the practice of moving monoliths even predates ancient construction challenges. In Maine, the largest boulder believed to have been transported by glacier is known as Daggett Rock. Deposited in the vicinity of what is now Phillips—a town of about a thousand people in the western part of the state—this boulder that measures roughly eighty by thirty by twenty-five feet is estimated to weigh about eight thousand tons. The rock's namesake was an early nineteenth-century woodsman who is said to have climbed atop the monolith during a raging thunderstorm and cursed the weather and the god who made it. A lightning bolt struck Daggett down and cracked the boulder into the three large pieces in which it is found today. Even in its divided state, or perhaps because of it, Daggett Rock is a tourist attraction.

Though perhaps not an attraction to anyone but me, there is a boulder of modest size in front of our house that has been split into two parts. Chipmunks and squirrels use the resulting little gorge, which fills up with leaves each fall, as a shortcut into the bushes. A 1950s photo of the house shows this boulder intact in the foreground, indicating that it was split just yesterday in geological time. I have often wondered how this happened, and how the halves came to be moved apart. Did lightning split the rock suddenly? Or did a small fissure grow slowly over many seasons as the water that collected in it froze and wedged the rock apart little by little to fracture? Whatever created the crevice in the first place, does the space between the parts grow each year? To the eye it does not, but to my foot, which used to get caught in the gap but now does not, the opening does widen—at a glacial pace. How long can the space continue to grow before the half closer to

The split rock beside the river

the river loses its footing and rolls into the water? Or will it stay put for ages, like Daggett Rock?

The largest boulder anywhere ever to have been transported by man also has a name: Thunder Stone. Its origin was Finland and its destination Saint Petersburg, Russia, where it was to be used as a pedestal for an equestrian statue of Peter the Great that had been conceived by the French Rococo sculptor Étienne Falconet. There was need for a base in keeping with the scale of the twenty-foot-tall *Bronze Horseman,* as the piece of commemorative sculpture commissioned in 1766 by Catherine the Great came to be known. Falconet wanted to carve the stone to his specifications where it was found, but Catherine wished it be moved to Russia immediately, which was accomplished in part by employing a sledge supported by bronze balls riding on tracks laid on the frozen ground to transport the stone the four miles from where it was found to the Gulf of Finland, where it was loaded onto a barge for passage to Saint Petersburg. The estimated 1,600-ton boulder, which measured about forty by twenty by twenty-five feet tall, began to be carved in transit to shape it into the cliff upon which the equestrian now stands.

In its more familiar form, the problem of moving great masses has been one of lifting large pieces of shaped stone to build pyramids, relocate obelisks, and construct cathedrals. In most of these cases, there was little but the power of men, animals, and ingenuity to assist in the task. What machines that were devised were typically human- or animal-powered. However, much heavy lifting was likely done by direct muscle power involving large numbers of men, in which case the agreement on a procedure of who lifted when and who pushed and who pulled when was critical to the success of the endeavor. On large projects such as building a monumental structure, in which there was an enormous amount of repetitive moving of similarly shaped pieces of stone, there no doubt were set procedures followed. These procedures most likely evolved by trial and error from ad hoc solutions devised, studied, and executed by master builders, engineers, and the workers themselves.

The same process can still be observed at work today. In Maine, I once witnessed two workmen wrestle with the problem of moving a heavy piece of stone from the ground to the top of our chimney—a problem that brought to mind the Middle Ages, if not ancient times. When the roof on the house was altered, Phinney's original stone chimney would have become concealed between the old flat roof and the new peaked one had the flue not been extended above the new roof within brickwork that is now the house's visible chimney. It emerges from the front portion of the steeply pitched roof and marks the position beneath the roof of the large stone fireplace. The chimney is located about midway up the front slope of the roof, about equidistant from the gutter and the ridge, and it is positioned about fifteen feet from one gable and twenty-five from the other. The dimensions of the brick chimney projecting upward from the roof are about two feet by three and a half feet in cross section, and it projects from about six feet to about eight feet above the roof. In other words, the top of the chimney is just a little above the level of the ridge, but it is about eight feet away from it. The cap on this chimney had been made of some unidentified synthetic material, and its underside had begun to deteriorate badly, dropping residue into the flue. Because we were told that the white chalky stuff leaching down the stone facing of the fireplace had its origin in this deteriorating chimney cap, we wanted to replace it with one more resistant to erosion. We also wanted a cap that would overhang the chimney a little more, so that rain was less likely to find its way into the fireplace. How to take off the old cap and replace it with a new one involved designing a procedure to deal with the moving of heavy objects.

A mason told us that to accomplish the task he would have to erect a scaffold to establish a working platform around the chimney. The entire job, including building and disassembling the scaffolding, might take days to complete. A chimney sweep we asked said that he would not need any scaffolding and so could do the job in about an hour. Rather than spending considerable time setting

Chimney on steeply pitched roof

up and tearing down a lot of ancillary equipment, he would follow an ad hoc scheme to accomplish the task. As a replacement for the deteriorating chimney cap, he proposed a piece of granite about an inch and a half thick, which meant that it would weigh at least 150 pounds, but he expressed little doubt that he and his helper could handle the job without scaffolding. It was only later that I learned that their full-time job was as firemen in the Topsham area, and so they could be expected to be able to carry the weight of a good size person, in addition to their own fire-fighting gear, across a bare roof. Still, removing the old chimney cap, which itself must have weighed at least seventy-five pounds, and getting the new one in place all in an hour seemed like an ambitious schedule.

On the appointed day, the chimney sweep and his helper arrived in a pickup truck, with a beautiful piece of polished granite in the bed. The sweep explained that the granite was of a much higher quality than the situation demanded, but that he had by chance found the odd-sized slab available for a price he could not refuse. The truck also carried three ladders on its elevated rack, and at least the makings of a plan in the back of the sweep's mind. How else would he have known how many ladders to bring? One of them was a standard extension type, and it was leaned against the end of the house closer to the chimney. A second ladder could not be extended, but it had large hooks at one end that enabled it to be secured over the ridge of the roof and thus provide a stairway of sorts up the steep slope.

The sweep climbed up to the ridge of the roof and walked across it toward the chimney. He carried the third ladder—a common aluminum stepladder—with him and parked it open straddling the ridge, presumably at the ready for some future use. Unencumbered by the ladder, he scooted down the slope to the chimney, the top of which was over his head. In a move as effortless and as graceful as a gymnast mounting a pommel horse, the sweep pulled himself into a kneeling position atop the flat chimney cap and proceeded to hacksaw through and remove the few bolts that secured it to the open brickwork. This being done, he dismounted the chimney and called for his helper to join him. The two men, standing on the sloped roof on either side of the chimney, and reaching well above their heads, slid the old cap off and took it to the ridge, where all by himself the helper lifted it and carried it over to the long ladder. He placed the burden across the rails of the ladder and slid it down the slope of the roof as he himself backed down rung by rung before it. When he reached the juncture of the roof ladder with the one against the gable, the sweep came over and held the old chimney cap on the ladder rails while the helper mounted the second ladder. Working together, the two of them repositioned the cap in the crooks of the helper's arms, which held onto the ladder rails. He backed down the ladder to the ground and carried the old cap over to a tree, against which he leaned it intact.

The sweep called down for a rat-tail brush, a term with which the helper said he was not familiar. After it was described to him, he said that was what he called a fox-tail. After some banter, the sweep had what he wanted. With the brush in hand, he returned to the chimney and again mounted it, this time kneeling across two of its brick piers to brush clean the mortar wash that covered the top course of bricks on the chimney proper. The wash was configured to slope outward and so direct water away from the flue. The sweep had determined on his first visit that the wash needed to be repaired, and he was preparing the surface before the new cap was installed. Balanced on one hand and two knees across the chimney top, he used the brush vigorously and raised a considerable amount of dust, which made him sneeze. With the bricks cleaned of dust and loose pieces of old wash, the sweep shouted down that he could see a long hole reaching well into the bricks of the chimney, which he surmised had allowed water into the fireplace. When he finished brushing the wash surface, he backed down from the chimney top and returned to the ground. He would plug the hole and apply a new mortar wash only after the new cap was in place, so that while struggling with the heavy piece of granite he and his helper would be able to have the freedom to grab a handhold anywhere on the chimney. Experience had evidently taught the sweep that foreseeing what should not be done, and when, is as important to designing a successful procedure as seeing what should be done and when.

Removing the old cap had been practice of sorts for installing the new, but the large flat stone to be lifted and installed would be at least twice as heavy as that which had been taken down. The team would be working against rather than with gravity, and the consequences of a misstep could be a broken piece of tabletop-quality granite, or worse. The two men huddled and spoke quietly about how they would get the granite cap up onto the roof, over to the chimney, and set atop it. They considered possibilities and weighed options, taking into account the constraints and trade-offs in their problem and contemplated solutions. The steep pitch of the roof and the location of the chimney on it presented a situation that was not standard, and so they knew they would have to proceed with a degree of uncertainty and be prepared to change their plan as conditions demanded. All they could be sure about were their own strength and ingenuity and, perhaps equally important, the limits of their strength and ingenuity.

Since the polished granite gave little sure purchase for their hands, the sweep directed his helper to get an old rope from the back of the truck. The half-inch-diameter line appeared to be made of nylon and was dirty red in color, perhaps from years of use on a working boat or in chimney-cleaning work. The sweep talked quietly to his helper about the rope, seeming to give its provenance and explaining how it had been well stretched and would not give during use. He inspected the rope with the intensity that a diamond cutter does a rough stone. Then the sweep tied the rope around the piece of granite as carefully as if he were wrapping a special birthday present. He circled the rope around the slab first one way and then another, tying knots with the practiced speed and precision of a surgeon. The entire length of rope, which must have been at least fifty feet, was used, and the loose end was tied multiple times to finish the package in what resembled a bulky bow. The sweep hefted the granite by the rope several times, testing his wrapping and declaring it good. A second rope, one that the sweep had carried in a black nylon pouch up to the roof, was already secured near the top of the ladder anchored there and thrown over the edge. At first the free end of the rope hung down over the gutter along the front edge of the roof, but that was clearly not the way the granite would be raised, as direct a path as it would have provided. The gutter would have been crushed under the weight, which was why the ground ladder had been positioned at the gable. (The sweep knew that design is as much about rejecting as selecting alternatives.) The rope was repositioned to hang down over the gable, and the sweep secured a large mountain climber's carabiner to the crossed ropes on the package of granite. This piece of mountain-climbing equipment, through which the hauling rope could move freely, added a new dimension to the personality and experience of the sweep.

With the granite secured to the hauling rope, the sweep climbed up to the roof and positioned himself near the bottom of the roof ladder, where it met the top of the ground ladder. The sweep pulled from above and the helper pushed from below, and between them they got the granite cap balanced on the top of the extension ladder, giving them a chance to rest and plan their next move. Getting the granite from the one ladder to the other was done by sheer muscle power, with the sweep braced against the bottom rung of the roof ladder and the helper against the top of the ground-based one. When the slab had been transferred successfully, it was centered across the inclined ladder rails and held in place by the helper, who was no doubt aided by what little friction there was between the old nylon rope and the aluminum ladder. Now, the sweep climbed to the ridge of the roof. From there, he again pulled while the helper pushed the granite up the incline. When the cap reached the ridge, a new maneuver was required to reposition it for the trek across the roof, which had to be done unaided by any ladder footholds or pulling ropes. The two men had to work together, the helper moving backward and the sweep forward, lifting the granite slab between them and setting it down at intervals to reposition it and themselves until they were directly uproof from the chimney.

While the helper sat straddling the roof's peak and holding the piece of granite balanced there like a teeterboard on the ridge, the sweep inched down to the chimney and looked up at it. He held onto the back of the chimney with one hand while he leaned his body down the slope to analyze the task before them one last time. The stepladder that earlier had been parked across the peak of the roof was now positioned against the uproof side of the chimney, not reaching its top but providing a prop or shelf for one end of the granite to be placed on while it would be aligned for the final lift and push into place. The sweep and the helper conferred again, quietly and at length, about how they would lift the heavy granite cap up to the top of the chimney. The sweep took one corner of the slab and the helper one side, and the two men lifted its front edge by sheer muscle power onto the waiting stepladder and rested. After a minute, they lifted the edge of the granite onto the brick chimney top and placed it across the four columns of bricks that formed one edge of the crown of the chimney. This movement was one of a lift and shift as opposed to a slide, for pushing the slab across the brick piers might have opened up cracks in the mortar and damaged the brickwork. Besides, the sweep and his helper had the encircling rope to contend with.

With the cap more or less in place, the rope had to be removed before the final positioning of the cap on the chimney. The helper had remarked when the sweep was tying the multiple knots in it that they would all have to be removed later, but the sweep had seemed to take no heed. He had evidently had it in his mind from the beginning that he would sacrifice the dirty red rope, for he did not hesitate when he took a knife from his pocket and sliced the rope in several places. The helper lifted up one side of the slab so that the pieces of rope could be removed and thrown off the roof. (Nothing was ever left underfoot up there.) The sweep then repositioned himself directly behind the chimney, from where he sighted along its sides to gauge the slab's overhang. He directed the helper where to lift the piece of granite and nudge it left and right. The entire job of removing the old and installing the new cap took less than an hour, as promised.

With the new cap in place some thirty-odd feet in the air, a seat from which no wind or rain would budge the heavy slab of granite, the sweep returned to the ground to mix a small pail of mortar for forming the new wash. Compared to the cap work, repairing the wash was not a strenuous task, but it did require some contorting to apply the trowels of mortar to the six distinct openings framed by the brickwork of the chimney, the brick piers, and the new granite cap. The job took another half hour, and the sweep and his helper had the truck all packed up and ready to go barely ninety minutes from when they drove down the driveway.

The installation of the chimney cap was a real-life, real-time illustration of the timelessness of invention, design, and ingenuity. Except for the mountain climber's carabiner, the sweep and his

New chimney cap in place

helper used no tools, power, or scheme that would not have been available to those who toiled on Egyptian pyramids, Greek and Roman temples, or Gothic cathedrals. Even the aluminum ladders were but a version in modern material of some climbing device that should have been familiar to the pyramid engineer Imhotep. The chimney cap installers wore no work gloves, no safety harnesses, and no hardhats. The helper did not even wear long pants, and his knees were exposed to the gritty surface of the composition shingles. Indeed, the two men joked about hoping that no representative of the Occupational Safety and Health Administration—the dreaded OSHA—was watching, for they had installed no guardrails and were not tethered to anything. They were, in effect, working in another time.

However, in the modern context, the problem consisted of more than just moving a piece of granite into place on the chimney top; it also involved the issues of worker and user safety, which were addressed by thought and care rather than the imposed rules and tools of modern construction practice. There was likely little concern for the safety of ancient or medieval workers, save for how an accident might have disrupted work and lowered worker morale. Even as late as the early twentieth century, there appears to have been considerable disregard for human worker life, with construction workers wearing little more than soft caps on their heads, providing no real protection from projecting beams and falling tools and debris. It was not until the great construction projects of the 1930s, notably those of the Hoover Dam and the Golden Gate Bridge, that hardhats became routinely worn and mandatory on job sites. The construction of the Empire State Building took place on the verge of this revolution; the famous Lewis Hine photographs of ironworkers high above New York City streets show that they did not wear hardhats or safety harnesses. Nevertheless, no worker lives were lost on the project, which came in under budget and ahead of schedule, being completed in less than fifteen months.

That the chimney sweep and his helper were casual in their street clothes and dismissive of safety equipment is not to say that they were careless. At all times they moved deliberately and with a sureness of step. There was never more than one tool at a time in the sweep's hand, and what was not in his hand was in his pocket or in the hands of his helper. When the sweep sawed off one of the rusty bolts holding the old chimney cap down, he tossed it to the helper, who put it in his pocket. When one of the bolt shanks was stubborn in coming loose, the sweep used a mallet to persuade it. The piece of metal flew across the roof and rolled down onto the grass in front of the house. All the time it was moving, the sweep watched it from his precarious perch. The helper was sent down to retrieve it from the ground, directed by the sweep to walk this way and that until it was picked up and placed safely in the helper's pocket. "That would not be a good thing to hit with a power mower," the sweep shouted down to me on the ground, where I had been watching them work from a safe distance.

Though the granite cap now sitting on top of our chimney is a beautiful piece of stone, I am sure that over time it will suffer many indignities under the wings of the seagulls, ospreys, eagles, and other birds that fly over the house. Fortunately, I will not be able to see the polished top dulled by the passage of time and the droppings of birds. Rather, whenever I look up at the chimney or even just watch the smoke rise into it from the fireplace, I invariably recall the hour of the cap's installation, not only as a triumph of mind and muscle over gravity but also as a striking example of occasional design. The slab of granite may not cap a pyramid or crown a cathedral, but the process of getting it into place will always symbolize to me the importance of design as procedure as well as of product. It is thinking about the problem that lifts the thing into place, as much as it is the idea of the thing that pulls out of the mind the thought about how to do it. Thinking about how to accomplish something is in fact the essence of design. The plan is as important as the path. When the consequences of a misstep can be fatal, the avoidance of an unchecked slip along the way can be as important to success as the final push to the summit. As far as understanding the process, as opposed to just appreciating the product, the journey of a chimney cap is more important than the chimney cap itself. It was a fitting lesson played out atop the vertical extension of the house that Phinney built. And it helped me understand how he may have been able to lift the house's roof timbers and mantel pieces into place, perhaps with a helper.

 *Fourteen*

WORKING SPACE

ONE OF THE OBJECTIVES of spending summers in Maine was to escape the North Carolina heat and humidity. I also wanted a place where I would be able to work on extended writing projects without the unpredictable interruptions that can walk through a doorway off a busy university hallway. It was not that I was trying to escape routine itself, for I thrive on a work regimen, and in our first summer in Maine I had soon set about to establish one in the building behind the garage.

The front room of the former workshop was furnished with a sofa bed, a swivel chair, a rocking chair, and a few occasional tables, none of which was large or steady enough to provide a suitable working surface. So my first challenge was to find a desk or a table that would serve the purpose. Catherine and I visited new and used furniture stores, flea markets, and antique shops looking for something small enough to fit in the trunk of our Volvo—with its back-seat folded down flat, if necessary—and yet large enough to give me the working space that I wished to have. It proved not to be an easy task, since we also did not want to spend a great deal of money on something that might be fancier than everything else in the cabin. Finally, in one of Bath's several antique and used-furniture stores, we came across a gateleg table that looked like it might do the trick. It was covered with a display of glassware, which the proprietor gladly removed to reveal a nicely finished cherry top sitting on eight spidery turned legs painted black. Two of the legs swung out to support large drop leaves. When the leaves and legs were folded out, the table provided an ample thirty-six-by-forty-two-inch working surface; with the leaves down, the table became a compact package measuring thirty-six by fourteen by twenty-nine inches, something that was easy to carry out of the store and fit into the car.

Neither of the chairs in the cabin could serve as a suitable desk chair, and the main house had none to spare. So on our outing we looked also for a chair and found one on the Phippsburg peninsula in a store full of furniture odds and ends. It was as small and simple (and hard-seated) a chair as I would ever work in, but it seemed to fit perfectly with the Spartan surroundings in the cabin, and it fit easily into our car. In the same shop, we also found a matched pair of wooden armchairs in a style and finish that we knew would go nicely with the décor in the house's living room. However, we would have to make a separate trip to transport these.

When we got everything back to Arrowsic, I opened up the table and set it in front of the guest cabin's large window facing the river, whose boat traffic was visible through the trees but distant enough to have its sound muffled and distraction diminished by the underbrush. Unfortunately, there seem always to be unanticipated complications with things we bring home, and the table was no exception. I would have preferred to work sitting at a longer side of the table, but this was supported under its center by a pair of legs set eleven inches apart with a short stretcher between them. To work at the table in that orientation would have required me to sit uncomfortably with my legs spread apart for hours at a time. Besides, I liked to cross my stretched-out legs at the ankles while working. So I turned the table to make a shorter side face the window. This gave me a narrower working space, but certainly enough to accommodate my laptop computer and a book or article or manuscript or two on either side. There remained a problem, however,

The gateleg table: leaves down, and up

for the gateleg supporting the open leaf still prevented me from pulling the chair under the table and crossing my legs. So, for the years that I worked in the guest cabin, I straddled the table leg and leaned across the gap between the chair and table to type.

Certainly all of these impediments could have been foreseen, but even choosing so simple a piece of technology as a table is complicated by distinct objectives and competing constraints. Our overarching concern, whether the table would fit in the car, was irrelevant once we got the thing home. But without satisfying the transportation requirement, we did not think I could have a piece of furniture. After all, the common concept of a table is something with a flat, horizontal, rectangular working surface supported by four vertical legs, one at each corner. This is so fundamental that we take it for granted. It is our mind's picture of a table, even when the one we are looking at does not conform to it. Thus, when examining the gateleg table in the store I focused on the size and height and condition of the working surface when opened to full size, and on the compactness of the table when fully closed. The mechanism of how the top and legs folded down and up, in and out, was of no immediate concern. Likewise, the location and number of the legs was a detail, or two, or four, or six, or eight. It was not until I had the table in the intended workplace and set up for use there that these details became conspicuously important. The experience made me appreciate all the more Bob Phinney's achievements in building his house, anticipating problems the way he did.

We humans are remarkably adaptive creatures, and once we get immersed in our work we can do it in the most awkward and uncomfortable positions. The phenomenon is clear to me every time I fly and watch a business person typing one-handed on a laptop that he is holding up with his other hand while standing in line at the gate, his boarding pass in his mouth and his luggage slung over his shoulder. Even on the airplane, where one would expect a tray table to provide support enough to allow two-hand typing, a reclining passenger in the seat ahead can so restrict the space that the laptop keyboard can only be used in a virtually vertical position. We make do with the tools we have, tables included.

I wrote a couple of books working at my gateleg table by an arm of the sea. The cabin had no phone line, which was fine with me, since it meant that I could work during the day uninterrupted by phone calls or e-mail. There was electricity, of course, which was essential not only to power my computer when the battery was drained but also to provide baseboard heat in the morning chill. Since the cabin had its own bathroom, I could work in voluntary solitary confinement until lunchtime, after which I would usually work a little more in the cabin and then do yard work and chores around the house and property.

When the cabin was being used by guests, which also meant more activity in the house itself, I was pretty much out of even a semiprivate working space. It was then that we began looking seriously at finishing the attic. We did it in three stages, each time giving Rob Shultz an entire winter to work on a convenient indoor job just down the lane from his home.

Without a level floor, the attic had been virtually unusable for anything but storage. We were not bothered having boxes and bins resting on an incline like ships on the ways, but I did not want to sit and work out of plumb. So the first stage of the finishing work was obvious. Installing a level floor extending out eight feet or so on each side from the ridge of the old roof required building up a framework of joists made horizontal by properly placed struts, wedges, and shims. Two-by-fours were used for the short-span joists to keep the floor height as low as possible over the roof ridge, thereby maintaining as much headroom as possible. But this left the riser of the last step up the attic stairway shorter than the rest. The uneven risers do take some getting used to going up and down the stairs, but my legs have adapted. Still, I do warn rare visitors to the attic to watch their step.

The floor-leveling procedure created wedge-shaped hollows on each side of the roof ridge, and it was natural to fill these in with insulation. Installing a level and continuous floor also necessarily involved covering over the old skylights. Originally illuminating the boys' half bath and the hallway, the skylights had become largely ineffective anyway after the pitched roof was constructed over the flat one.

The formerly unusable space was now a study, albeit a rudimentary one. For a desk I used a large, sturdy kitchen table, which we assembled from a kit after hauling the flat but heavy box of parts home in a rented van and up into the attic. This table gave me a good-size work surface and uninterrupted legroom. To turn the table into an L-shaped desk of sorts, I used the old gateleg as a left return on which to pile bankers boxes, files, papers, and books. An occasional table that the Moniers had used for a television stand downstairs sat to the right of the desk itself and held a printer and supplies of stationery. For the time being, the hodgepodge of furniture sat on the unfinished but level plywood floor between and beneath exposed wall framing and rafters. Finally, I had a room (of sorts) of my own. From the north windows, near which I had set the table, there was a great view upriver toward Fiddler's Reach, but I soon forgot that it was there.

The next winter, we had the attic walls finished. The knee-wall framing that was already in place surely was put in at the same time as the pitched roof. It would have been done to help support the long rafters, and possibly also in anticipation of one day finishing the attic. In any case, the studs were there, leaving a distance between the knee-wall framings of sixteen feet three inches. At first I thought that the walls should be paneled to mimic what is downstairs, that is, with vertical boards set atop a horizontal baseboard. This would have required that horizontal furring strips first be nailed across the vertical studs, and the thickness of the furring and panel boards would have made the paneled-wall-to-paneled-wall distance exactly sixteen feet, meaning that the floor between could be covered with sheets of standard four-by-eight-foot plywood with virtually no waste. The wall framing may well have been positioned with this in mind.

But Rob pointed out that it might be wiser to install the knotty-pine boards horizontally along the long knee walls in order to better stiffen the roof structure against racking in the wind. This was an excellent suggestion, and one whose structural advantage I preferred over the perceived aesthetic imperative. Since the horizontal boards could be nailed directly to the vertical studs, no furring strips would have to be added, thus saving materials and time and hence some expense. But this would have meant that the floor distance between paneled walls would have been one and a half inches greater than sixteen feet. To avoid that gap, one-by-two strips were nailed to the face of each stud, thereby providing vertical furring of a sort to which the horizontal paneling was attached.

I did insist that the end walls be paneled vertically, however, with a flush baseboard following the downstairs model, thus carrying that theme upstairs to at least some extent. Five access doors were fitted into the long walls, and we finally could store things out of sight, even if still on an incline. (Since the doors were made to harmonize with the horizontal paneling, each Z-brace was turned on its side to appear to be an N-brace.) The next summer I felt I had a real study in which to work, one that was sixteen feet wide and forty feet long (640 square feet!), an expansive rectangle interrupted only by the stairwell more or less in the middle of the floor and the chimney of the fireplace jutting out from the west wall. It was certainly more private space than I had ever had and probably should ever need. The area in which I actually work measures maybe five by ten feet—a space of my own in a room of my own.

In the time since Phinney built his house, and even in the time since the stairway to the attic was installed, the automatic nail gun had become increasingly popular. This innovation has changed not only the way carpenters work but also the way we hear them at work. Instead of the sound of a few deliberate pounds followed by a brief silence while the hammerer reached into his apron for another nail and held it in place before resuming pounding, now we hear staccato pneumatic impacts that repeat until the wielder of the weapon must reload, reach for another piece of lumber, or reposition himself for another foray into the wood.

It may have been my express desire to have Phinney's style replicated as much as possible in the attic paneling that led to all the boards up there being nailed directly through their face rather than being toenailed. Thus, the attic wall paneling boldly displays the distinct artifacts of machine-gun nailing, which by its action had set the nails deep into the wood, a reminder of the violent nature of the tool. The ragged scars left behind are square-cornered because, in order to load as many nails as possible into the gun's magazine, their heads came clipped into a somewhat rectangular shape, an ironic throwback to the time of wrought nails. The vertical boards at the ends of the room are attached with two (to Phinney's three) nails, and since two points define a line, it cannot be said that they do not form a straight line on each board. However, unlike Phinney's careful alignment from board to board, the new nail lines generally zigzag up and down from board to board, a pattern that does not hold up to close aesthetic scrutiny. It does, however, follow the natural drift of a carpenter's arm wielding an unwieldy nail gun. Regardless, the machine-driven nails will never be mistaken for small knots in the wood.

It had originally been our intention to stain and varnish the attic paneling to make it consistent with the original walls downstairs. I began with the stairwell, because the bare treads and risers picked up scuff marks very easily and the steps were beginning to look dirty. After sanding off the marks, I began staining the stairs, the newer paneling bordering them, and the railing around the stairwell. This proved to be a much more time-consuming project than I had anticipated, and I did not want to see an entire summer of afternoons taken up by staining the walls also. So we decided that we would leave the wall paneling unfinished, anticipating that sunlight would darken the wood in time, just as it had in the guest cabin. Since the walls would not get nearly the abuse that the stairs and railing would, we expected them to stay clean and darken uniformly, because we had hung nothing on the walls. So far, we have not been disappointed in our decision, and the different look that the attic working space has from the downstairs living area makes for an appropriate change of atmosphere, with the stained stairwell providing a nice transition between the two levels. Like the kitchen, the attic is a working space marked by its mostly horizontal paneling.

View from top of attic stairs

The final stage of finishing the attic involved considerable thought. The otherwise open volume beneath the peaked roof was interrupted about a foot above head height by a series of horizontal two-by-sixes connecting pairs of rafters. Such collar ties are intended to hold the tops of rafters together against uplift forces caused by strong winds, but their structural necessity is debated for steeply pitched roofs. In any case, I wished the ties to remain in place and be designed around. The easiest solution would have been to nail boards across the bottoms of the collar ties, but this would have produced a forty-foot-long room with a seven-foot ceiling—an unacceptably tunnel-like space. For some time, we puzzled over what to do about the final finishing of the attic and eventually came up with a solution: The horizontal paneling on the knee walls would be carried up along the incline defined by the rafters to a foot or so past the ties before being taken across the room on a plane parallel to the floor. In this way, there is effectively a nine-foot ceiling, with the volume of the room interrupted every two feet by a six-inch-deep tie at the seven-foot level. Rob

Finished attic ceiling above exposed collar ties

took on the winter work, and we were very pleased with the effect when we saw it the next spring.

Like the vertical paneling at each end of the attic, the horizontal boards along the side walls are generally held with two nails defining each fastening line, but the boards on the incline typically are pierced by three nails each where they are attached to a rafter. This may have been done in recognition of the fact that gravity wants to pull the boards off to a greater extent, or just to better hold them in alignment under difficult working conditions. Another explanation might be that the different sets of boards show signs of a different hand working at a different stage of improvement; there can certainly be telltale signs of the human touch even when an advanced mechanical tool is being used. Whatever the reason, the nails are unevenly spaced and often misaligned. This is what can happen when work is done with a powerful tool in a confined space interrupted by obstacles like collar ties. The nail-gun operator cannot maintain the same rhythm that he can in an open area. Efficiency, not aesthetic satisfaction, was likely the goal of the workers in the attic.

The finishing details in the upstairs room are not quite Phinneyesque. Gaps left where panel boards meet rafters and ties seem to have presented the most difficulty. The distance up the wall from floor to rafter or up the incline from wall to tie could not be filled with an exact number of boards. Ripping a sixteen-foot-long board in a perfectly straight line should not be impossible to do with a power saw, but even if done to perfection the altered board would not likely fill the gap uniformly along its entire length because of small preexisting irregularities in the roof structure. Phinney in his patience would likely have ripped, trimmed, and notched boards to fit neatly into gaps and around each individual collar tie, but Phinney worked in a different time at a different pace. So, whatever narrow gaps were left in the newer work were covered over with quarter-inch-thick slats that so closely match the paneling in color that they are only noticeable upon close scrutiny. A two-inch-wide slat covers the gap between the top of the wall paneling and where the incline begins, another between the board just under the ties and the ties themselves, and still another between the top inclined board and where the horizontal ceiling begins. Boards nailed onto the incline directly above the ties were notched where they cross the tops of ties, but the notches were not made as carefully as Phinney surely would have done. The gaps left around the sides and top of the collar ties are covered over with flat molding strips, which stick out physically and aesthetically because their grain runs counter to that of the paneling. I was greatly disappointed in this detail when I first saw it, but after reflecting on the difficulty of fitting forty feet of boards around twenty or so ties, I realized that I should be grateful that the overall effect looks as good as it does.

A few other details also point to how differently things can turn out when they are conceived and executed by the same person as opposed to one person having an idea in his head trying to communicate it to another who is expected to execute it or pass the

A space of my own

instructions onto still another person. When we had asked that three ceiling-light receptacles be installed on designated collar ties at the same time that the attic floor was being leveled, we found that the wiring between each two fixtures was run down the center of the open attic space via holes drilled through the intermediate ties. Perhaps the electrician expected that we would finish the attic by nailing ceiling boards across the bottoms of the ties, in which case the electrical cables (and holes) would have been concealed, but at the time we requested the electrical work to be done we wanted to keep our options open about whether or not the ties would be exposed. We asked that the wiring be rerun, carrying it behind the side-wall studs and bringing it out along the back (as seen from the stairwell) of each of the three relevant ties.

In our own nod to speed and convenience, we soon installed track lighting on the three wired collar ties, had the floor covered with carpeting, and had a second telephone line installed. When I expressed displeasure with the one-inch holes the electrician had initially made in the ties, Rob fixed the problem nicely by plugging each of them with a disk of wood cut off a one-inch-diameter dowel rod. That the crosscut circles of wood did not exactly match the longitudinal grain of the ties did not bother me, because from a distance the plugs looked like knots. One wood disk fell out and was lost, but the single hole left behind looks just as if a loose knot had once been there.

Fifteen

NAME
AND
ADDRESS

THE MAILBOX WE INHERITED on Spinney Mill Road was labeled with a simple "98." We were in fact Box 98 of Highway Contract 33, which was delivered out of the Bath post office. The form of our mailing address, HC 33, Box 98, was confusing to people accustomed to RFD or simple P.O. box numbers. The idea of an HC route was that the mail was delivered not by a postal employee but by someone under contract to the Post Office, preferably someone who had intimate knowledge of the roads and houses along the route.

Our first mailman was somewhat infamous hereabouts. George Moore had taken over the responsibilities from his father, Fenton Moore. George was very dependable, working as many as twelve hours a day, six days a week, during which time he listened to unabridged books on tape, going through a book and a half a week. In three decades of delivering mail, he recalled missing only six days. According to a local report, "One was when his wife died. One was when he had a stroke, although, as he recalls, 'when I came out of the stroke, I finished my route.' It was the next day he took off. Even on the day he got married, he delivered the mail." According to the same newspaper account in which this tally occurred, one day in 1999 George was called to a meeting about changes in emergency procedures that would affect his route. As soon as he arrived at the meeting place, he knew "he had been set up" to be presented with a "plaque, present and cake" in appreciation of his thirty years of service to Arrowsic and Georgetown, whose mail he also delivered. He left after the twenty-minute ceremony to finish delivering his route.

Our mail was reliably delivered, and whenever we received a package too large to fit in the box he drove in on Spinney Mill Road and left it with a neighbor or brought it down to us. Thanks to George, our mail always got through, even when it was addressed in the most unorthodox, incorrect, or incomplete way. Though there may have been a ceremony marking his service, when George ceased delivering the mail it was abrupt and unceremonious.

Shortly after George's departure, the replacement who took over the mail route left a note informing us that he was a "small man" and could not easily reach our mailbox from where he sat in his car. The fact that our box was set a bit higher than the others was the result of a combination of factors: The post on which it was mounted was on the tall side to begin with, and when we replaced the standard-size box that came with the house with a larger one to accommodate the volume of mail that we anticipated to be forwarded from our home and my office in North Carolina, the box's latch towered a good six inches above the others. The small man's note was not a clear order, nor was it an overly polite plea. We worried that the power vested in the mailman, even if only a contractor, might enable him to stop delivering to us, and so we considered what we might do. As it turned out, the complainant was soon replaced by one who sat taller in his seat, and so we have just left the mailbox as it was. Its sticking up above the others makes it easier for us to pick it out of the lineup.

Giving our address to someone unfamiliar with the highway contract numbering system was often very frustrating. The address that we believed to be correct, and so the one we recited, was:

HC 33, Box 98
Spinney Mill Road
Arrowsic, ME 04530

Spinney Mill Road's mailboxes

Like the designation of Navy warships, this and virtually all mailing addresses contained a superfluity of information. Strictly speaking, the road, town, and state added nothing to the numbers, and a letter addressed to HC 33, Box 98, 04530—or even to just 33 98 04530—might have reached us. In fact, it might have arrived more efficiently, since there was no unnecessary information competing for the mail sorter's attention. However, the five-digit zip code is also Bath's, and so without an additional four digits or the town Arrowsic, a letter or parcel in the hands of a novice sorter might go astray.

Of course, FedEx, UPS, DHL, and other express or courier services do not deliver to post-office boxes or mailboxes, and so they had to have a street address. This is where the Spinney Mill Road designation was necessary, but it was not always sufficient. It is true that when we looked at the house with the realtor, it did appear to have its own driveway, but since that direct access had been sealed off, the way to our place, via the right-of-way through the Shultz property, continued to be a source of confusion. Whereas we had anticipated putting up a Petroski sign where the driveway met the Road, we were reluctant to do so at the head of the right-of-way. We felt that it was ours to use but not necessarily to mark.

At first, many a delivery person looked in vain for some hint of where the Petroski residence was. The seasoned driver who knew the names of all the old-timers looked for a new house or some sign that one of the two rental properties had changed tenants. The difficulty of finding us on (or, rather, off) Spinney Mill Road only emphasized a common problem of finding residences throughout Maine generally. The highway-contract box number was not alone sufficient for locating the physical house, and the street or road name was useful only to a degree. Few if any houses or driveways displayed a number corresponding to the highway-contract box number. All too many Mainers and summer-Mainers did not have signs of any kind on their driveway. Of those that were there, many were cryptic at best, and many others had long faded or rotted away and fallen into the oblivion of undergrowth. Besides, emergency respondents such as ambulances did not have the time to drive slowly down a road in the pitch dark looking for a whimsically designed slab of wood nailed to a tree announcing who lived down the drive. The situation led to an imperative to assign unique names to previously unnamed roads, to assign in a rational way unique numbers to houses on those roads, and to use uniform signage to identify all of a town's roads. The idea was, of course, old hat to city folk, but it was new to rural Mainers.

Houses on the left side of Spinney Mill Road, as you drive in from Route 127, were given even numbers; those on the right, odd. The first house encountered on the road is easy to miss, in part because it is off to the left, and the marsh to the right so commands one's attention. This house sits on the side of a hill overlooking the marsh and is reached via a steep driveway. For years, a house trailer sat on the land, largely obscured in the summer by foliage. The property was bought some years ago by a couple who spent what seemed to be an inordinate amount of time trying to accommodate a new legal home design to the existing trailer's footprint, and expanding that footprint as much as the code would allow. Perhaps in order to maximize the livable space inside, and to break it up with as few obstacles and space-consuming structural features as possible, they ended up with a house with virtually no interior walls and a banister-less stairway leading up to a loft storage space and, beyond, a small bedroom. After (or perhaps because of) all their work on the house, the couple divorced, and 22 Spinney Mill Road went on the market.

The number of a house correlates with how far down the road it is located. Thus, the Stafford house, which after you pass through the marsh is the first one encountered on the right, was given the number 75, indicating that it is about three and a half times as far as number 22 from the start of the road. The Pieh place, the second house on the right, and some ways from the Stafford house, is number 87. The next on the right, the Shultz house, was assigned number 111, and ours was to be 113, a number Catherine did not like. More importantly, according to the numbering scheme, the house number 113 might suggest to an emergency responder that it is the green-roofed barn, the next structure after Rob's house visible from the road. The potential confusion that this could cause during an emergency led to the conclusion that the Shultz driveway, our right-of-way, should be given a name of its own, and then our house could be assigned a number indicating how far down that road it is located.

After we talked it over with Rob, he agreed that it was up to us to come up with a name for the road leading to our house. Thus, we revisited an issue that we had talked about on and off since acquiring the place: Should it have a name and, if so, what should that be? We were not being pretentious, nor did we think we were naming a Camp David or a Biltmore. Like a lot of people of modest means, we had referred to the houses in which we had grown up and lived not by names but by their address numbers. Catherine grew up in 1906 (West Main Street); the first house we owned was 2501 (Tower Drive). We referred to our daughter's erstwhile place in New York City as 10Q, an apartment number to which wiseacre New Yorkers invariably responded, "You're welcome; tenk you, too."

Since our house on, or rather off, Spinney Mill Road came with no street or apartment number, we did not have a shorthand number by which to refer to it. It just didn't seem right to call it by its mailbox number, 98. So we began to play a little part-time parlor game. I proposed calling our property "Pencil Point," but even had Catherine agreed I doubt I would have had the nerve actually to do that. (It was bad enough being called the "Pencil Professor.") Her preference was Pine Ledge, which was self-descriptive, and which she eventually began to write as one word. However, we could not come to a final agreement on what to name the place, so the matter was more or less dropped until the issue of naming the road to it arose—with a deadline for responding to the authorities.

After tiring of the mandatory and stale jokes that invariably arise in such a situation ("One Lane Road," "Dirt Road," "Road Way"), we settled down to serious business. Early on, Catherine pushed for Pineledge Road. We checked in our DeLorme and on the Web and found that there were no roads named Pineledge in the vicinity, though there were some in other areas of Maine. We agreed that the road should be named Pineledge, but we could not come to a final decision on whether it was a road, a way, a lane, a trail, etc. We got out our dictionaries and discussed the fine distinctions between the different designations, differences that seemed to be regularly disregarded. In the end, we agreed that "lane" best described what the road leading to our house was, and I liked the fact that it alliterated with "ledge" and rhymed with "Maine," giving the address some poetic justification. We ran it by Rob, who had no objection, and submitted our entry for an address, hoping to preempt it being assigned the number 13. We proposed what sounded to me almost like part of a haiku:

15 Pineledge Lane
Arrowsic, Maine 04530

After checking that it had the proper uniqueness and no detectable unacceptable innuendo, the authorities approved our choice. Our house had an address, which meant that we could give it a shorthand name. But we do not call it "15." That is for the emergency responders. We call our place "Pineledge" and like to think that mail could reach us addressed simply as:

> Pineledge
> Arrowsic, Maine

Of course, when ordering merchandise on the Internet, something more extended is expected for the delivery address. Here, when we enter the full address with zip code, the software automatically changes "Arrowsic" to the town of our parent post office, and the address becomes:

> 15 Pineledge Lane
> Bath, ME 04530-7320

Although not as poetic, it does scan more like a true haiku.

In addition to each house having a unique street address, it had to have a visibly displayed street number, and so just before leaving for the summer we posted a "15" on the tree where the drive splits. In addition, each road had to have a street sign, which the town would supply. This was to be done in our absence. When we returned the next summer, we found the town's neat brown-and-white sign installed on the power pole at the Y where Rob's driveway angles off Spinney Mill Road. This resolved the problem we had wrestled with for years: whether to ask Rob if he minded if we erected a discreet sign pointing visitors to our place—or even if we wanted such a sign. That was no longer necessary.

In the years after it was put up, the Pineledge Lane sign became obscured behind flourishing junipers. But regular visitors have long since learned the way to our house, and now even first-time

Right-of-way signage

delivery people seldom need to call ahead for directions. Nevertheless, the sign eventually had to be raised in the event that someday
emergency responders may need to find us quickly. Even though
Pineledge Lane is now in most GPS systems, they seem to think
the little road ends near the green-roofed barn, which has no number on it.

Once someone gets that far we hope they will guess that number 15 is just a bit further down the lane. But not everyone does.
Now that they can punch "Maine, Arrowsic, Pineledge Lane, 15"
into their GPS, the act of doing so gives first-time visitors a false
sense of confidence that they can find us. But they tend to question that confidence when they reach the end of the blacktop in
front of Rob's barn, which bears no number. Since it looks like
the road itself ends there, at that point we still get telephone calls

from people unsure of whether the barn is our place, or whether they should continue off the brink and onto the dirt track before which they are stopped. We tell them, "Yes, we are at the end of the lane."

After the Pineledge address was official, we had to change the number on our mailbox. It was an opportunity to install a brand-new one, something we had wanted to do since the last time vandals used the line of Spinney Mill boxes for batting practice. Just about every one of them had been struck, causing the loss of flags and handles and properly functioning doors. None of the neighbors seemed to be rushing to replace a damaged mailbox, however, electing rather to paste new road numbers over the old box numbers. We assumed it was just another Maine frugality, until we returned the next summer to find our new mailbox battered into submission. We have not replaced it.

Since all the other mailboxes at the entrance to the Road represent houses with Spinney Mill numbers, most of them have just the appropriate number on them. Because ours is not a Spinney Mill Road address, however, we could not do that. Rather, we labeled the large black box "Pineledge 15," but the numbers did not stick. So for a while it just read "Pineledge," which was fine with us. Recently, however, with the advent of still another new mailman on the route, we found a faint "15" had been inscribed in black magic marker above the word. To the mail carrier, our house was more a number than a name.

Sixteen

THE WALLS
HAVE EYES

Knots, as natural as they may be, are normally considered undesirable in lumber. These blemishes have their origin where a branch has grown out of the trunk of a tree, leaving a hard round inclusion enveloped by subsequent trunk growth. When the timber is cut up into boards, a knot shows up as a round or elliptical section whose grain is in a cross-direction to that of the board proper. Knots can weaken lumber and complicate its cutting. They also make wooden products more difficult to finish because knots take paint and stain differently than does the surrounding wood, and the resins that can exude from a knot are sticky. Knotty fir and pine are woods especially prone to this problem.

Still, in the 1950s at least, knotty pine was considered to have a high decorative value. The more knots the better, since they gave some interesting features to an otherwise flat and weak-grained wood. The paneling in our place has very prominent knots, but few of them have oozed over the years. This can probably be attributed to the fact that the wood was harvested in the winter, when the sap was not active, and to the fact that the boards were properly prepared for varnishing, a detail to which Bob Phinney would certainly have attended.

Wood from pine trees that sprouted a lot of small branches naturally contains a lot of little knots. When pairs of branches grow close together around the circumference and at about the same level in the tree trunk, they leave inclusions that can converge within the trunk. When boards are cut from such a tree, the knots occur in closely spaced and sometimes coalescing pairs aligned across the width of the board. Many of the knotty-pine boards that were used to panel the walls of our place in Maine were cut from such trees.

At first glance, the paired knots in the paneling look like little more than that. But upon reflection, when the wood was lit up and brought to life by a late afternoon sun or a nighttime reading lamp, we began to see the paired knots not as remnants of branches but as the eyes of animals peering out as if they belonged to spirits locked in the wall. In rare cases, by some magic of the woods, the eyes appeared on separate boards that were fortuitously juxtaposed. Catherine and I each identified our private menageries in the pine, watching us in our silent thoughts.

Pineledge has eyes everywhere, and once we saw they were there we noted their character change from room to room throughout the house, from hour to hour throughout the day, from shadow to shadow throughout the evening, and from day to day throughout the season, as the natural and artificial light and the mood behind our own eyes played differently upon them—and on our perceptions of them. I had identified the eyes of birds and of baby seals and of foxes and of less familiar critters high on the walls of the living room and low on the walls of the bathroom. Catherine, who reads in bed at night, was surrounded by eyes peering out at her from the dimly lit walls of that room, including the eyes and one ear of what she thinks is a zebra. In one bathroom, she sees a koala bear just above the door-latch mounting.

I don't recall exactly when or how we revealed our common perceptions to each other, but once we began to talk openly about the eyes in the wood we happily shared our latest finds. Some of the eyes were close to the floor in places so dark at night that we needed a flashlight to reveal them. Some were so high on the wall that to communicate their position to each other we had to give directions by counting boards from one end of the wall or from a doorway. To make it easier to zero in on the knot-eyes, we bought a small laser pointer. When we had guests whom we trusted not to think us completely nutty, we used the pointer to introduce them to some of our favorite pairs of eyes and made it a parlor game to find more and identify the kind of animal to which they might belong. We are still discovering new pairs of eyes.

While Catherine reads among the creatures watching her in the bedroom in the evening and into the night, I read in the living room amidst the stares of my own familiars. Outside the picture windows on moonless nights there is pitch blackness, save for the distant island of light thrown upon the clouds in the sky above the city of Bath. When the lights are on in the house, there is also the reflection of my reading lamp and the occasional searchlight or running light of a boat finding its way up the river to Bath or down the river toward Phippsburg. Regardless of conditions, I seldom look up from my book to peer outside, for there is nothing much else to see, yet I wonder if from time to time there have been pairs of eyes out there looking in at me. But why would any nocturnal creature, other than the moths that smack into the window, be attracted to this house full of daylight in the middle of night?

We don't think our cats have noticed the eyes in the knotty pine, but we can't be sure. They do seem more relaxed when they are in the attic, where the newer pine boards have many fewer and less distinct pairs of eyes; the knots up there are mostly monocular. And because most of the boards are horizontal, the pairs of knots there are aligned vertically and so do not look so much like eyes at all. Still, we all know that we are surrounded by wildlife, inside and outside the house. We know that there are plenty of creatures in the woods out there, and unlike our knotty-pine residents they are not frozen in place. We do know there are mink, because one morning we saw one cavorting across the lawn, coming home from a late night out, perhaps looking for a chipmunk to snack on before retiring for the day. There are also foxes, for once we saw one walking toward the garage, the most regal creature I had ever seen. There are deer, as we know from the marsh, and wild turkey and porcupines, which we have seen waddling up our driveway. There are bats and squirrels and, we have been told, moose, though we have yet to see one of those. The closest we did come to seeing a moose was early one morning when we were occupied on our respective computers. Being online then meant that we were offline to telephone calls, and so when Rob tried to ring us up to alert us to look out the window for the moose strolling down our lane, he could only leave a message that we retrieved hours after the opportunity had passed.

One summer evening I was sitting reading a book under watchful eyes high in the living-room wall. It had been quite windy after an afternoon rainstorm, but otherwise it was a normal night. The quiet was disturbed only by what sounded like a bird flying into one of our large windows. This would not be an unusual occurrence during daylight hours, but it was not something I expected to hear at night. I continued to read, and after a short while the sound was repeated, this time seeming to come from the direction of the kitchen window. It was unlikely to be the same or a second bird. Maybe it was a bat, I thought.

I continued to sit and tried to continue to read, but the noise continued to continue, eventually changing to an intermittent fluttering alternating with periods of what sounded like scratching on metal. Now the sound seemed to me to be coming from the front door, which is metal-clad. I imagined (that is, I hypothesized) that perhaps something had gotten caught between it and the aluminum screen door—which was not a Phinney product and is not always tightly latched—and was trying to escape. The fluttering and scratching continued, seeming at times to grow more frantic. But there were also periods of silence, during which I assumed that the creature was resting. I tested every sound and silence in the context of a hypothetical bat or bird, and my mind fluttered between them.

I did not want to open the front door, lest something fly inside. The resulting louder commotion would surely have awakened

Catherine, who was asleep in the bedroom. Besides, if it were a bat, I feared that it might be rabid, not knowing for sure even if such was a likely possibility for the area. I wrote a Post-it note to Catherine and stuck it prominently on the door, alerting her not to open it should the sound awaken her after I had gone to bed. In the morning, I planned, I would climb out a back window, go around the house, open the screen door, and let the creature free, expecting to catch a glimpse of it in the daylight.

After a while, the noise resumed, but this time it sounded as if it was coming from the fireplace, which is near the door. I got up from my chair quietly and stood beside the hearth, my ear toward the chimney. My proximity appeared to silence the creature, but in time it resumed its activity. Now the flapping and scratching sounds were clear and distinct, and I knew that something was in the flue. I had to reframe my problem-hypothesis-and-solution scenario.

Our fireplace has a steel casing fitted with a damper that is operated by a lever. I can never remember which position of the lever signals an open damper, and so I usually stick my head into the fireplace and look up before starting a fire. This night I expected that the damper was closed, given that nothing was flying around in the fireplace itself. I was confident that no small animal could open the heavy damper, and so I decided that this problem also would be better dealt with in daylight, if it did not resolve itself during the night. Surely the creature would eventually fly up the chimney to freedom. I took the note off the front door and wrote a new Post-it to stick on the front of the mantel. Since the noise was keeping me from concentrating on my reading, I turned off the lights and went to bed. The noise was barely audible from the bedroom. Before falling asleep, I weighed the evidence for the bird and bat hypotheses, and found each of them equally plausible.

Sometime in the middle of the night new and much louder noises woke me up. Somehow the creature must have gotten out of the chimney, for it seemed to be flying around in the living room and kitchen, crashing into windows and generally making a ruckus.

Still fearing something rabid, and not knowing how in our sleepy state we would ever capture a flying creature, I closed the door to our bedroom and hoped for the best. Catherine had been awakened by the commotion too, and now we both lay listening to the noises and wondering how we would get rid of our unwelcome visitor. Were there a cat in the house, it might have helped. Unfortunately, we did not have a cat living with us that summer.

I became preoccupied with how the visitor got out of the chimney. Had the damper been open after all? Had the creature earlier been flailing around in the baffle before finding its way out through the damper? The steel-cased fireplace had a large flat screen in front of it, but the screen did not fit flush against the rustic stone façade, and so there were numerous gaps. But the presence of the screen also meant that it would not be easy for the flying animal to find its way back up the chimney.

Wide awake, Catherine and I lay in bed listening to the goings on. The noises became increasingly varied, sometimes sounding like they were coming from the living room and kitchen, other times seeming to emanate from the basement. How did the creature get down there? At one point there was a very loud noise, which sounded like a piece of metal dropping onto a concrete floor, which lent credence to the idea that the thing was indeed in the basement. I had earlier heard noises that sounded like those made when the heat comes up, and so I wondered if the creature had somehow gotten itself into the furnace, perhaps through the large return duct beneath the grating in the floor behind the fireplace. This might also explain how it got into the basement. Rather than applying Occam's razor to the situation, I was haphazardly multiplying hypotheses as the variety of sounds multiplied.

As the dark of night gave way to the light of dawn, the noises began to grow more frantic, but they soon disappeared entirely. Had the creature, which based on the absence of chirpings I was now convinced was a bat, found a dark corner in which to spend the day? I imagined that this could easily be done in the basement, but on exiting the bedroom I still looked up in the dark hallway so as not to be surprised from above. With some reluctance, I removed the screen and stuck my head into the fireplace to check the damper—and found it open! I now assumed that the creature had somehow clawed the delicately balanced gate open to escape into our house and then escaped back out through the opening. I closed the damper, making note of the lever handle's position.

Catherine and I walked around the kitchen and living room, where we found a heavy vase full of cattails on the floor in front of the bookcase on which it had sat. Its falling must have been the loud noise we had heard, I thought, the hollow ceramic vase hitting the maple bookcase making a sound that I confused with metal hitting concrete. I rolled the vase into the bookcase to test this idea, and convinced myself that the sounds were the same. From her study, Catherine called out that she found evidence that the creature had been in there also, for the small clock that she kept on the windowsill was upset onto her desk, its battery loose on the floor beside the heating vent. Perhaps in falling and rolling the battery had produced the sound that, conducted through the ductwork into our bedroom, appeared to have come from the basement. I modified my hypothesis still again. We looked with flashlights in the dark corners of the house, but found nothing. I looked down at the return air register and decided that a small bat could indeed squeeze through its grille and so find its way into the basement. We covered the register with a large newspaper weighted down with an upside-down step stool and kept the basement door closed until we could get help in exterminating the bat.

We had had trouble with bats a few years earlier. We had discovered droppings on a ledge of the chimney just below where it passed through the roof in our then-unfinished attic, and so we called the state extension service seeking help in identifying the intruder or intruders. Within hours, an extension worker who is known throughout Maine as "the Bat Man" had come and looked at the situation. He confirmed that there indeed had been bats in our attic, but in spite of his disturbing pounding on the underside of the roof could find no sign of them on the day of his visit. He suggested that we use fine steel wool to block even the most narrow of crevices leading into the attic and hope that we could close off any access point. It seemed to work, and in the years since we have had no further evidence of bats in the attic.

In fact, it had been so long that we had forgotten the Bat Man's name. So this time Catherine called the general information number for the state offices in Augusta and just asked for "the Bat Man." The woman answering the phone knew immediately whom we were seeking, and she transferred the call to his phone. Catherine left a message on the answering machine. Throughout the morning there was silence in the house, and we hoped that we were correct in thinking that the bat had somehow escaped the way it had gotten in.

When the Bat Man called back that afternoon, I described what I had heard the night before and told him I assumed that we had a bird or a bat in the house, telling him why I favored the latter. He assumed just the opposite. In his experience, he informed me, it was extremely rare for bats to crash into anything, since the creatures have excellent sonar. In fact, the expert was sure our visitor was not a bat; he thought a bird had gotten into our house. With the bat hypothesis shot down, I tried to reconcile the sounds I had heard with the flight of a bird.

A welcome silence continued throughout the day and into the evening. There was a spectacular sunset over the river, and night came slowly. I was tired after the previous night's activity and was halfheartedly watching some Congressional committee hearings on C-SPAN. The first noise I heard behind me was a quiet rustle, which I attributed, more out of hope than reason, to some of the day's newspapers settling in the large copper kettle into which we place them after reading. A louder, scratching noise soon got me out of my chair, however, and just as I was turning around I caught sight of something scurrying toward the kitchen. It was long and low and in the dim light looked like a chipmunk, of which we had many in our yard. Was this the culprit? It certainly challenged the bird hypothesis.

I called Catherine, who was as disappointed as I to learn that we were not alone. We both wielded flashlights, looking for the animal in the dark corners of the hall. Catherine caught a glimpse of it and thought maybe it was a mouse or a rat. My beam caught it coming around a corner, and it froze briefly, then retreated from the light. It seemed rodent-like and resembled a very small squirrel. Noting its aversion to light, we turned on lights in the back of the house. I opened the front door to give the intruder an escape route, and we tried to herd it with flashlight beams out toward the dark. Our light sabers did work somewhat, but instead of going toward the door the creature ran into the living room and up onto the back of a chair. Chased off there, it ran for the fireplace, climbing the stones as easily as if they were the bark of a tree. It rushed across the mantel and up around the corner, always seeming to want to get away from the light. At this point it froze momentarily, and it clung spread-eagled to the fireplace, straddling the corner. With its legs so stretched out, its folds of skin were extended to reveal its true identity as a flying squirrel, something I had never seen and so had not hypothesized. I had imagined the creature to be something I knew, not something I did not.

Catherine went into the kitchen, so she could keep an eye on the squirrel if it went out there. Driven by my flashlight, the intruder did go in that direction, and Catherine saw it dive into an empty vase on the topmost shelf behind the fireplace. I went around to see, and the squirrel looked out at me Kilroy-style over the rim of the vase. It had found a place of protection and escape from the light, I imagined. Catherine handed me a towel, which I threw over the top of the vase and grasped around its sides. With the squirrel trapped, I carried the vase to the door, Catherine closed the door behind me, and I let the animal out on the lawn.

Neither of us had guessed that it was a flying squirrel that had invaded our house. My assumptions that it had been a bat or a bird were reinforced in my own mind by my imagining that I heard wings flapping and interpreting the squirrel's behavior in the context of a mental image of how familiar flying animals would behave. Even the Bat Man did not suggest that it could be a flying squirrel, but in his defense he was presented nothing more than my assumptions and inferences about wings and windows. Only in retrospect, when Catherine and I had the bulging eyes of the evidence staring us in the face, did we abandon our false models of its behavior.

We learned from a field guide that our visitor was most likely a southern flying squirrel: "nocturnal; gregarious; sleeps by day in hole in tree (or attic); can glide 125 ft. given a high enough takeoff point. Lands with an audible thump, as on a camp roof." The creature had not been flying around our living room and kitchen. It had been gliding, probably from a perch on the fireplace or a chair back, perhaps hitting the floor hard rather than the windows. It was probably preying on crickets, which frequently find their way into our house. Apparently it had caught some, because that morning we had found amputated cricket legs in pairs on the floor of the kitchen and in Catherine's study. They had seemed like further evidence to us that a bat had been the culprit, but even after that theory had been dismissed by the expert I did not rethink what might have devoured the tastier parts of the crickets. So firmly had I constructed the bat theory in my mind that I gave it up completely only when I was face to face with the flying counterexample.

Catherine and I wanted to believe the visit was a fluke. After all, we had spent many summers in this house without a prior incident. I imagined that the squirrel found its way down the chimney by accident, it being blown off course by strong winds. As the occasion receded into the past, we remembered it with more affection than seemed warranted. Catherine, who had been a devotee of the television cartoon series starring Rocky and Bullwinkle, christened our visitor Rocket J. Squirrel, and called him Rocky for short. We had not even imagined that such a creature existed in our area, even though we knew from the patterns of disturbed foliage around our house that all sorts of unseen animals must have browsed among it in the night. We related the story of our adventure with "our squirrel" at dinner parties, learning from neighbors that they too had had trouble with squirrels but not, to the best of their knowledge, of the flying kind, an example of which none of them had ever seen. We treasured our unique memories, which we did not expect to be repeated.

Almost four weeks to the day after the incident, I was awakened in the middle of the night by new noises. Had Rocky gotten in again? But these were not the sounds of Rocky, I was sure. I could hear no crashing into clocks, vases, or anything else. There were no thumping noises. What I did hear sounded like scurrying across the carpet, muffled, quiet sounds. I had heard no scratching in the chimney. I got up to close the bedroom door and then returned to bed and tried to sleep. At one point I believed that I heard something scurrying around in the bedroom, but I attributed it to my overactive imagination. As they had a month earlier, the sounds ended as the dawn arrived, and I tried to catch just a little more sleep.

We had had human company the night before—the writer Shelby Hearon and her husband, the inventor Bill Halpern—and we had all gone out to dinner. We returned well after dark and had talked at the open door for some time as our guests were leaving. Something could have sneaked into the house at that time, I imagined. Or perhaps it had come in through the fireplace again, this time the damper bouncing closed behind it. It could happen, I thought, for among the things we had discussed at dinner was an incident that Bill and Shelby had recently experienced. One day she went into their yard to do some gardening, but when she tried to get back into the house she found its screen door locked from the inside. Its hook and eye had somehow gotten engaged. She called to Bill, who was working elsewhere in the house, and he came and opened the door. He denied being mischievous and suggested that the hook had somehow fallen into the eye as the door slammed shut. They described trying to replicate the event by slamming the door many times, but with no success. She seemed to remain skeptical that such a thing could happen all by itself, but he and I, both engineers, thought it improbable but possible, given the kinematics and dynamics of a swinging door and its attached swinging hook. (A few days later, after Catherine and I had tidied up our guest cabin, she told me that when its screen door closed behind me she saw its hook almost fall into the eye on the jamb.)

Upon awaking after the new night of noises, I immediately looked into the fireplace to check the position of the damper. It was closed, and to be sure that it stayed closed I used a poker to wedge it shut. After all, if a hook and eye could come together by themselves, perhaps a precariously balanced fireplace damper could open by itself. I rustled the newspapers in the copper kettle, but nothing seemed to respond. Catherine and I looked around the living room, where we found a picture knocked over. We also found small droppings on the mantel and on some magazines near the window, something of which there had been no evidence last time. There also were no dismembered cricket legs to be seen, but then we had not been seeing many crickets lately. The evidence did not fit exactly with Rocky the Squirrel's visit, and we could reach no agreement over what was in the house this time. Catherine insisted it was Rocky, but I thought her argument sentimental. I argued for a chipmunk, on less evidence but perhaps with more hope. A chipmunk, I thought, should be easier to get rid of. (Recently, one had gotten into the local Staples, and a stock boy caught it easily with his bare hands. The dry weather in our area had apparently been driving many animals into houses and buildings.)

As usual, that evening Catherine went into the bedroom to read, and I read in the living room. After the last light of sunset, Catherine called from the bedroom, "He's baaack." Rocky had apparently spent the day beneath her nightstand, out from which he had just poked his head. She used a book to block him from going under the bed, as I shined a flashlight into his eyes. He remained still long enough for us to confirm that he was indeed Rocky, or a dead ringer for him, and then he darted past me out of the bedroom and into the living room. I followed and saw him run up the side of the fireplace, make an aborted move to get behind the screen, and then run up into a hollow between the stonework and a ceiling timber. We knew where he was, but how would we get him out?

I propped open the front door, which is just a few feet from where he was holed up, and turned on all the lights in the back of the house, reasoning that he would again avoid the light and seek the dark. With Catherine stationed in the kitchen behind the fireplace and I at the end of the living room, each of us with a flashlight, we held a vigil. At this point, we were not absolutely sure he was still in his hiding place, for he might well have run out the door as we were turning on lights and closing doors to the back rooms. Catherine worried that the open door would invite more creatures into the house, but I thought we had to accept the risk, for there seemed to be no other way that we were going to get rid of our unwelcome squirrel. The vase that had worked so well last time was now full of dried flowers.

From a chair at the far end of the living room, I watched the place into which I had seen Rocky disappear. I had never before

Rocky's cave

stared so intently and motionlessly at something; I imagined myself to be experiencing what naturalists or preying animals do. My head was in an uncomfortable position, because I had to look through the center part of my trifocals to see clearly. After a good twenty minutes or so, my patience was rewarded as I saw Rocky ease himself tentatively out of hiding, first his head and then his full body. He moved cautiously down the side of the fireplace and onto the mantel. I shined the light behind him and he ran across the mantel and behind the fireplace. Catherine was armed with a large towel and I with an empty wastebasket, hoping we could trap him. But the irregular stonework on the fireplace made the wastebasket useless, and the best we could do was corral him between the fireplace and the open front door. He faced freedom but inexplicably turned up the fireplace and ran back into his cave.

Catherine emptied the flowers out of the vase and placed it on the mantel underneath his hiding place. I returned to my observation post and waited some more. When he next inched down the fireplace, I shined my light behind him, reasoning that this would drive him further down and maybe into the vase or out the open door. He did neither, but rather ran right through the flashlight beam and back into his hole. Thus began a third vigil.

I returned to the chair and watched more intently than before. My eyes were growing tired and I was having a hard time focusing on the fireplace corner. I was trying to think of how we would get rid of him if he did not run out the door. Would we call the animal control officer? Would he be able to provide us with a trap? How would we sleep? How long would it take to return to normalcy?

After twenty or thirty minutes, Rocky reappeared. As before, he proceeded very slowly and tentatively. He inched down the fireplace and sat on the mantel, next to the vase. He faced away from it, however, towards the open door. I shined the light behind him, hoping to drive him to the door. It worked! He ran down the side of the fireplace and directly out the door, which we immediately rushed to close behind him. Sleeping was pleasant that night, indeed.

My approach to identifying and getting rid of Rocky was filled with assumptions, inferences, and hypotheses, none of which I can say was truly confirmed as valid. Because Rocky ultimately did run out of the house does not at all mean that his retreat was prompted by any of our actions. Rocky, if it was even he the second time, found his way into our house by ways still unknown to us. Perhaps he returned to find some more crickets, which he did not find. I still hypothesize on how he might have gotten back in, as I imagined scenarios of how to get him to leave. However, none of my hypotheses is incontrovertible or fully testable, nor are my exit schemes. My experience with Rocky was humbling, but his two visits—if indeed again they were both by him—gave me new perspectives on engineering and analysis, and on living and life. His first visit showed me how wrong I could be in interpreting data, evidence, and behavior. His second visit showed me how wrong I could be even in the face of past experience. In fact, we can fool ourselves into believing just about anything. Such are the lessons learned from a fable of errors involving a cute and furry creature. I assumed a lot about Rocky and his behavior, but in the end I confirmed little. In fact, he may even have been a she.

I don't know how close to or how distant from the truth are my assumptions and hypotheses about how Bob Phinney designed and built his house in Maine. Maybe more credit than I have given her should go to his wife, Billie. In 1978, she retired from her long-time job at the Pine Tree Society. About fifteen years earlier, she had looked into oceanfront property on Indian Point, which is located at the southeastern extreme of Georgetown Island, from which she claimed she had "god's view to Boothbay, Phippsburg and Portugal," presumably the one across the Atlantic. "Bob was not quite as adventurous," she admitted in her own obituary that she wrote when she was eighty years old, in order to tell the story of her "good life," just "in case a beer truck creams me." Admitting that "Dutch women are very strong minded," she related how she exercised her "Dutch independence" and took out a mortgage to buy herself, without her husband's knowledge, two lots for $2,500 each, making the $50 monthly payments out of her pin money.

Bob eventually did find out about the Indian Point land when a stranger approached him and asked if it was for sale. He had no choice but to accept what his wife had done, and together they put in a driveway at the beach property and puttered about on the land until he died suddenly in 1989. According to his obituary, "he was stricken while walking on the beach at Reid State Park with his wife," but a tribute to her life published two decades later said that he was "raking seaweed on the beach" at the time of his death. However exactly it happened, after Bob passed away Billie declared to the family, "We are under new rule"; she was finally going to build, with the help of her son Bill, a house on the Indian Point property. The structure was set atop a sand dune and elevated seven feet off the ground, no doubt to let storm surf run under it. She had probably had enough of water in the basement.

Her son Peter died just a couple of years after his father. After graduating from Bath's Morse High School, he had attended the University of Maine, the U.S. Air Force Academy, and the Academy School of Cooking in San Francisco, where he lived at the time of his death. Sandra Phinney Reed had followed her mother's profession and became a registered nurse. At the time of this writing she was living in Pennsylvania. Robert Phinney the younger was living in Bridgetown, Nova Scotia, a town with a population of under a thousand across the Bay of Fundy from where his grandfather was born. Bill Phinney stayed close to the Arrowsic home where he and his siblings once sat for a photo on a fireplace mantel in the middle of an unfinished home. Beginning in the mid-1970s, he worked as a landscaper based in Woolwich, and later ran his own site planning and landscape design business just up Route 1 in Wiscasset. One day shortly after Catherine and I had bought the house his father built, Bill Phinney came down the right-of-way and asked if he could show the person he was with where he lived and played as a child. Before leaving, he looked around in the underbrush behind the house for a long-lost but warmly remembered goldfish pond. He did not find it that day, but on a subsequent visit he did locate the concrete base, still surmounted by rocks but long overgrown with vegetation.

Billie Phinney, who lived till she was ninety, passed away only a few years ago at her home above the surf on Indian Point. What role she played in the design and construction of the River House I do not know, but being the strong woman that she said she was, she likely had at least some influence on how Bob Phinney designed and built the house we now call our summer home. Even if he was not fully satisfied with what he produced, she preferred it over his second effort, the Pond House.

Regardless of what the Phinneys individually thought of the River House, to us it is a thing of beauty and magnificently strong. It doesn't creak in the wind that howls down the Kennebec the way our frame house in the western suburbs of Chicago did when the wind blew in across the Illinois prairie. When we lived there, I swore I could feel that balloon-framed two-story structure racking and shaking and straining to stay in place, and I worried for its strength each time there was a tornado watch. Our place in Maine is as stiff and solid as the brick ranch of the same era that we call our home in North Carolina. Even though we have spent only a few winter months in Maine, they gave us the confidence to know that the house here is as steady as the ledge it is founded upon. And, on balance, based on the evidence, data points, and clues I have found, I cannot help but believe that Bob Phinney began it all by driving an iron stake into this hard point of land. And he finished the house with countless soft hammer blows to its grand expanses of knotty pine.

Many of my hypotheses about George Stafford were also never proven. They were based on neighbors' anecdotes and incidents that may or may not have been representative. After George returned our keys, I recall coming in or going out on the Road and seeing him driving his riding mower across his great lawn on the slope of the hill above the marsh. Catherine and I would wave at him and he would look up and wave back from the distance, but we hardly ever spoke. He was a taciturn man, and since he had no more business to transact with us, perhaps he thought there was nothing much left to say between us. Over time, George's hearing began to fade, and even polite conversation would not have been possible. He began to look the other way when we passed, not, I hoped, because of some memory of dirty gravel but perhaps because he did not want us to know how badly his hearing had deteriorated. He would not want to be embarrassed by a conversation in which he could not engage. George was a proud man. Gravel that was good enough for him should have been good enough for us. After all, he was born in Maine, on Arrowsic, and we only had a summer place here. It saddened us the spring that we learned that George's health had worsened badly and that he died just weeks before we left North Carolina to come up to Maine for another season.

George was in our thoughts as we drove down Route 127, still the spine of Arrowsic, on the last leg of our northward journey in 2012. Just after we passed the town office we noticed a new road sign, one reading Stafford Lane. The town had named the road leading to and from the new fire station in honor of George and Milly, in recognition of their long-standing dedication to the volunteer fire department and to the town generally. As we turned onto Spinney Mill Road and were greeted by the greening of the marsh, we

A sign of appreciation

Looking west across the marsh

missed seeing George riding his mower in the distance. It was too late for us to tell him how much we had learned from him in the short time he helped us get to know our place by the river.

We continue down the road, noting what had and had not changed since the previous summer. Liz and Doug Ware, who live in the smallest house on the road, have been adding a barn that looks to be about the same size as their house. A few years ago, in the tradition of Mainers, Doug had built a boat from scratch, and so he was well prepared to build a stationary structure. It sits on a rise that had been cleared of trees, their trunks and larger branches cut up for firewood and stacked neatly beside the road. The Stones' house is rented out to another young family, where the Arrowsic baby that attended Milly Stafford's birthday party was born just before Christmas. But the sight of the house also saddened us. Al Stone had passed away shortly after New Year's, and the not unexpected news brought back cherished memories of earlier days. The population of the Road, actual and virtual, ebbs and flows like the tides in the river and the sea.

The river beside the house

The Shultz place looks pretty much the same as it did last year, and we take the right fork into its driveway, which now that it is paved with asphalt looks more like a road to take. The lane down to our place is still unimproved, and we drop off the pavement onto it with a bump. The winter snow and ice and the spring rains and mud took a toll on the road, but it still leads to where we want to go. We find the grass high and the rhododendron bushes another year taller and heavy with blooms. The roof is the first feature of our house to come into view, and with its still-new shingles it is handsome. I no longer see the house's south-side fenestration as ungainly, since I have had many seasons not only to get used to it but also to know it for what its creator meant it to be.

We proceed to the edge of the drive and pause to watch the river flowing as it always does, with deliberateness and determination to and from the sea. The key fits tightly in the lock, feeling like it has not been used for some time. We enter the house, smell the naphthalene, and raise the Mylar shades. The view is as stunning as ever, and we know that we made the right decision when we took a road less traveled to get to this place in Maine.

ACKNOWLEDGMENTS

MUCH OF WHAT I have learned over the years about Maine and our place in it came of informal conversations with people—friends, neighbors, merchants, contractors, workers, clerks, librarians, and Mainers from all walks of life. I doubt that I can recall everyone I have learned from, but I would like to acknowledge the help, even if inadvertent or indirect, of some of those I do know by name. Although I never met Bob Phinney, I feel that I have gotten to know him through the remarkable house he designed and built, and I am grateful to him for it.

Al and Grace Stone, who were regular visitors when they lived across the Road, introduced us to people and places in Maine that they knew we should know. It was Grace who early on entrusted to us some old secrets and photos of the place. Years later, she came back from Atlanta to visit us, bearing memories, along with some helpful photos and slides taken by Al. Grace's brother David Woodbury and his wife Candy also contributed their memories of the place. It was Grace who introduced us to Gladys Monier, with whom we enjoyed dinner in Bath and dessert back home in Arrowsic, all the while talking about the place she so thoughtfully decorated. On occasion, other previous owners and residents of the house have come down the lane to have a look at the old place and share impromptu memories with us. Bill Phinney did this shortly after we had acquired the house. He returned when I was writing this book, and his recollection of things provided a reality check for some of my suggestions and speculations. He also provided a survey drawn by his grandfather and brought to my attention photographs that I had not known to exist. When Alan and Lauren Robinson showed up at the door one Saturday afternoon, I showed them around the house and we established an e-mail correspondence that helped fill in some additional details of the story.

I am also grateful to many other people for assistance and information. Andrea Galuza was the patient realtor who showed us Midcoast properties until we found the one that became ours. George and Milly Stafford took good care of the house for many years before we arrived, and they helped us get through our early months as remote owners of a summer place. Milly has especially shared her boundless knowledge of Arrowsic and the Road, and I have enjoyed my conversations with her about them. Rob Shultz has told us much about our house, and he has been there when we were not to do work that has greatly enhanced our enjoyment of the place. He has also been vigilant in watching for the red light that is set to go off in the window if our furnace fails in the dead of winter. Deirdre Barton has brightened our right-of-way with her horticultural skills and has been our trusted color consultant for paint and shingles. One Sunday afternoon, Larry and Betty Wilson graciously showed us around their nearby property, on which a young Bill Phinney had built a house and his father a barn, the latter of which still exhibits much of its original fabric. Bud Warren and Sam Manning provided information about tide mills and one afternoon walked me along the remains of the Spinney Mill dam. Bud also shared his informative PowerPoint presentation on Industrial Arrowsic. Our neighbors Doug and Liz Ware provided historical images of the old mill when it was still intact. Michael Kreindler and Mary McDonald helped regarding Arrowsic building records.

A number of painters and carpenters have provided insights into the nature of our house and its construction, including the painter Mark Geiger, who also owns a Phinney house on Arrowsic; Brendon Augustine, a house painter based in Brunswick, who brought to our attention some aspects of the picture-window construction of which we were unaware; and Damien Augustine, a Portland carpenter who shared his knowledge of the ways of Maine boat- and house builders. I am also grateful to the preservationist spirit of the previous owners of the house, all of whom were respectful and considerate enough of Bob Phinney's walls of knotty pine not to have painted over them. If I have made any errors of description or ascription relating to our house or to anyone connected with it, or to the neighborhood of which it is a part, I apologize. Any mistakes or misstatements are, of course, my responsibility.

Some of the ideas in this book were first tentatively explored in my "Engineering" column in *American Scientist*. Duke University Libraries and librarians, as they have with all of my research and writing projects, were of great help, especially by making available to me a wide range of electronic databases and services, including document delivery and Interlibrary Loan. In Bath, Maine, I have found indispensable information in the Patten Free Library's Sagadahoc History & Genealogy Room, where Peter Goodwin, its manager, and Robin Haynes introduced me to some of its unique resources and helped me learn to use them.

A sabbatical leave from Duke University, endorsed by Miguel Medina, as interim chairman of the civil and environmental engineering department, and Tom Katsouleas, as dean of the Pratt School of Engineering, and granted by Provost Peter Lange, enabled me to focus on this project. I am also grateful to Doron Weber, of the Alfred P. Sloan Foundation, for expressing enthusiasm for the project when I first shared its barest outlines with him, and to the Foundation's Public Understanding of Science and Technology program for providing summer support for the writing and photography. This marks for me a half century of association with the Sloan Foundation: My first year in graduate school was spent as an Alfred P. Sloan Teaching Fellow, an outstanding experience that helped shape my career.

I am very fortunate to have found a sympathetic editor for this book. When I sent her an outline, Alane Salierno Mason of W. W. Norton immediately embraced the idea of a book about a modest summer house. Her comments on reading the manuscript were enormously helpful to me in tightening and focusing the story. I am also grateful to Anna Mageras and to all the others at Norton who saw the book through production.

As usual, Catherine has been my first reader. In this case, she was also my first researcher, collecting information on real-estate transactions at the Sagadahoc County Courthouse and later poring over building permits and related documents at the Arrowsic Town Hall and Sagadahoc History & Genealogy Room. And, of course, for this project Catherine has also been my first photographer, with her images capturing features of our place that have eluded my thousands of words.

PHOTOGRAPHER'S NOTE

FOR SEVERAL YEARS, writing about Pineledge and Spinney Mill Road was my fantasy project. The fiction writer in me had found a fascinating cast of characters in Maine, far better than I thought I could make up, and in a setting that was beautiful and complex and mysterious. I imagined a roman à clef in which an academic couple from North Carolina tested the patience, generosity, values, and natural reticence of the Mainers amidst whom they had so casually dropped themselves, with the Mainers' ways conversely testing the Southerners. But impelling such a narrative with heightened, fictitious conflicts was not something I could do to the neighbors who had been so good to us folks "from away."

So when Henry decided to take on the writing of an engineer's book about Pineledge, I was greatly relieved, knowing that his approach would take the place's potential in a completely different direction. As it turned out, he did develop strong narrative elements within his Pineledge story, and guided by his vision and always-close observations, my camera and I discovered many new things about the place in which we had spent the previous fifteen summers. Though I have taken each of Henry's jacket photos and many photos for his books and articles, the photographic survey of Pineledge was a very exciting challenge.

To my eye, the geometry of our place on the river seemed custom-made for monochromatic images. Pineledge has plenty of color, but color is not the essence of the place. The monochromes of Tillman Crane, Lilo Raymond, and Frederick H. Evans have served as inspirations with their poetic, quiet spaces and gentleness, their spare geometries, and their reverence for simplicity. Over the summer of 2012 I captured thousands of digital images, so it humbles me to learn that upon being awarded a prize, Lilo Raymond said, "What have I done? Fifty good pictures, period!" These masters have been my teachers, along with a high school art teacher, Marjorie M. Murray, most of whose lessons in design have stuck with me for decades; Gordon Buck Jr., who on dpreview's Canon forum suggested a technical solution to bring light to Pineledge's summer-shaded dark interior spaces; and, at one remove, the elemental aesthetic of my writing mentor, William H. Gass. Our neighbor Doug Ware took me on an end-of-summer circumnavigation of Arrowsic in his handcrafted *Morgan*, providing the opportunity to take many shots from the water. Not least, I am grateful for the Sloan Foundation's support of this project. The majority of the photographs of Pineledge and its environs in this book were taken with a Canon G1X.

Like every photographer, I am continually "just looking," and perhaps like an engineer never completely satisfied but nonetheless continuing to process and refine what I am seeing. This Pineledge book may now be finished, but I know that the pictures I will take here are not. There is always more to see, if one just keeps looking.

LIST OF
ILLUSTRATIONS
& CREDITS

Photographs by Catherine Petroski, except as noted.

BIBLIOGRAPHY

Aladdin Co. *Aladdin Readi-Cut Homes,* annual sales catalogs, various years, 1908–1954.

Arrowsic, Town of. *Annual Reports,* 1998–1999 through 2012–2013.

Arrowsic, Town of. *Valuation Book and Tax Record,* 1950 through 1955.

Arrowsic Arrow, The. Various issues, 2005–2012.

Associated Press. "Towns Honor Dedicated Rural Letter Carrier," (Lewiston, Maine) *Sun Journal,* May 28, 1999, p. A5.

Baker, Emerson W. *The Clarke and Lake Company: The Historical Archaeology of a Seventeenth-century Maine Settlement* (Augusta, Maine: Maine Historic Preservation Commission, 1985).

Baker, Emerson W., and John G. Reid. *The New England Knight: Sir William Phips, 1651–1695* (Toronto: University of Toronto Press, 1998).

Baker, John Milnes. *American House Styles: A Concise Guide* (New York: W. W. Norton, 1994).

Bath (Maine) *Directory.* 1950s, 1960s, and 1970s.

Bath Historical Society. *The Sesquicentennial of Bath, Maine* (Bath, Maine: Bath Historical Society, 1997).

Bath (Maine) *Independent.* Various issues.

Bell, William E. *Carpentry Made Easy; or, The Science and Art of Framing, on a New and Improved System. With Specific Instructions for Building Balloon Frames, etc.* (Philadelphia: Howard Challen, 1857; reprint, Whitefish, Mont.: Kessinger Publishing, [2013]).

Bryson, Bill. *At Home: A Short History of Private Life* (New York: Anchor Books, 2011).

Busch, Akiko. *Geography of Home: Writings on Where We Live* (New York: Princeton Architectural Press, 1999).

Carlsen, Spike. *A Splintered History of Wood: Belt Sander Races, Blind Woodworkers, and Baseball Bats* (New York: Collins, 2008).

Carlton, George M., Sr., comp. and ed. "Tide Mills of Maine and Beyond." Http://www.dorchesteratheneum.org/pdf/Tide-Mills%20of%20 Maine%20and%20Beyond.pdf (accessed Feb. 18, 2013).

Cavanagh, Ted. "Balloon Houses: The Original Aspects of Conventional Wood-Frame Construction Re-examined," *Journal of Architectural Education* 51 (1997): 5–15.

Christie, Deborah Carnes. *Green House: The Story of a Healthy, Energy-Efficient Home* (Durham, N.C.: privately printed, 2009).

Coastal Journal, The (Bath, Maine). Various issues, 1997–2012.

Coffin, Robert P. Tristram. *Kennebec: Cradle of Americans* (New York: Farrar & Reinhart, 1937).

Cole, John N. *Maine Trivia* (Nashville, Tenn.: Rutledge Hill Press, 1998).

Colt, George Howe. *The Big House: A Century in the Life of an American Summer Home* (New York: Scribner, 2003).

Condit, Carl W. *American Building Art: The Nineteenth Century* (New York: Oxford University Press, 1960).

Crane, Tillman. *Structure* (San Francisco: Custom & Limited Editions, 2000).

de Botton, Alain. *The Architecture of Happiness* (New York: Pantheon Books, 2006).

Dolan, Michael. *The American Porch: An Informal History of an Informal Place* (Guilford, Conn.: The Lyons Press, 2002).

Fisher Body Craftsman's Guild. *Plans and Instructions: 1932–1933 Competition.* (Detroit: Fisher Body Corp. [1932]).

Field, Walker. "A Reexamination into the Invention of the Balloon Frame," *Journal of the American Society of Architectural Historians* 2, 4 (October 1942): 3–29.

Finney, Howard. *Finney-Phinney Families in America; Descendants of John Finney of Plymouth and Barnstable, Mass., and Bristol, of Samuel Finney of Philadelphia, Pa., and of Robert Finney of New London, Pa.* (Richmond, Va.: William Byrd Press, 1957).

Giedion, Sigfried. *Space, Time and Architecture: The Growth of a New Tradition* (Cambridge, Mass.: Harvard University Press, 1941).

Gilman, Stanwood C. and Margaret C. *Georgetown on Arrowsic: The Ancient Dominions of Maine on the Kennebec, 1716–1966.* (Privately printed, 1966).

Goodwin, Peter. "Newtown on Arrowsic Island: The 18th Century Hub of Georgetown," DVD, PowerPoint Presentation, Town History Series, Patten Free Library (Bath, Maine, 2006).

Goodwin, Peter. "19th Century Arrowsic: Farms, Families and Roads," DVD, PowerPoint Presentation, Town History Series, Patten Free Library (Bath, Maine, 2005).

Green, Harvey. *Wood: Craft, Culture, History* (New York: Viking, 2006).

Greene, Fayal. *The Anatomy of a House: A Picture Dictionary of Architectural and Design Elements* (New York: Doubleday, 1991).

Hildebrand, Grant. *Origins of Architectural Pleasure* (Berkeley: University of California Press, 1999).

Hoadley, R. Bruce. *Understanding Wood: A Craftsman's Guide to Wood Technology,* second edition (Newtown, Conn.: Taunton Press, 2000).

Jacobus, John L. *The Fisher Body Craftsman's Guild: An Illustrated History* (Jefferson, N.C.: McFarland & Co., 2005).

Kahrl, Fred. "West of Woolwich: The Second Colonization of Maine," *The New Maine Times,* November 16, 2011. Http://www.newmainetimes .org/articles/2011/11/16/west-woolwich-second-colonization-maine-or (accessed Aug. 30, 2012).

Kidder, Tracy. *House* (Boston: Houghton Mifflin, 1983).

Kniffen, Fred, and Henry Glassie. "Building in Wood in the Eastern United States: A Time-Place Perspective," *Geographical Review* 55 (1966): 40–66.

Knoblock, Glenn A. *Historic Iron and Steel Bridges in Maine, New Hampshire and Vermont* (Jefferson, N.C.: McFarland & Co., 2012).

Koenig, Seth. "State Scuttles Route 1 Bypass," (Brunswick, Maine) *Times Record,* August 2, 2011, p. 1.

Kreindler, Michael. "Fiddler Reach: Arrowsic's Dangerous Double Dogleg." DVD, Local History Series, Sagadahoc History Room, Patten Free Library (Bath, Maine: Ferret Productions, [2007]).

Kuprenas, John. *101 Things I Learned in Engineering School* (New York: Grand Central, 2013).

Lank, David M. "Freedom Form and Movement: Robert Phinney's Sculptures Take Flight," *Nature Canada* 9, 1 (January-March 1980): 46–53.

Le Corbusier. *Towards a New Architecture,* translated by Frederick Etchells (London: John Rodker, 1931; republication, New York: Dover Publications, 1986).

Lehmann, Gary Paul. "Inventors and Inventions: The 2 x 4," *Forest History Today,* 1995, p. 23.

Lenik, Edward J. *Picture Rocks: American Indian Rock Art in the Northeast Woodlands* (Lebanon, N.H.: University Press of New England, 2002).

Locke, Jim. *The Well-Built House,* revised edition (Boston: Houghton Mifflin, 1992).

Longley, Diane G., and Arthur H. Young. *Steel over the Kennebec: Building a Maine Bridge* (Bath, Maine: 1978).

Maine Atlas and Gazetteer, 32nd ed. (Yarmouth, Maine: DeLorme, 2011).

McAlester, Virginia and Lee. *A Field Guide to American Houses* (New York: Alfred A. Knopf, 2011).

McLane, Charles B. *Islands of the Mid-Maine Coast, vol. 4: Pemaquid Point to the Kennebec River* (Rockland, Maine: The Island Institute; Gardiner, Maine: Tilbury House, 1994).

Michor, Daniel J. *People in Nature: Environmental History of the Kennebec River, Maine.* M.A. thesis, University of Maine, 2003.

Mitchell, H. E., and E. K. Woodard. *New Vineyard and Strong Register, 1902* (Reprint, North New Portland, Maine: Western Somerset Historical Society, n.d.).

Morgan, James. *If These Walls Had Ears: The Biography of a House* (New York: Warner Books, 1996).

Nelson, George, and Henry Wright. *Tomorrow's House: How to Plan Your Post-War Home Now* (New York: Simon and Schuster, 1945).

Oldenziel, Ruth. "Boys and Their Toys: The Fisher Body Craftsman's Guild, 1930–1968, and the Making of a Male Technical Domain," *Technology and Culture* 38 (1997): 60–96.

Owen, David. *The Walls Around Us: The Thinking Person's Guide to How a House Works* (New York: Villard Books, 1991).

Paddleford, Clementine. "The Joys of Fishing—at 10 Below!" *This Week Magazine,* February 25, 1962.

Palladio, Andrea. *The Four Books of Architecture.* Republication of 1738 Isaac Ware edition, with a new introduction by Adolf K. Placzek. (New York: Dover Publications, 1965).

Peters, Tom F. *Building the Nineteenth Century* (Cambridge, Mass.: MIT Press, 1996).

Petroski, Catherine. *A Bride's Passage: Susan Hathorn's Year under Sail* (Boston: Northeastern University Press, 1997).

Phinney, Dale. "Phinney's Place." Http://www.phinneysplace.com (accessed Aug. 23, 2012).

Phinney, Robert. "Robert Phinney (b. 1942)," *Masterpiece Online*. Http://www .masterpieceonline.com/bio.php?artistId=10000089&id=10BD-DBFH -6E59&name=Robert%20Phinney (accessed July 19, 2011).

Pillsbury, Richard, and Andrew Kardos. *A Field Guide to the Folk Architecture of the Northeastern United States*. Geography Publications at Dartmouth, No. 8, Special Edition on Geographical Lore.

Piper, Linda J., ed. *The Millennium Bridge: Crossing the Kennebec River* (Vancouver, Wash.: Pediment Publishing, 2000).

Pollan, Michael. *A Place of My Own: The Education of an Amateur Builder* (New York: Delta Books, 1997).

Rybczynski, Witold. *Home: A Short History of an Idea* (New York: Viking, 1987).

⸻. *Last Harvest: How a Cornfield Became New Daleville: Real Estate Development in America from George Washington to the Builders of the Twenty-first Century, and Why We Live in Houses Anyway* (New York: Scribner, 2007).

⸻. *The Most Beautiful House in the World.* (New York: Viking, 1989).

⸻. *One Good Turn: A Natural History of the Screwdriver and the Screw* (New York: Scribner, 2000).

⸻. *The Perfect House: A Journey with the Renaissance Master Andrea Palladio* (New York: Scribner, 2002).

Sanders, Michael S. *The Yard: Building a Destroyer at the Bath Iron Works* (New York: HarperCollins, 1999).

Schenker, Alexander M. *The Bronze Horseman: Falconet's Monument to Peter the Great* (New Haven, Conn.: Yale University Press, 2003).

Schuler, Stanley. *The Illustrated Encyclopedia of Carpentry & Woodworking Tools, Terms & Materials* (Chester, Conn.: Pequot Press, 1973).

Sears, Roebuck and Co. *Sears House Designs of the Thirties* (Mineola, N.Y.: Dover Publications, 2003).

Smith, Henry Atterbury, comp. *500 Small Houses of the Twenties* (New York: Dover Publications, 1990).

Smith, L. W., and L. W. Wood. "History of Yard Lumber Size Standards," U.S. Department of Agriculture, Forest Service, Forest Products Laboratory, September 1964.

Snow, Ralph Linwood. *Bath Iron Works: The First Hundred Years* (Bath, Maine: Maine Maritime Museum, 1987).

Sprague, Paul E., "The Origin of Balloon Framing," *Journal of the Society of Architectural Historians* 40, 4 (December 1981): 311–19.

Stone, Albert E., and Richard P. Horwitz, "American Studies As a Way of Life," *American Studies* 43, 3 (Fall 2002): 83–104.

Thoreau, Henry D. *Walden; or, Life in the Woods* (Boston: Ticknor and Fields, 1854).

Times Record (Brunswick, Maine). Various obituaries, various dates.

Todd, Carolyn F. "Georgetown Island: A Brief Historical Perspective." Http://www.georgetownhistoricalsociety.org/Georgetown%20History%2010-07.html.

Townsend, Gilbert, and J. Ralph Dalzell. *How to Plan a House* (Chicago: American Technical Society, 1942).

U.S. War Department. *Carpentry*. Technical Manual TM 5-226 (Washington, D.C.: War Department, 1943).

Ureneck, Lou. *Cabin: Two Brothers, a Dream and Five Acres in Maine* (New York: Viking, 2011).

Varney, Geo. J. *A Gazetteer of the State of Maine* (Boston: B. B. Russell, 1886).

Viollet-le-Duc, E. *How to Build a House: An Architectural Novelette*, second edition, translated by Benjamin Bucknall (London: Sampson Low, Marston, Searle, and Rivington, 1876; reprint, [Hong Kong]: Forgotten Books, 2012).

Vitruvius. *The Ten Books on Architecture,* translated by Morris Hicky Morgan. (Cambridge, Mass.: Harvard University Press, 1914; reprint, New York: Dover Publications, 1960).

Warren, Bud. "The Salt Water Mills of Maine in Context," manuscript, c. 2012.

Woolf, Virginia. *A Room of One's Own* (New York: Harcourt Brace, 1929).

INDEX

Place names refer to locations in Maine when no state is specified; house parts refer principally to those of the structure on Arrowsic; and italicized page numbers refer to illustrations and their captions.